We hope you enjoy this book.
Please return or renew it by the due date.
You can renew it at **www.norfolk.gov.uk/libraries**
or by using our free library app. Otherwise you can
phone **0344 800 8020** - please have your library
card and pin ready.
You can sign up for email reminders too.

NORFOLK COUNTY COUNCIL
LIBRARY AND INFORMATION SERVICE

D0784173

DK Delhi
Senior editors Bharti Bedi, Rupa Rao
Senior art editor Pooja Pipil
Jacket designer Juhi Sheth
DTP designer Mrinmoy Mazumdar
Pre-production manager Balwant Singh
Managing editor Kingshuk Ghoshal
Managing art editor Govind Mittal

DK London
Project editor Vicky Richards
Senior art editor Spencer Holbrook
Jacket editor Claire Gell
Jacket design development manager Sophia MTT
Production editor Gillian Reid
Senior production controller Jude Crozier
Managing editor Francesca Baines
Managing art editor Philip Letsu
Publisher Andrew Macintyre
Associate publishing director Liz Wheeler
Art director Karen Self
Publishing director Jonathan Metcalf

Content previously published in *It Can't Be True!* in 2013,
True Or False? in 2014, *Strange But True!* in 2015, and
It Can't Be True! 2 in 2016

First published in Great Britain in 2020 by
Dorling Kindersley Limited
One Embassy Gardens, 8 Viaduct Gardens,
London SW11 7BW

A CIP catalogue record for this book
is available from the British Library.
ISBN: 978-0-2414-4058-2

Printed and bound in Latvia

A WORLD OF IDEAS:
SEE ALL THERE IS TO KNOW

www.dk.com

Strange but true!

CONTENTS

It can't be true!

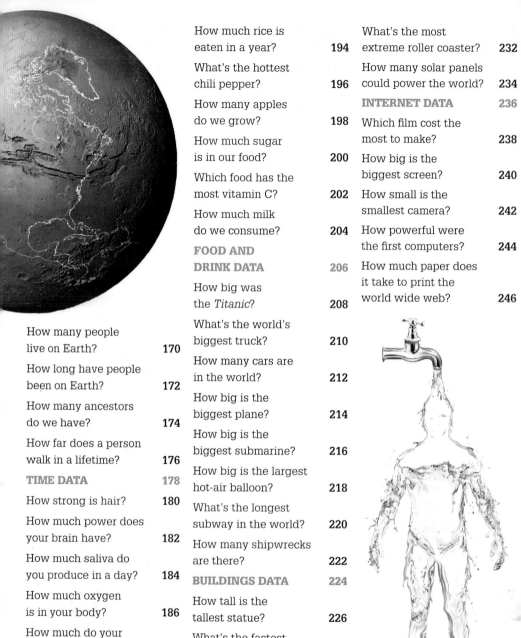

True or false?

STRANGE BUT TRUE!

Did you know there are rainbow-colored rocks, plants that eat mice, and spiders that dance? No? It may sound strange, but it's all true. Read on to discover many more bizarre beasts, incredible places, and peculiar phenomena in our wonderful, but sometimes weird, world.

Antelope Canyon in Arizona is famous for the strangely beautiful spiral formation of its rocks. Created by flooding and then erosion, the canyon's stunning, swirling forms are a popular tourist attraction.

Door to hell

Welcome to **hell on Earth**. More than 40 years ago, in the desert of north Turkmenistan, workers drilling for gas got a surprise when a **humongous hole** suddenly opened up. The resulting **crater of fire** still burns today, with locals naming the hot spot the "Door to Hell."

SUDDEN SINKHOLES

Sinkholes occur where supporting structures break down, most commonly in limestone areas. Water trickles underground, dissolving rock and creating caverns. When a cavern roof weakens, the ground opens, forming a sinkhole like this one in Guatemala.

The temperature of the burning gas is so hot, it can melt rock.

The Derweze crater is **66 ft (20 m) deep** in the center and **230 ft (70 m) wide**.

FAST FACTS

Sea sinkholes can occur in coastal areas. Water cuts through limestone to form caverns, into which the sinkhole collapses. If the cavern meets the sea, the level of the water in the hole rises and falls with the tide.

Sinkhole   Land   Sea

Cavern

Light produced by the burning gas is visible many miles away.

In 1971 drilling for gas in Derweze, Turkmenistan, went badly wrong when the ground collapsed and swallowed the drilling equipment. Workers set fire to the exposed gas reservoir to stop the poisonous gases leaking out. They assumed the fire would burn out, but it still rages today.

Salt of the Earth

This eerie and endless **expanse of nothingness** is the **world's largest salt flat**—a dry lake bed with a perfectly flat salt crust. High on a Bolivian plateau, **Salar de Uyuni** gets covered in water when it rains. Most of this water soon evaporates, turning the surface into a **magnificent mirror**.

Stretching across 4,085 sq miles (10,582 sq km), the salt flat can be crossed on foot or by car because it is either dry or flooded by only a few centimeters of water.

SALTY STAY

Salt is so plentiful that a hotel has been built from salt in the Salar. Called Palacio de Sal ("Palace of Salt"), it dissolves in water and must be repaired every time it rains.

🖼 FAST FACTS

The Salar has a bed of salt because it has no outlet. Water collecting on the surface evaporates, leaving behind any minerals it was carrying as salts.

Ocean water
Water in the open ocean is about 3.5 percent salt.

3.5% salt

Salar de Uyuni
As the Salar dries up, its water becomes eight times saltier than the sea.

28% salt

Dead Sea
Some salt lakes, such as the Dead Sea, are even saltier than the Salar.

33.7% salt

A thin covering of water lies over a crust of salt up to 33 ft (10 m) thick.

Highlands within the Salar become islands when the lake bed floods. The islands are never drenched, so they have no salt crust. Plants such as cacti can survive on the islands' slopes.

Beneath the salt is about **half the world's supply of lithium,** which is mainly used in **computer** and **cell phone batteries**.

The dry lake bed that forms Salar de Uyuni was once part of a much larger prehistoric salt lake. Occasional rainfall covers the salt briefly in water, which dissolves the surface. As the water evaporates, the salt recrystallizes in a perfectly flat plain.

A time and a place

Some places serve as reminders of the **past**. These **eerie sites** bear the scars of moments that **changed the landscape** forever.

Beach bomb
At the turn of the 20th century, the Mexican government bombed the uninhabited Marieta Islands for target practice. One bomb blasted out Hidden Beach, a postcard-picture paradise beach tucked underneath the shore.

Religious ruins

All that is left of the Mexican village of Parangaricutiro is the Church of San Juan. In 1943 the Parícutin volcano started smoking and eventually erupted, burying all the buildings except the church under rock and ash.

Unforgettable forts

In World War II, defensive forts were constructed off the UK's Kent coastline to protect the Thames estuary. The Maunsell Sea Forts are now open to the public, with boat trips to the forts offered every summer.

Lake **spotting**

Canada's Okanagan Valley is home to a lake **like no other**. Its dazzling dots are caused by **high levels of minerals**. For centuries **Spotted Lake** has been a **sacred site** for the First Nations (Canadian native peoples), who harnessed the **healing properties** of its mix of minerals.

WATER THERAPY

First Nations people used the lake's mud and water to treat aches, pains, and other medical problems. Legend has it that two warring tribes signed a truce so both groups could treat their injured warriors with the waters. In 2001 the Okanagan First Nations bought the site in order to protect it from development.

The lake's spots can range from green and blue to white and yellow depending on the mixture of minerals they contain.

By the city of Osoyoos in British Columbia lies Spotted Lake. Its waters contain an unusually high concentration of minerals, especially magnesium sulfate, calcium, and sodium sulfates, along with lower levels of at least 10 other minerals. In summer the water evaporates, leaving more than 300 individual pools in an array of different colors.

📊 FAST FACTS

British Columbia, Canada

Washington, USA Epsom, UK

Arizona, USA Wyoming, USA

Stassfurt, Germany

Mount Vesuvius, Italy

New Mexico, USA

Hérault, France

South Africa

This map shows the main places where magnesium sulfate occurs naturally.

Magnesium sulfate is commonly known as Epsom salts, named after the town in Surrey, UK, where the mineral also occurs naturally. It has a range of medical uses, from treating boils to relieving constipation. Many athletes bathe in Epsom salts to soothe sore muscles and speed up recovery times.

During **World War I**, the lake's **minerals** were used in Canadian **ammunition factories**.

Magnesium sulfate crystallizes in summer to form pathways around the lake's spots.

Mysterious wells

The **cenotes** ("sacred wells") of Mexico are **secret pools** with beautiful, clear waters. These developed naturally around the Yucatán Peninsula when **cavern roofs collapsed**. The ancient Mayan people believed cenotes were entrances to the **mysterious underworld** of the gods.

ALL THAT REMAINS

Underwater archaeologists exploring Mexico's cenotes have found human skulls and bones, suggesting that the Mayan people performed human sacrifices to honor their gods. The discoveries have scared villagers living near the cenotes today, who steer clear of these pools.

The Yucatán Peninsula is known for its porous limestone. Over time heavy rainfall caused the rock to give way in places, revealing spectacular groundwater pools underneath. The Mayans set up home nearby, making use of the pristine water supply. They thought the gods communicated at cenotes, so religious ceremonies were also performed there.

📊 FAST FACTS

1,112 ft (339 m)

1,063 ft (324 m)

The deepest water-filled cenote in the world is also in Mexico. El Zacatón is 1,112 ft (339 m) deep—deeper than France's Eiffel Tower (1,063 ft, or 324 m) is high.

Tree roots dangle through the surface opening into the clear water of the cenote.

There are about **7,000** cenotes in the **Yucatán Peninsula.**

Fairy chimneys

These **magical stone structures** transform the Turkish terrain of Cappadocia into a fairy kingdom. Carved by the **forces of nature**, countless **ancient rock formations** tower over the surrounding valleys and villages.

The body of each chimney is made up of layers of limestone and volcanic ash.

Fairy chimneys are named for their seemingly magical shapes.

Fairy chimneys have explosive origins. Millions of years ago, volcanic activity resulted in layers of soft sedimentary rock, topped by a hard layer of basalt. At the mercy of wind and rain, the soft rock eroded gradually, transforming the landscape into distinctive shapes, including cones, columns, and mushrooms. Local people turned the chimneys into buildings, shaping houses, churches, and monasteries out of the rock.

FAIRYTALE HOTELS

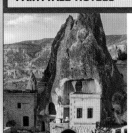

Some of the larger fairy chimneys have been hollowed out and sculpted into unique boutique hotels. With cave-like rooms offering views of the colossal chimneys, visitors can enjoy the most authentic experience of Cappadocia.

The "capped" chimneys have a tough head of basalt, which protects the soft rock below.

FAST FACTS

Rivers of rainwater eroded the soft rock.

Several million years ago, volcanoes covered the area with volcanic ash, which was compressed into soft sedimentary rock. Rainwater and wind eroded this rock, leaving behind chimney-like formations protected by hard basalt caps. If a fairy chimney loses its basalt cap, it will eventually disappear completely.

Rainbow **rocks**

There's no need to roll out the red carpet at **Danxia** in **China's Gansu Province**. The jaw-dropping rocky landscape is **naturally red** from a buildup of sandstone over many millions of years, while the **rainbow effect** comes from **colorful mineral deposits**.

LIFE ON MARS

Another red world is Mars. It is called the "Red Planet" because of the dusty surface layer of orange-red iron oxide. Alien life-forms may have lived on Mars three billion years ago when it was warmer and had flowing water.

The name **Danxia** means "rosy clouds" in Chinese.

Danxia's crumpled landscape comes from movement in Earth's crust, combined with wind and rain carving out ravines and pillars in the soft rock.

Covering 154 sq miles (400 sq km), Danxia's rock formations have eroded naturally by wind and rain. This has created today's steep cliffs, solitary peaks, and textured layers. Danxia is the generic term for red sandstone landforms, but kaleidoscopic streaks of yellow, green, and blue from various mineral deposits add to the palette.

FAST FACTS

Over millions of years, sandstone and mineral deposits were compressed into multicolored layers of rock. Movement of the giant plates that form Earth's crust pushed, cut, and folded the layers.

Rain and wind gradually erode the surface, revealing more colored layers.

Bands of sandstone colored by different minerals are laid down.

Plate pushes in

Plate pushes in

The layers fold up as the plates push together.

On the rocks

Wind and water constantly **batter** the planet's rocky regions, sculpting **unusual formations** that must be seen to be believed.

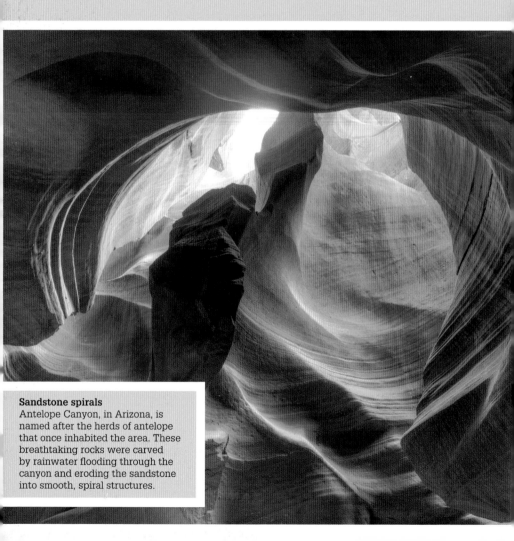

Sandstone spirals
Antelope Canyon, in Arizona, is named after the herds of antelope that once inhabited the area. These breathtaking rocks were carved by rainwater flooding through the canyon and eroding the sandstone into smooth, spiral structures.

Hobgoblin's playground
Little Finland, in Nevada, is named for the fins adorning the desert's red sandstone. The area is also called the Hobgoblin's playground because of its fantastical formations.

Seaside seat
Norway's Kannesteinen rock is the eye-popping result of years of coastal erosion. With its sea view overlooking Vågsøy Island, this distinctive formation is called "the Kanne chair" by locals.

Wipeout wave
The surf's always up at Wave Rock in Hyden, Australia. Stretching 46 ft (14 m) high and reaching 360 ft (110 m) wide, the huge rock resembles a breaking wave and is a sacred spot for Aboriginal locals.

Glorious geyser

Fly Ranch in Nevada's Black Rock Desert is no ordinary geyser. A **faulty well** drilled in the early 1900s caused **geothermally heated water** to burst through surface cracks. Repeated eruptions have left behind **mineral deposits**, forming a multicolored mound.

Each time Fly Ranch Geyser erupts, it releases minerals that have dissolved in the scalding water. These minerals solidify when the water cools, creating an ever-growing mound surrounded by terraced rock pools. Vibrant red and green streaks over the mound are the result of thermophilic (heat-loving) algae thriving in the steamy surroundings.

SPOUTS IN SPACE

Geysers are not only found on Earth. Saturn's moon Enceladus (above) hosts 101 geysers, while geysers of water vapor were seen on Jupiter's moon Europa in 2013 and 2016.

Water erupting from the geyser is a piping hot 200°F (93°C) and spills into up to 40 separate pools.

⛰ FAST FACTS

Geysers occur where underground water comes into contact with hot rocks. Under pressure, the water becomes superheated before reaching boiling point and making its way through cracks in the rock to erupt explosively through a surface vent.

Groundwater soaks through layers of rock.

The geyser erupts.

Water is heated further under pressure and rises to the surface.

Water is heated by contact with hot rocks.

Minerals in the water react with oxygen in the air to create a layer of colorful algae.

The mound continues to grow, adding new layers to its height each year.

🖼 FAST FACTS

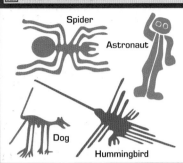

Spider
Astronaut
Dog
Hummingbird

The mysterious lines are found on a coastal plain between two river valleys. There are hundreds of individual designs, and many more shapes and straight lines. They were created over several centuries, with some newer geoglyphs overlapping or obscuring older ones. Previously unknown geoglyphs are continually being discovered.

Crafted between 500 BCE and 500 CE, the Nazca lines include images of animals, birds, and human-like figures. The reason for their construction remains uncertain. Some historians believe the lines were art created for the gods to enjoy, while others speculate that they were maps of underground water sources or an early form of calendar.

The **geoglyphs** cover a **vast area** of about **174 sq miles (450 sq km).**

The huge lines were created by removing the dark top layer of gravel to reveal the lighter-colored earth underneath.

NAZCA WORSHIP

The Nazca people believed that worshipping the gods was key to survival. Their expertly crafted pottery features depictions of their gods, as well as nature spirits and mythical creatures. The Nazca had no writing system, so painting pots would have been one way of communicating their beliefs.

Desert **drawings**

Aircraft pilots flying over Peru's **Nazca desert** in the 1930s were amazed to see huge drawings **scratched into the landscape**. These **geoglyphs** are called **Nazca lines**, after the ancient Nazcas who made them, and they are a fascinating tribute to a **lost people**.

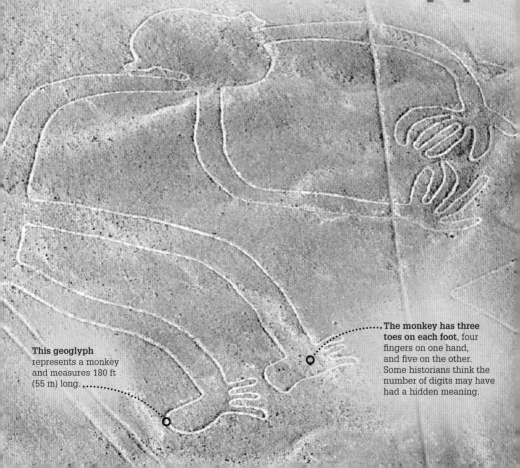

This geoglyph represents a monkey and measures 180 ft (55 m) long.

The monkey has three toes on each foot, four fingers on one hand, and five on the other. Some historians think the number of digits may have had a hidden meaning.

Clay corps

A **chance discovery** of a hidden pit in Xian, China, led to an incredible find—nearly **8,000 life-size soldiers** sculpted **2,200 years ago**. Called the **Terracotta army**, these clay figures were crafted to protect the tomb of China's **First Emperor**, Qin Shi Huang.

Statues were modeled in clay and originally painted in bright colors.

EXTENSIVE EXCAVATIONS

Four pits were found, but the last was empty, suggesting the mausoleum was incomplete when the emperor died. Many warriors lay in pieces and were painstakingly restored. They had been preserved due to the consistent temperature from burial until excavation.

▥ FAST FACTS

One of the warriors' huge crossbows could fire an arrow the length of seven and a half soccer fields.

The warriors' weapons were real, but never used in battle. Thousands of bronze spears, battle-axes, crossbows, and arrowheads have been uncovered in great condition. One crossbow found was about 5 ft (1.5 m) long, and was capable of firing an arrow as far as 2,600 ft (792 m).

The **emperor's tomb** lies 0.93 miles (1.5 km) away at **Mount Li** and remains **undisturbed.**

Each warrior is unique, with its own hairstyle, facial features, and expression.

Attention to detail is remarkable—even shoe soles, where visible, have their own intricate patterns.

In 1974 Chinese farmers were digging a well when they uncovered the pit housing the Terracotta army. Lined up according to rank, there are archers, charioteers, officers, generals, and horsemen. A production-line approach was used to make each warrior, with every body part crafted separately before the figure was fully assembled at the end.

Happy endings

Funerals in the West African country of Ghana are **upbeat gatherings**. Innovative coffins **celebrate** the deceased's work or interests.

Flight of fancy
Two brothers created this wooden aircraft coffin for their grandmother, who had never been in a plane but dreamed of flying.

Snap-happy
Many coffins reflect the deceased's career, such as this camera-shaped coffin for a photographer.

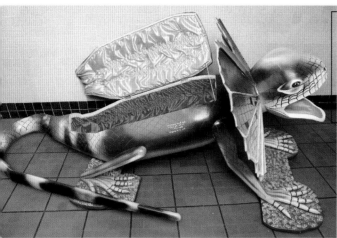

Coffin art
Examples of the handcrafted, ornately decorated caskets have been displayed all over the world. This lizard coffin was created for an exhibition in Melbourne, Australia.

Final fizz
No need to guess the deceased's drink of choice. Favorite foods can also be reflected in the shape of a coffin.

Luxury at a price
Fantasy coffins offer lavishly lined interiors, as this open leopard coffin shows, and cost about $750 each. This is equivalent to about a year's wages, so usually only the wealthier Ghanaians can afford them.

Secret **city**

Turkey's ancient underground caves of **Cappadocia** were once **inhabited cities**. Steep, hollowed hillsides mask a **secret subterranean world**.

Derinkuyu is about **279 ft (85 m) deep** and carved out of **volcanic rock**.

Derinkuyu had **11 floors** and a network of random tunnels to deter would-be invaders.

The deepest of Cappadocia's underground cities, Derinkuyu had sleeping quarters, communal rooms, bathrooms, cooking pits, wells, ventilation shafts, churches, and stables for animals. Historians believe this was the hiding place for early Christians trying to flee persecution from the Roman empire. At its peak, the city may have housed up to 20,000 people.

📷 FACT FACTS

One of about 40 cities, Derinkuyu had at least 600 entrances, hidden in the courtyards of houses above ground. The city's inhabitants used heavy circular stone doors to block tunnels from the inside in the event of an attack.

The stone was rolled into the narrow passage and wedged from behind to block attackers.

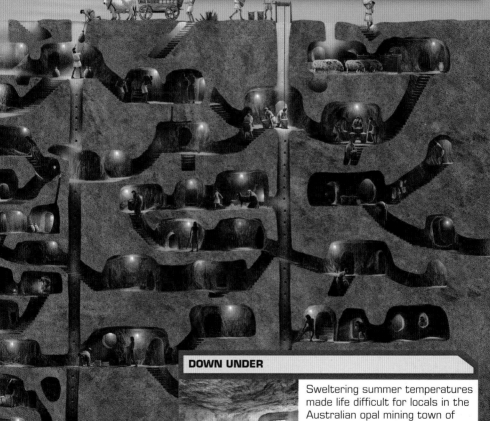

DOWN UNDER

Sweltering summer temperatures made life difficult for locals in the Australian opal mining town of Coober Pedy—so, in 1915, they decided to retreat underground. About half of the town's 4,000 inhabitants still live underground in homes known as "dugouts."

Mysterious moai

Standing head and shoulders above the volcanic land of **Easter Island** are moai—huge human heads carved from rock more than **500 years** ago. Created by the **ancient Polynesians**, the sculptures are still **sacred** to today's islanders

Each moai has been carved out of soft volcanic rock.

FAMOUS FACES

Mount Rushmore, in South Dakota, is famous for its cliff carvings of four US Presidents— George Washington, Thomas Jefferson, Theodore Roosevelt, and Abraham Lincoln. From 1927 until the carvings' completion in 1941, about 400 people worked on the faces.

Easter Island is **1,100 miles (1,700 km)** away from its nearest island neighbor.

The average height of a moai is 13 ft (4 m) and the average weight is 14 tons. ⋯⋯⋯⋯

The moai are testament to the extraordinary capabilities of the ancient Polynesians because they were difficult to construct and tough to transport around Easter Island. There are 887 statues, all of them male. Most experts believe the moai were meant to honor the spirits of deceased ancestors, existing chiefs, or others special to the Polynesians, but nothing has been proven.

FAST FACTS

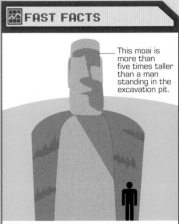

This moai is more than five times taller than a man standing in the excavation pit.

A large part of each moai is unseen because it is buried underground. The height of the tallest statue ever erected on Easter Island is about 33 ft (10 m).

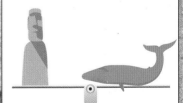

The biggest statue, nicknamed "El Gigante," was found in a quarry. This mega moai is 72 ft (22 m) tall and weighs about 180 tons—as much as a large blue whale.

MARKET MAYHEM

Maeklong Train Market in Thailand sits right along a train line. Eight times a day vendors collapse their awnings and pull back produce just enough to let a train through. As soon as the train is gone, business gets back on track!

More than **30 million people** live in **Chongqing** municipality.

The **train** sounds only as loud as a dishwasher to the building's residents, due to soundproofing.

Tower block train

Some **high-rise householders** in China's "mountain city" Chongqing can **board a train** without even stepping outside their building.

Located between the sixth and eighth floors of the 19-story building, Liziba Station was opened in 2004. It was part of an innovative new monorail line seen by city planners as a solution to finding space in the heavily built-up city.

FAST FACTS

Shinjuku, Japan

Penn, US

The busiest train station in the world is Shinjuku Station in Japan. Around 3.6 million passengers pass through it in a single day. Penn Station in New York City—the busiest station in North America—sees only 430,000 passengers.

Deep breath

The depths some people dive will **take your breath away**. From the earliest times, people have taken the plunge, but today **free diving** (diving without breathing equipment) is an **extreme sport** that pushes the human body to its **absolute limit**. Participants dive the depths on just one **deep breath**.

As the depth increases, so does the amount of water pressing down on free diver Pierre Frolla from above. Free divers must learn to cope with the extreme conditions.

FREE DIVING FOR FOOD

The Bajau people of Borneo are real water babies. Their houses stand on stilts in the sea, and they free dive in search of fish to eat. The best Bajau free divers can stay submerged on a single breath for up to five minutes, diving to the bottom of the reef 66 ft (20 m) below.

At a depth of **328 ft (100 m)** water pressure **compresses human lungs** to the size of **fists**.

FAST FACTS

Constant weight without fins world record: 334 ft (102 m)

Constant weight with fins world record: 419 ft (128 m)

No limits world record: 702 ft (214 m)

Competitive free diving has different disciplines depending on what equipment the diver uses. "No limits" free diving involves using a weight and cable to descend very quickly. "Constant weight" free divers descend and ascend under their own power. They can use a weight to help them descend, but must return to the surface with the same weight.

This wreck of an aircraft is in the Bahamas.

Holding their breath for minutes at a time, free divers plunge to depths of more than 328 ft (100 m). Divers train themselves for the challenge mentally and physically, but in some ways the human body is hardwired to undertake this amazing aquatic activity. When submerged in cold water, the heart rate slows to conserve oxygen. The blood moves away from the arms and legs to protect the vital organs.

Wet and **wild**

Crossing the raging rapids of Asia's **Mekong River** on a precarious rope bridge is part of the daily routine for **local Lao fishermen**. However high the water, they must navigate the **dangerous currents** to secure a top spot and net a big catch.

More than **1,100 species** of fish inhabit the **Mekong River**.

SCHOOL'S OUT

The school run is a challenge in some parts of the world. These pupils must walk for two hours each day to attend their school in the mountains of Bijie, Guizhou Province, China. As well as passing through narrow tunnels in the rock, they must travel this treacherous cliff path, which is only 1 ft 7 in (0.5 m) wide.

With swirling rapids and crashing waterfalls, the Mekong River is unpredictable, experiencing huge fluctuations in flow throughout the year. But the river's wild waters contain a large variety of fish, making fishing the most common occupation for Mekong's riverside dwellers. This fisherman is risking a treacherous trip over a makeshift bridge to reach a prime fishing spot.

This precarious tightrope was built by a local fisherman using bits of rope and old cable.

The Chinese name for Mekong translates as "turbulent river," while the Thai and Lao name means "mother water." The Vietnamese call it "nine dragons" after the delta's many tributaries.

📊 FAST FACTS

China

Myanmar (Burma)

Mekong River

Vietnam

Laos

Thailand

Cambodia

Stretching about 3,000 miles (4,800 km), the Mekong is the world's 12th longest river. It flows through China, Myanmar, Thailand, Laos, Cambodia, and Vietnam.

Honey hunters

The **Gurung tribesmen** of Nepal make a living by collecting honeycomb from **gravity-defying** Himalayan cliffs. They put themselves in the **stickiest** of situations, dangling from rope ladders to access the sweet treat.

Blisters and bee stings are common complaints, but honey hunting can be fatal.

RISKY BUSINESS

Honey hunters in the Sundarbans forests of Bangladesh run the risk of tiger attacks. They light fires beside cliffs to smoke the bees out, but many hunters are injured or killed when the big cats come to investigate.

Balancing precariously up to 300 ft (90 m) above the ground, honey hunters use thick smoke to sedate huge swarms of angry bees. This tradition has been going on for thousands of years. Some of the honey is shared among the villagers to make tea, and the rest is sold.

Honey hunters use "tangos"—tools adapted from bamboo sticks—to cut the honey from the cliff face.

🖼 FAST FACTS

Measuring up to 1⅛ in (3 cm) in length, the Himalayan honey bee (*Apis laboriosa*) is the largest honey bee in the world. It lives at high altitude and builds its large, precarious nests on the sides of vertical cliffs.

The Western honey bee is just ½ in (1.2 cm) long.

Himalayan honey bee

Tower of strength

Since the 18th century a **fascinating festival** has taken place in Spain's Catalonia region. Here, **human tower building** is a competitive sport, in which **courageous castellers** (builders) attempt to create a formation that stands head and shoulders above the rest.

At this twice-yearly arena event, teams of castellers work together to build the most impressive human towers as quickly as possible. The last member in position raises one hand with four fingers outstretched to represent the Catalan flag. The best score goes to the most intricate tower to be assembled and dismantled successfully.

Children climb up to form the higher levels.

Dismounting is the hardest part, so a **medical crew** must be standing by.

FAST FACTS

The top section, or *pom*, must be assembled rapidly.

The main section of the tower is called the trunk, or *tronc*.

The solid base, or *pinya*, provides support and cushioning if the tower collapses.

The tallest castell on record was 10 tiers high, with three people at each level. It was built by local castellers at the annual Vilafranca festival in Catalonia. More than 500 people provided support at the base of the tower.

DOUBLE CELEBRATION

Everyone loves a party! Inhabitants of the town of Bérchules in Spain celebrate the new year twice a year. A power outage on December 31, 1994, ruined the usual festivities, so they had another New Year's Eve party in August. The tradition continues to this day.

Fleeting flower

The supersized Titan arum is an **absolute showstopper** of the horticultural world. Taking many **years to flower**, botanists wait with baited breath for this unpredictable giant to bloom in **brief but breathtaking** glory.

This rare species grows in Sumatran rain forests, but its spectacular size has made it a favorite at botanical gardens. Its single flowerhead consists of a spadix (flower-bearing spike) surrounded by a leaf-like spathe. Flowering occurs only occasionally and lasts just days, accompanied by the rancid smell of rotting meat. When the flower dies, a single leaf the size of a small tree takes its place. This builds up food stores so the plant will eventually flower again.

The fleshy spadix heats up as the plant flowers and emits a powerful odor that attracts pollinating insects.

The protective spathe unfurls to reveal rings of flowers at the base of the spadix.

The flowerhead emerging from the tuber adds 4 in (10 cm) to its height per day.

POISON IN PARADISE

While Titan arum is smelly but harmless, *Daphne mezereum* is the opposite. Nicknamed the paradise plant, this species produces fragrant flowers, hiding the fact that it is deadly poisonous. Swallowing any part of this plant would lead to sudden sickness or even death.

The flower emerges from a huge tuber (underground stem) that can weigh more than 154 lb (70 kg).

FAST FACTS

The sizeable Titan arum flower is not a single flower—it is an inflorescence, or flower spike, bearing hundreds of flowers.

The century plant has a taller flower spike than the Titan arum, which it sends up every 20–30 years.

The talipot palm has the largest flower spike of all. Its flowers form an 26-ft (8-m) structure on top of the tree, which itself can be up to 82 ft (25 m) tall.

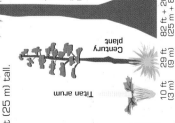

Talipot palm   82 ft + 26 ft (25 m + 8 m)

Century plant   29 ft (9 m)

Titan arum   10 ft (3 m)

Hot lips

This plant may look like it is puckering up for a **big smooch**, but it's really saving all its love for **hummingbirds** and **butterflies**. The vibrant lip-like parts are actually **special leaves** designed to draw these feeders to its **sweet nectar**.

SNAPDRAGON SKULLS

Blooming in the sunshine, snapdragon flowers are colorful and beautiful, but things take a sinister turn when their seed pods dry out to resemble tiny skulls.

In this gap, the plant will grow its small white flowers. As butterflies and hummingbirds land on the flowers to drink nectar, they transfer pollen from flower to flower. This is essential for the plant's reproduction.

In **Central America**, this attractive plant is often given as a **token of love**.

FAST FACTS

The hot lips plant is not the only plant to resemble something else. The bird of paradise plant looks just like its namesake, complete with colorful plumage, while the bleeding heart has bright pink, heart-shaped flowers. The yellow, orange, and red flowers of the flame lily resemble a roaring fire.

Each petal is crimson red at the tip and yellow at the base, just like a flame.

Flame lily

The outer pink petals look like a heart.

Bleeding heart

The pointed stalk looks like a beak.

The flowers spike out like a bird's crest.

Bird of paradise

Psychotria elata **is the scientific name** for the hot lips plant, which flowers in the humid forests of Costa Rica, Panama, and Colombia. Called bracts, the glossy red leaves are the perfect color to catch the eye of pollinators because butterfly and hummingbird eyes are very sensitive to red light.

The plant's "lips" measure about 2 in (5 cm) from top to bottom.

Posturing petals

Some flowers can make you **look twice**. Although their **real identities** are floral, they resemble something **entirely different**.

Monkey business
The flowers of *Dracula simia*, or the monkey orchid, are a dead ringer for a mini monkey face. Preferring high altitude habitats in Ecuador, Colombia, and Peru, this unique flower has also been grown in captivity by orchid experts.

Budding baby
The *Anguloa uniflora* is a short orchid native to Peru and Chile, with each flower mimicking a baby swaddled in a blanket. The creamy, scented petals open in the summer months.

Buzzy bloomer
At first glance, this looks like bees drawing nectar from flowers. But look again. Growing around the Mediterranean and Middle East, this is the Woodcock Bee-orchid, a flower that closely resembles a bee.

Parrot petals
Native to Burma, Thailand, and India, the rare *Impatiens psittacina* is better known as the "parrot flower" because its pretty pastel petals look just like a parrot in flight.

Attack of the
killer plants

There are at least 500 species of **carnivorous plant** on planet Earth, but nature's most famous meat-eater is the **Venus flytrap**. These jaws of death prey on **vulnerable insects**—and when they **snap shut**, there's no escape.

Unscrupulous collectors dig up the wild plants, putting the Venus flytrap at risk.

An unsuspecting cricket moves closer to the sweet nectar secreted from the Venus flytrap's open leaves.

FAST FACTS

The Venus flytrap's lightning reflexes are not well understood, but they may be the result of electrical impulses. When the trigger hairs are touched, a signal causes water to move rapidly between the leaf's cells; the cells on the outside of the leaf swell up, making the trap snap shut.

Touching a second hair increases the charge and triggers the trap.

Cells on the outside of the leaf swell with water and the trap snaps shut.

Brushing a hair stimulates a tiny electrical impulse, but not enough to shut the trap.

Formally known as *Dionaea muscipula*, this predatory plant grows in the wetlands on the east coast, in North Carolina and South Carolina. A carnivorous plant is one that lures, traps, kills, and digests its victims, and the Venus flytrap does all of these in quick succession, thanks to its special touch-sensitive leaves. Trigger hairs on the leaves detect prey, but withstand false alarms such as drops of rain.

Snap! In less than a second, the leaves close tight. Glands on the leaf release digestive fluids that break down the cricket's soft tissues, then reabsorb the nutritious insect soup.

The cricket touches trigger hairs on the leaves, and the plant's touch-sensitive mechanism responds instantly.

MIGHTY MOUSETRAP

One of the largest carnivorous plants in the world is *Nepenthes attenboroughii*, native to the Philippines. Reaching 16 ft (5 m) tall, its leafy jaws can trap and digest mice and rats.

TREE ART

Tree shaping transforms plants into living art. Bending, weaving, and twisting help these sculptures take shape. The art form takes advantage of a process called inosculation—where tissue from two different plants, or parts of a plant that are touching, knits itself together.

Tree **bridges**

In the **forests of northeastern India**, rivers and streams are crossed using structures crafted from **ancient banyan trees**. Forged by tangled roots and vines, these living tree bridges are both a **natural wonder** and a master class in engineering

The roots of the *Ficus elastica*, a type of banyan tree, twist into strong lattices.

Some of Cherrapunji's **tree bridges** are thought to be more than **500 years old.**

Cherrapunji is one of the world's wettest places, so normal wooden structures would rot and break. Living bridges avoid this problem, enabling these children to get to school. By carefully guiding the strong, thick tree roots across rivers and voids, local Khasi people have grown permanent crossings that only get stronger over time. Patience and planning are required: they take 10 to 15 years to grow.

FAST FACTS

Some tree bridges are up to 100 ft (30 m) long, and can support the weight of 50 people or more at once. Local people use hollowed-out tree trunks to guide new roots into position and ensure the structure is strong.

Tree of **blood**

It can't fly and it doesn't breathe fire, but the **dragon's blood tree** can make one extraordinary claim to fame. The **bark of the tree bleeds**, leading to its use in magic and **medicine** since ancient times.

The dragon's blood tree (*dracaena cinnabari*) has an unusual appearance, with branches like white bony fingers reaching up to a crown of evergreen leaves. The blood-red sap is secreted naturally from cracks and cuts in the trunk. Harvesters open the existing fissures to collect the oozing sap, which has a variety of uses.

Legend claims the "blood" is an effective ingredient in **love spells**.

This slow-growing species is unique to the islands of Socotra in the Indian Ocean, off the coast of Yemen.

NEW BLOOD

The deep-red sap of the dragon's blood tree is an effective ingredient in dyes, varnish, adhesive, and incense. It has also been successful in treating cuts, bites, burns, and sores because the resin's healing properties reduce redness and swelling.

The dragon's blood tree grows up to 33 ft (10 m) in height.

📊 FAST FACTS

Long, waxy leaves catch droplets of water from clouds of mist.

Water droplets run down the branches and trunk to the roots.

Although the dragon's blood tree looks like an umbrella, it is designed to collect, rather than repel, water. The long, waxy leaves gather moisture from the air and transport it down to the branches, trunk, and roots, enabling the tree to survive in Socotra's hot and dry climate.

Crab army

Every year up to **100 million red crabs** inhabiting Australia's **Christmas Island** migrate from their forest home to the Indian Ocean. This convoy of crustaceans travels 5 miles (9 km) with **only one goal**—reproduction.

Christmas Island red crabs can measure up to 4½ in (11.5 cm) across.

BAT CAVE

Another huge concentration of creatures can be found at Bracken Cave in Texas, home to the world's largest bat colony. About 20 million bats exit the cave each day at dusk searching for insects to feed on. It's one of nature's most amazing aerial sights.

Amorous male crabs will fight one another during the annual migration, competing for the attention of the females.

FAST FACTS

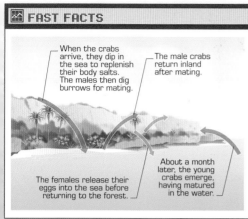

When the crabs arrive, they dip in the sea to replenish their body salts. The males then dig burrows for mating.

The male crabs return inland after mating.

The females release their eggs into the sea before returning to the forest.

About a month later, the young crabs emerge, having matured in the water.

The migration starts in early November and ends in January. Male crabs set off first, followed by the female crabs. It takes about a week for them to reach the shore. After mating, the males head back inland, followed soon after by the females.

The crabs are making their way to the sea. Mating takes place on the shore because the larval form of the crab has primitive gills that function only in water. Female crabs release eggs into the sea. The larvae hatch and grow in the water for about a month before congregating at the shore, ready to become mini air-breathing crabs. The tiny baby crabs then head back to the forest.

Male crabs reach the beach first and dig the burrows where mating will take place.

Jumbo **jitters**

It's every elephant's worst nightmare—
just when you're chilling out by a
watering hole, a **swarm of thousands
of squawking birds** comes and spoils
the serenity. **Overwhelmed by the
frenzy**, this jumbo soon backed away.

Red-billed quelea
are the world's
most plentiful wild
birds, with an adult
breeding population
of about 1.5 billion.

These tiny birds are red-billed quelea. They weigh just ½–¾ oz (15–20 g) each, but their huge number meant the total weight suddenly snapped a tree branch at Kenya's Satao Camp water hole in 2012. Taking to the skies, their deafening call and ferocious flapping of wings was too much for the big-eared elephant, who made a hasty retreat.

FAST FACTS

Flocks of red-billed quelea are a menace for farmers in Africa. One swarm can eat several fields of grain (56 tons) in a day—about the weight of seven elephants.

The **African elephant** is the world's **largest** living land animal.

SCAREDY CATS

Despite being king of the beasts, lions have also been known to scare easily. A pack of lions was seen stalking an adult giraffe and baby in Kenya's Maasai Mara. Fearing for her offspring's safety, the giraffe charged and the pack ran away.

Dream teams

Teaming up works wonders in the animal kingdom. From aerial attacks to making mounds, there is definitely **strength in numbers**.

Golden jelly
Jellyfish Lake sits on a remote island of the Palau archipelago in the Pacific Ocean. This saltwater lake is the perfect home for millions of jellyfish because there are plenty of algae to feed on and no predators to avoid.

Spanish swarm
In 2004 the skies over the Spanish island of Fuerteventura were plagued by swarms of pink locusts from Africa. Their collective power wiped out one-third of the crops in some African countries, before 100 million of them flew on to Fuerteventura.

Wonder weavers
Named after their huge woven nests standing up to 13 ft (4 m) tall, sociable weaver birds of southern Africa work together to gather twigs, stems, and grass for their carefully constructed homes.

Massive mounds
There's no slacking in the termite team. Like ants and bees, this insect knows the power of many. Termite builders in Africa, Australia, and South America (above) create enormous mounds, with diameters stretching 98 ft (30 m). These homes can take five years to complete.

The journey south takes two months. The butterflies travel up to 100 miles (160 km) per day.

Marathon migration

It's a journey that would leave most of us exhausted: **Monarch butterflies** cover **3,000 miles (4,800 km)** on their annual flight from **Canada to Mexico.** The skies fill with millions of **monarchs** in the world's longest **insect migration.**

Monarch butterflies can't survive the cold Canadian winter, so they fly south to warmer climes. Most monarchs live for a maximum of eight weeks, but the generation that hatches at the end of the Canadian summer is different. Instead of mating and dying, they put all their energy into the migration, and can live for up to eight months. After spending the winter in Mexico, the migrating generation reproduce and their offspring

The butterflies return to the same small area, and often the exact same trees, as previous generations.

In Mexico the monarch **butterflies** roost on the trunks and branches of fir trees to conserve energy.

SUPPORTING THE SPECIES

Monarch butterflies only lay their eggs on milkweed plants because they are the sole food of the newly hatched larvae. However, herbicide use has decreased the number of milkweed plants in North America. Conservationists are encouraging people to plant milkweeds at home, to create the habitat the monarchs need to survive.

⬛ FAST FACTS

Like all butterflies, monarchs go through four distinct stages in their life cycle. They are laid as eggs, which hatch into larvae, or caterpillars. The larva feeds, shedding its skin four or more times as its body gets bigger.

The larva then becomes a pupa, or chrysalis. Inside the pupa, the larva turns into an imago—an adult butterfly. The whole process from egg to butterfly is called metamorphosis.

Larva

Egg

Pupa

Imago

World's wild webs

If **millions of spiders** congregate in one place, they can work as a team, spinning **enormous sheet webs** that **cover trees**, **hedges**, and **fields**. These wonder weavers transform the landscape with their **intricate designs**.

These webs are so dense that trees appear to be covered in nets. ....

When water levels rose several yards above Sindh's normal levels, wildlife headed for the trees to survive. ....

🖼 FAST FACTS

The spider with the longest legs is a species discovered in a cave in Laos in 2001—the giant huntsman spider. It measures 12 in (30 cm) from the tip of one leg to the tip of its opposite leg. The biggest spider by weight is the Goliath bird-eater, a species of South American tarantula that weighs in at 2½ oz (70 g).

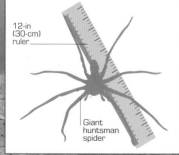

12-in (30-cm) ruler

Giant huntsman spider

Spiders made these webs when a decade's worth of rain dropped on Sindh in a week.

In 2010 many trees were blanketed by giant webs in Sindh, Pakistan, when heavy monsoon rains flooded large areas. Spiders and other web-spinning creatures living on the ground had to seek shelter. They climbed trees to escape the flood waters, and their handiwork was visible for all to see.

ANIMAL ORACLES

Some creatures can predict natural disasters. Birds take flight when they sense a storm coming, and researchers in Florida found sharks swim into deeper water before a hurricane.

Strutting
spider

Australia's **peacock spider** makes all the right **moves** in a bid to impress the ladies. Getting into the groove is easy with **eight legs** and a multicolored stomach flap to shake.

Peacock spiders have six eyes and can see fine details in color from yards away.

🖾 FAST FACTS

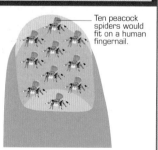

Ten peacock spiders would fit on a human fingernail.

Peacock spiders are tiny—adults grow to only about 1/10 in (4 mm) long. Despite this, these aptly named jumping spiders are capable of pouncing more than 20 times their body length.

The colorful stomach flap of the male spider is lifted like a fan during the courtship dance. At other times it remains folded away out of sight.

The courtship dance of the male peacock spider involves a series of attention-grabbing jumps, sways, and struts to attract partners. His colors and moves are studied by the female before she decides if he is a suitable mate. If she isn't interested, she may attack and eat her suitor instead!

After mating, the peacock spider will get up and moving again to find more females.

This spider gets its name from the equally flashy peacock bird.

PLUMAGE OF PARADISE

The mating efforts of the bird of paradise are hard to ignore. The male is transformed by showcasing his big, brilliant blue frontage before he performs an impressive courtship dance. His performance must be perfect to win over the drably colored female.

Bloated
bloodsuckers

Ticks are the **vampires** of the bug brigade, gorging on blood for survival. The **Rocky Mountain wood tick** swells to many times its original size after a grand feast. **Bloated on blood**, the sucker drops off its weakened host.

At home in the higher ground of Colorado, the Rocky Mountain wood tick (*Dermacentor andersoni*) is a three-host species. It feeds three times in its three-year lifetime—as a newly hatched larva, as a nymph, and as an adult. While small creatures suffice for its first two feeds, this tick's last supper features deer, sheep, or even people!

> An adult wood tick can **live for up to 600 days** without feeding.

The adult wood tick is armed and dangerous, with a hard shell and a ruthless bite. ......

Before

📷 FAST FACTS

Eggs → Larva → Nymph → Adult

Rocky Mountain wood ticks are best avoided. At all stages in their life cycle, they can transmit tick-borne diseases to humans, cats, and dogs. In most cases, the victim has just 24 hours to remove the tick from the skin (by grasping it with blunt tweezers) before the body is infected

The tick feeds on its host and grows until it is fully engorged with blood.

Ticks are arachnids— closely related to spiders. There are up to 900 species of tick.

After

MIGHTY MICROBUG

The tardigrade is only 0.04 in (1 mm) long, but virtually indestructible. Dropped in boiling water or left in frozen ice, this little fighter won't flinch. Remove its water supply for a decade or launch it into space, and there's still no harm done.

Pouncing parasites

Parasites need **no invitation**. These organisms find a **host organism**, attach themselves to it, and **reap all the benefits**.

Tongue-tied
Inside the mouth of this pink anemonefish is a tongue-eating louse parasite. *Cymothoa exigua* enters through the fish's gills, latches onto its tongue, and settles in for a feast. When the tongue is all eaten up, the louse itself serves as a replacement.

The frog and the flatworm
Parasitic flatworms give tadpoles a terrible time, forcing themselves into the tissue that will later become frog's legs. The adult frog ends up with deformed, missing, or extra limbs.

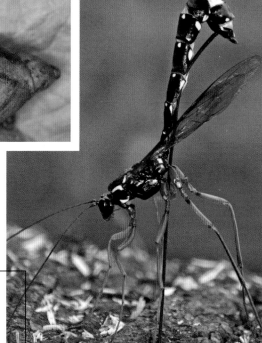

Shell shock
The *Leucochloridium paradoxum* flatworm infests the digestive systems of birds and passes to snails feeding on bird droppings. The parasite moves to the snail's tentacles where it is mistaken for caterpillars by hungry birds, and the cycle continues.

Hatching a plan
The female sabre wasp lays its eggs on the larvae of the wood wasp using its large ovipositor to drill into infested wood. When the eggs hatch into larvae, they eat their hosts alive.

Parasite for sore eyes

Blink and you'll miss them, but **minuscule parasites** have taken up residence on your **eyelashes**. Here, they've found a comfortable home and an **endless food supply** without even an invite. And the older you get, the more mites come to stay!

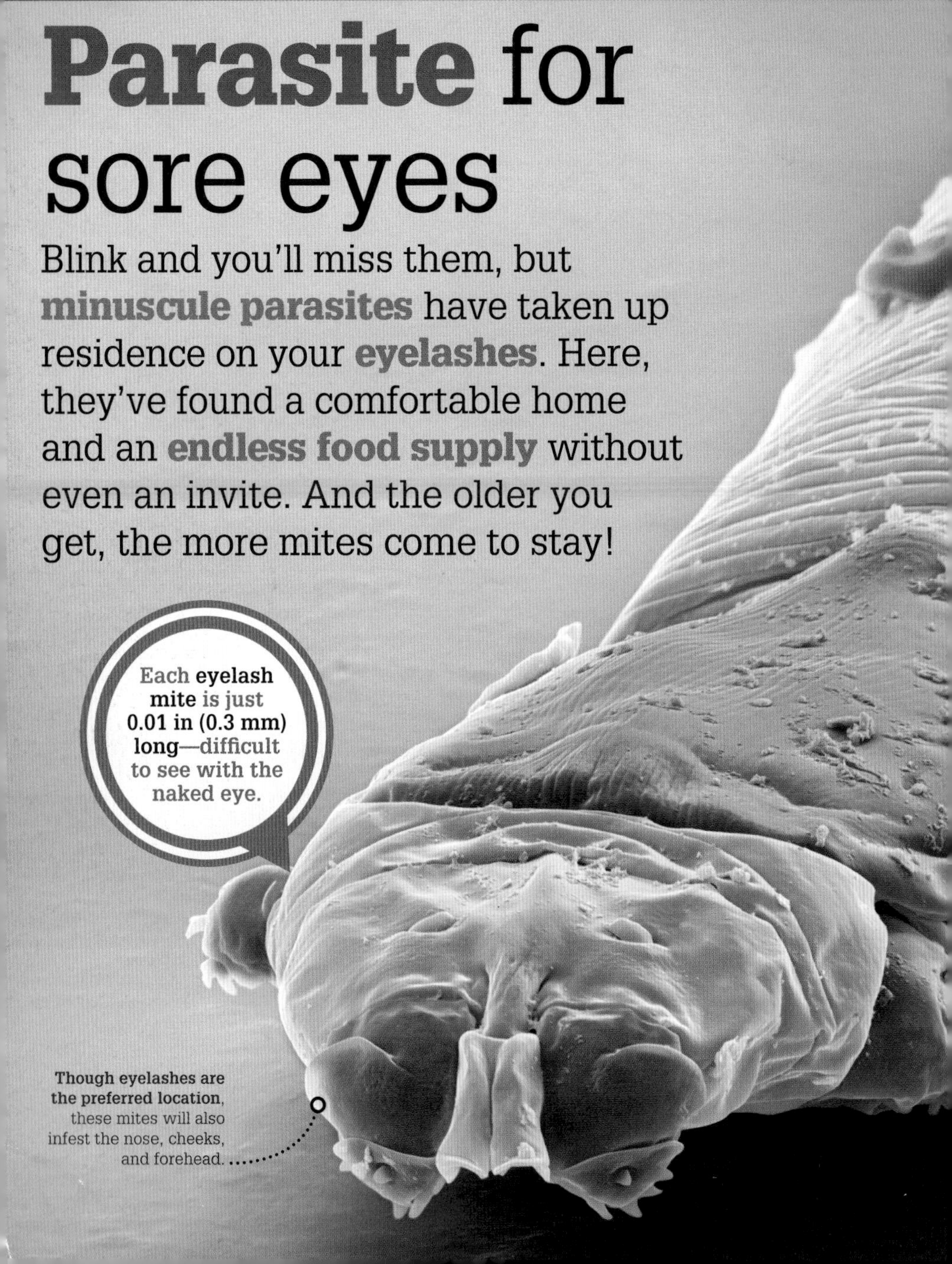

Each **eyelash mite** is just **0.01 in (0.3 mm) long**—difficult to see with the naked eye.

Though eyelashes are the preferred location, these mites will also infest the nose, cheeks, and forehead.

FAST FACTS

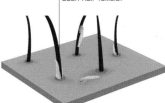

Several mites occupy each hair follicle.

Despite its grim appearance, this worm-like mite is harmless. Some scientists claim eyelash mites actually do good because they keep follicles clean. The mites spend most of their time facedown in hair follicles, clearing harmful dirt.

Eyelash mites, or *Demodex folliculorum*, are skin scavengers that bury themselves facedown in hair follicles to feast on the dead cells and oily secretions. Older people have oilier skin and weaker immune systems, so greater numbers of mites congregate on their eyelashes. Babies are born with no parasites, but impurities build up on the skin over time.

SKIN STALKERS

Another uninvited guest is the dust mite. Visible as tiny specks of dust, these mites thrive on dead skin flakes, which constantly fall off people. These troublemakers are a common cause of sneezes and asthma.

When ice attacks

Forget the **thunderous roars** of a violent storm—a less dramatic storm produces the most **spectacular** scenes. **Ice storms** happen when **supercooled rain** freezes as it hits the ground, transforming the landscape into a **frozen fairy-tale world**.

This storm only lasted **five minutes**, but it was enough to turn **cars and trees** into ice statues.

STORM DAMAGE

The crust of frozen rain that coats everything after an ice storm can be so thick and heavy that it makes structures like these electricity pylons collapse.

FAST FACTS

Warm air

Cold air

Rain
When frozen precipitation passes through warm air, it melts and falls to the ground as rain.

Freezing rain
If frozen precipitation melts in warm air, but cools rapidly as it nears the ground, it freezes on contact.

Sleet
If frozen precipitation thaws in shallow warm air, it re-freezes as sleet before it hits the ground.

Snow
When frozen precipitation falls through cold air, it reaches the surface as snow.

Icicles dangling from these tree branches follow the direction of the wind blowing in from Lake Geneva.

Roads and pavement become a treacherous ice rink.

Ice storms are rare events that occur when rain falls through warm air and meets cold air near the ground. The rain freezes on impact, covering everything in a thick, frosty coating. Switzerland's Lake Geneva experienced this ice storm in 2012.

Sailing stones

Death Valley is the US's hottest spot. This remote desert landscape provides a **perfect backdrop** for science-fiction blockbusters such as *Star Wars*, but something stranger than fiction happens here. Heavy rocks **inexplicably move around**. From magnetic fields to alien activity, theories abounded. Finally, we learned the truth.

Since 1948 scientific research has left no stone unturned. The breakthrough came in 2014, when stones were seen moving on camera. Floating ice proved to be the mischief-maker. On cold nights, thin sheets of ice develop, which then melt down into smaller pieces in the daytime sunshine. Wind pushes the ice along, carrying the rocks with it and depositing them elsewhere.

Each rock travels 6–20 ft (2–6 m) per minute, but in the desert this motion is hard to notice with the naked eye.

STONE COMMANDMENTS

These granite slabs in Elbert County, Georgia, are a mystery set in stone. Known as the Georgia Guidestones, they appeared in 1979 engraved with 10 guidelines for people to follow, which include avoiding useless officials and leaving room for nature. No one knows who wrote the list or who placed the stones.

Despite its name, Death Valley is home to more than 400 species of animal.

Early theories suggested that **strong winds** were responsible for moving the stones. But hurricane-force gusts would be needed to overcome the weight of the heavy rocks.

Racetrack Playa is a dry lake in Death Valley, dotted with large rocks that have fallen onto the plain from the surrounding mountains.

The moving stones can weigh more than 660 lb (300 kg), with some making tight turns and switching direction.

FAST FACTS

A floating sheet of ice is pushed along by wind.

Caught in the ice, the rock moves forward.

Wind

The weight of the stone leaves a trail behind.

Shallow water

Rainfall creates a shallow pool in the playa, which then freezes over as the temperature drops. A swift rise in temperature breaks up the ice into smaller, floating sheets. Wind then pushes the ice sheets over the pond. Any rocks caught in the ice sheet are easily carried along by the buoyant ice, inscribing a trail in the mud as they go.

Whipping up a dust storm

The incredible **power of nature** is seen when a violent dust storm blows up, filling the skies with inescapable banks of **suffocating cloud**. Tons of whirling sand or soil are swept along by high winds, leaving a **trail of devastation** behind.

FAST FACTS

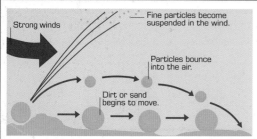

Fine particles become suspended in the wind.

Strong winds

Particles bounce into the air.

Dirt or sand begins to move.

Strong winds whip up particles of dust or sand. The pieces move along the ground, then begin to jump into the air. As they break up into smaller pieces, they are carried off by the wind.

Dust storms are most likely to occur during droughts, when sand or soil is loose and dry. Carried on the wind, billowing dust clouds can envelop entire cities, choking the inhabitants and damaging buildings. This huge dust cloud engulfed the desert city of Riyadh, Saudi Arabia, in March 2009. After the storm passed, parts of the city were left beneath several tons of sand.

DUST DEVILS

Resembling mini tornadoes, dust devils are small-scale whirlwinds, spinning dust in a vertical column of air over the ground. They are less dangerous than their name suggests, usually lasting only a few minutes and rarely causing any damage.

This massive storm on **March 10, 2009,** reduced **visibility** in Riyadh to **zero**.

Flights were grounded at Riyadh's airport as the control tower and runways were blanketed in thick dust.

When lightning strikes

No matter how long you keep staring and guessing, these **oddball objects** are almost impossible to fathom. Called **fulgurites**, they are the **remarkable and rare** result of what can happen when lightning strikes planet Earth.

ETERNAL STORM

There is never any calm before the storm at Venezuela's Catatumbo River. Thanks to a unique bank of storm clouds, an "everlasting storm" rages here, producing 1.2 million lightning strikes a year. Known as Catatumbo lightning, this incredible light show is visible 250 miles (400 km) away.

A fulgurite is formed when a lightning bolt with a minimum temperature of 3,270°F (1,800°C) strikes sand or rock. Heat melts the substance on impact, fusing the grains into natural glass tubes that follow the branching structure of the lightning bolt deep underground. Over time, the sand around the fulgurite shifts, exposing the fragile tube. Most fulgurites are made from sand, reflected in the unusually high number in the Sahara Desert.

With its branch-like formation, this sand fulgurite has a rough exterior covered in sand particles, but its interior is smooth and resembles glass.

Fulgurite comes from the Latin word for "thunderbolt."

Sand cools and solidifies quickly after the lightning strike to create the fulgurite. Its size depends on the power of the strike and the depth of the sand.

FAST FACTS

The longest fulgurite on record was dug up by researchers from the University of Florida in 1996. This impressive tube had two branches, the longest of which was about 16 ft (5 m) long.

Fulgurites are very fragile, so great care must be taken when digging them up.

The fulgurite is formed underground.

The forked shape of the fulgurite shows the lightning's path.

Super storms

Most thunderstorms develop from **updraughts of rising air**, with the most violent and speedy ones called **supercells**. These long-lasting storms are rare but deadly—they can **unleash havoc** in the form of whirling tornadoes, giant hailstones, punishing winds, and flash floods. Take cover!

Earth experiences about 45,000 thunderstorms a day, but only a few of these are supercells, the worst of all storms. Created by rapidly rotating updrafts of warm, moist air, these super storms carry huge amounts of water and bring extreme weather. The top of the thunderclouds can reach as high as 10 miles (16 km) into the air, while the base may be only 1,640 ft (500 m) above the ground.

Foreboding dark cumulonimbus clouds congregate in the skies before a supercell storm.

A supercell storm can last for two to six hours, often leaving behind considerable damage.

FAST FACTS

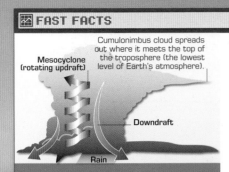

Mesocyclone (rotating updraft)

Cumulonimbus cloud spreads out where it meets the top of the troposphere (the lowest level of Earth's atmosphere).

Downdraft

Rain

Thunderstorms are formed by warm updrafts rising to create cumulonimbus clouds. Cold rain drags air down, creating a cold downdraft. When there is more downdraft than updraft, the storm fizzles out. In a supercell the updrafts and downdrafts are in balance, so the storm can keep going for hours. The mesocyclone (rapidly rotating updraft) at the storm's core carries huge amounts of water upward so the cloud grows bigger and bigger.

Lightning is about **54,000°F (30,000°C)**—hotter than the surface of the sun.

BALL LIGHTNING

During a supercell storm, other odd things can happen. Luminous, ball-shaped objects have appeared a few yards above the ground, bouncing around in a random pattern. Scientists can't agree on the reason for this phenomenon, known as ball lightning.

Weird weather

Extreme weather can be **challenging** for meteorologists to predict, and the consequences are often **devastating**.

Twisting tornado
More than 1,200 tornadoes rip across the US every year, traveling up to 200 mph (320 kph) and leaving trails of devastation behind them. Canada has the second highest number—this one is twisting across Elie, Manitoba.

Killer Katrina
When Hurricane Katrina tore across Florida in 2005, it became the US's costliest natural disaster. Winds topped 175 mph (280 kph) and nearly 2,000 people died.

Wild waves
Triggered by a huge offshore earthquake, the Indian Ocean tsunami on December 26, 2004, occurred without warning and heaped havoc on southern Asia. Giant waves devastated coastal communities and killed more than 200,000 people, displacing thousands more.

Heavy hail
In 2003 a thunderstorm in Moses, New Mexico, produced hailstones the size of golf balls. Huge hail can easily smash car windshields and injure people on the ground.

Deadly shower
All sorts of things have fallen from the skies, including frogs, bats, fish, insects, jellyfish, and worms. Strong winds can take creatures from shallow ponds and carry them until they fall back down to Earth. In 2011 about 1,000 dead birds mysteriously rained over Arkansas.

Lava and lightning

One of nature's most **explosive** combinations occurs when an **erupting volcano** generates an **electrical storm**. The reason for this **lightning bolt** out of the blue is still not fully understood.

EXPLODING PIZZA

The most explosive place in the solar system is Io, one of Jupiter's moons. The crater-faced surface earned Io the nickname "pizza moon." Io has hundreds of active volcanoes, and volcanic plumes can rise up to 186 miles (300 km) above its surface.

At least **150 episodes** of **volcanic lightning** have been documented over the last **200 years.**

Lightning is caused by a build up of static electric charges. Scientists are not sure what creates the charge during a volcanic eruption, but they think that hot ash particles in the volcanic cloud may rub together, producing a charge of static that triggers sparks of lightning. This is similar to what happens inside storm clouds, where ice particles collide and create a charge.

Volcanic lightning illuminates a cloud of ash and lava spewing from Japan's Sakurajima volcano in January 2013.

FAST FACTS

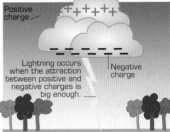

Positive charge

Lightning occurs when the attraction between positive and negative charges is big enough.

Negative charge

The negative charge at the base of the cloud causes a positive charge on the ground.

When ice particles in a storm cloud rub together, they gain electrons (becoming negatively charged) or lose electrons (becoming positively charged). The positively charged particles accumulate at the top of the cloud, while the negatively charged ones settle at the bottom. When the difference in charge becomes great enough, the energy is discharged as lightning.

UFO clouds

Hovering like a **flying saucer** in the sky, these amazing **layered** cloud formations are called **lenticular** (lentil-shaped) **clouds**. They form near **mountain ranges**, where mountains disturb the airflow and create **pressure waves**.

As air flows through and exits the rear of the cloud, the cloud droplets in the air evaporate, becoming water vapor. Because water vapor is an invisible part of the air, the cloud vanishes here.

CLOUD COVER

One of the world's cloudiest places is South Africa's Prince Edward Islands, with about 800 hours of sunshine all year. Sun lovers should go to Yuma in Arizona, which has more than 4,000 hours of sunshine annually.

The cloud's layers reveal the different layers of air flow in the atmosphere. Each layer of air forms a layer of the cloud.

Stacked like **pancakes**, each **lentil-shaped** layer of cloud forms on top of **layers of air**.

Locals in Yorkshire, England, were stunned when this curious lenticular cloud appeared in 2011. It was created by the Pennines—the hills forming the country's backbone. Lenticular clouds are a common sight in very mountainous areas, such as the Himalayas, Andes, and Rocky Mountains.

The cloud's base forms where the temperature is cold enough for moisture in the air to condense and form cloud. Below this level, the air is warm, so its moisture stays as invisible vapor.

FAST FACTS

Pressure waves form as air flows over mountains and is forced upward. This creates waves in the same way as a pebble creates ripples in a pond. Lenticular clouds form at the top of the waves, where the air is cool.

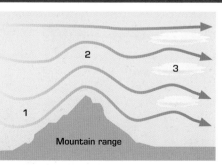

Mountain range

1 Air is forced up and over the mountain range.

2 Air from below disturbs air above and creates waves.

3 Clouds form at the crest of each wave.

IT CAN'T BE TRUE!

Have you ever wondered how big the hugest hailstone is? Or which chili pepper is the hottest? Discover the answers to the important questions about the tallest, biggest, most extraordinary objects in our universe, all explained using eye-popping visual comparisons. You'll never see the world the same way again.

Along the Tateyama Kurobe Alpine Route in Japan the snow is so deep it forms towering cliffs an incredible 66 ft (20 m) high when diggers cut through in the spring.

How **big** is the **Sun?**

The average **diameter** of the **Sun** is **864,337 miles** (1,391,016 km). It is more than **333,000 times** the mass of the **Earth.**

You could fit **109 Earths** across the diameter of the Sun.

SUNSPOTS

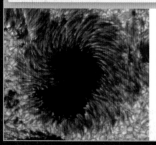

Sunspots are areas where a strong magnetic field stops hot gas reaching the surface. When sunspot numbers increase every 11 years, the Sun's intense magnetic activity can affect radio signals on Earth.

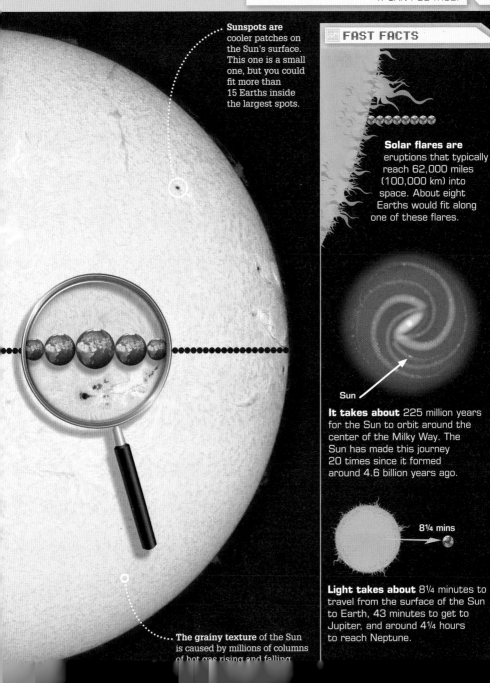

Sunspots are cooler patches on the Sun's surface. This one is a small one, but you could fit more than 15 Earths inside the largest spots.

Solar flares are eruptions that typically reach 62,000 miles (100,000 km) into space. About eight Earths would fit along one of these flares.

Sun

It takes about 225 million years for the Sun to orbit around the center of the Milky Way. The Sun has made this journey 20 times since it formed around 4.6 billion years ago.

8¼ mins

Light takes about 8¼ minutes to travel from the surface of the Sun to Earth, 43 minutes to get to Jupiter, and around 4¼ hours to reach Neptune.

The grainy texture of the Sun is caused by millions of columns of hot gas rising and falling.

6

How **big** is the **Moon?**

The **Moon's diameter** is **2,159 miles** (3,475 km), **one-quarter** the size of **Earth's**. Its surface area is **13 times smaller.**

The Copernicus Crater, one of the Moon's largest, measures 58 miles (93 km) across.

Australia

A PERFECT FIT

The Sun is 400 times the diameter of the Moon, but, by an amazing coincidence, it is also 400 times farther from the Earth. This means that seen from the Earth during an eclipse, the Sun and the Moon appear to be exactly the same size.

The Moon is the fifth-largest satellite in the solar system, after three of Jupiter's moons and one of Saturn's. It is the solar system's largest satellite relative to its planet. It doesn't usually hover above Australia, but orbits at a much more distant 238,854 miles (384,399 km) from the Earth.

The Sea of Tranquility is a flat plain of lava that solidified around 4 billion years ago. It is a little larger than the British Isles.

The **Moon** is almost as wide as **Australia**, which is 2,475 miles (3,983 km) across at its widest point.

Earth measures 7,926 miles (12,756 km) across at the equator. Four Moons could line up across it.

If there were no gaps, 50 Moons could fit inside the globe.

It would take 80 Moons to balance the scales against one Earth. The Earth is so much heavier because its core is solid iron and as wide as two Moon...

How **big** are the **planets?**

The **planets** in our solar system **vary in size.** Some are **small and rocky**, while others are **enormous balls of gas.**

POISONOUS VENUS

Venus is almost the same size and mass as Earth, but it is very different. Venus has a thick, poisonous atmosphere and a surface temperature of 867°F (464°C), which is hot enough to melt lead.

Jupiter, the biggest planet, measures 86,888 miles (139,833 km) across. It is made mainly of clouds of swirling gas.

The Earth is 7,918 miles (12,742 km) in diameter on average, although like most planets, it is slightly fatter around the equator. It is the largest of the rocky planets.

~~ FAST FACTS

Venus and Uranus spin in the opposite direction from the other planets. Uranus also rotates on its side, so it appears to spin clockwise or counterclockwise, depending on which pole you're looking at.

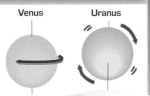

Venus   Uranus

Saturn is the second biggest planet, at 72,367 miles (116,464 km) in diameter. It is made mainly of the gases hydrogen and helium.

Saturn's rings are made up of dust, rock, and ice. They extend 174,000 miles (280,000 km) out, but are just over half a mile (1 km) thick.

Uranus is 31,518 miles (50,724 km) in diameter and is the farthest planet you can see with the naked eye. It is mostly made of gas, but possibly has an icy core.

Neptune is made of very cold gas. The farthest planet from the Sun, it has a diameter of 30,598 miles (49,244 km).

Venus is a rocky planet and, at 7,521 miles (12,104 km) across, is nearly as big as the Earth.

Mars measures 4,225 miles (6,799 km) across. It is known as the "red planet" because of the color of its rusty, iron-rich rocks.

Mercury is the smallest planet, just 3,032 miles (4,879 km) across. It lies the closest to the Sun and is made of rock.

Mercury is 29 times smaller around its equator than **Jupiter**.

How **big** are the **planets' moons?**

The two **largest moons** in the **solar system** are just over **3,100 miles** (5,000 km) across.

Titan is the only place in the solar system other than Earth to have lakes—although they are made of liquid methane and ethane.

Our **Moon** is the fifth largest, after Jupiter's **Ganymede, Callisto, and Io** and Saturn's **Titan.**

Titan
3,200 miles
(5,150 km)

Rhea
950 miles
(1,529 km)

Iapetus
914 miles
(1,471 km)

Dione
698 miles
(1,123 km)

Tethys
662 miles
(1,066 km)

Enceladus
313 miles
(504 km)

Mimas
246 miles (396 km)

SATURN

The Moon
2,159 miles (3,475 km)

EARTH

📊 FAST FACTS

So far, 67 moons have been discovered around Jupiter—the most of any planet. Saturn is second with 62. Uranus has 27 moons, Neptune has 13, Mars has two, and Earth has just one. Venus and Mercury have none.

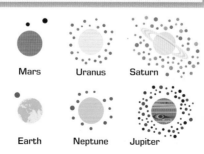

Mars

Uranus

Saturn

Earth

Neptune

Jupiter

Ganymede is the largest moon in the solar system— it is bigger than Mercury and three quarters the size of Mars.

Ganymede
3,270 miles
(5,262 km)

HYPERION

Larger moons usually have enough gravity to pull their material into a sphere, or ball shape. Saturn's small moon Hyperion does not have enough gravity, and so its shape is more like a potato.

Callisto
2,995 miles
(4,821 km)

Triton
1,682 miles
(2,707 km)

Europa
1,940 miles
(3,122 km)

NEPTUNE

Io
2,264 miles
(3,643 km)

JUPITER

Titania
980 miles
(1,578 km)

Oberon
946 miles
(1,523 km)

Both of Mars's tiny moons are possibly ex-asteroids, captured by Mars from the nearby asteroid belt.

Ariel
719 miles
(1,158 km)

Umbriel
726 miles
(1,169 km)

Miranda
293 miles
(472 km)

Deimos
8 miles (12 km)

Phobos
14 miles (22 km)

MARS

URANUS

There are 173 moons orbiting the major planets in the solar system, although new ones are being discovered all the time. Pictured here are each of the planets' major moons. Moons also orbit some dwarf planets, such as Pluto, and even some asteroids.

FAST FACTS

Although Saturn is the second biggest planet, it is not very dense. If you could fill with water a bathtub big enough, Saturn would float. All the other planets, including Jupiter, would sink to the bottom.

Ganymede   Mercury   Moon

Jupiter has at least 67 moons. The biggest, Ganymede, is also the largest moon in the solar system. It is bigger than the planet Mercury and our own Moon.

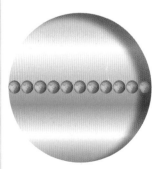

Around 11 Earths would fit across Jupiter's diameter.

Jupiter is made largely of gas, with a small rocky core. It is around two and a half times the combined mass of all the other planets put together.

Bands of cloud are created as Jupiter spins. It rotates once every 10 hours, faster than all the other planets.

How **big** is **Jupiter?**

More than **1,320 Earths** would fit inside **Jupiter.**

The **biggest planet** in the solar system is **Jupiter.** It has a **diameter** of **86,888 miles** (139,833 km), a **circumference** of **272,967 miles** (439,298 km) and its total **volume** is **343 trillion cu miles** (1,431 trillion cu km).

GREAT RED SPOT

The Great Red Spot is an enormous storm raging in the atmosphere of Jupiter. It is more than 12,000 miles (20,000 km) wide. You could fit two or three Earths inside it.

How **big** is an **asteroid?**

This mountain **is** one of the tallest peaks in the solar system.

Asteroids range from rocks a few **hundreds of feet** across to the giants **Vesta** (**356 miles**/573 km across) and **Ceres** (**590 miles**/950 km across). **Ceres** is now also classed as a **dwarf planet.**

United States

CHELYABINSK METEOR

If an asteroid enters the Earth's atmosphere, it is called a meteor. In 2013, a meteor about 56 ft (17 m) wide exploded over Russia, shattering windows and damaging buildings with its shock wave.

The chances of something the size of Vesta being on a collision course with Earth are very slim. If it did hit our planet, the impact would be so catastrophic that no life would survive. The asteroid that killed the dinosaurs 65 million years ago was no more than 9 miles (15 km) across.

The surface of Vesta was studied in detail when the *Dawn* spacecraft spent a year orbiting the asteroid in 2011. Dawn revealed the surface to be covered in grooves and craters.

This row of three big craters has been nicknamed the "snowman craters." The snowman's head is facing downward here.

Vesta is as wide as the entire Florida peninsula is long.

Florida

The Bahamas

1 Ceres
2 Pallas
3 Juno
4 Vesta
5 Astraea
6 Hebe
7 Iris
8 Flora
9 Metis
10 Hygiea

The Moon

The first 10 asteroids to be discovered were given the numbers 1–10 as part of their name. Even the biggest, Ceres, is much smaller than the Moon.

Asteroid Belt
Jupiter
Mars
Earth
Mercury
Venus

The Asteroid Belt between Jupiter and Mars contains millions of different-sized asteroids orbiting the Sun.

Dactyl 4,600 ft (1.4 km) across

Ida 33 miles (54 km) long

Some asteroids have moons. In 1994, for instance, scientists discovered that the asteroid Ida had a small moon, which they named Dactyl.

How **big** is a **comet?**

A comet's **nucleus** is **small**, but the **dust** and **gases** that surround it (the **coma**) can be **60,000 miles** (100,000 km) across. Amazingly, the **tail** can be many **millions of miles** long.

CRASH-LANDING

Most comets go around the Sun, but some are captured by Jupiter's massive gravitational pull. In July 1994, comet Shoemaker-Levy 9 broke into pieces and the fragments slammed into Jupiter, leaving a line of dark spots where they hit its atmosphere.

Jupiter
86,888 miles
(139,833 km) across

The tail is made of very thin, glowing gas. There is more matter in 1 cu mm of air than there is in ¼ cu mile (1 cu km) of a comet's tail.

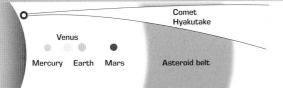

Venus

Mercury   Earth   Mars

Comet
Hyakutake

Asteroid belt

Jupiter

The longest tail ever seen was that of comet Hyakutake in 1996. It was at least 360 million miles (570 million km) long and reached to the outer limits of the asteroid belt.

The nucleus of a comet usually measures less than 6 miles (10 km) in diameter. However, it is surrounded by an enormous coma of dust and gases.

A comet's **coma** can spread nearly as wide as **Jupiter, the solar system's** largest planet.

Comets spend most of their lives as small, icy bodies orbiting in the outer regions of the solar system. The orbits of some comets, however, send them hurtling inwards. As a comet gets close to the Sun, its ice turns into gas and is blown away from the nucleus by the solar wind, forming a tail.

Where is the biggest canyon?

The Valles Marineris on **Mars** is up to **4 miles** (7 km) **deep** and more than **2,500 miles** (4,000 km) **long**. The **Grand Canyon** would fit along its length **nine times**.

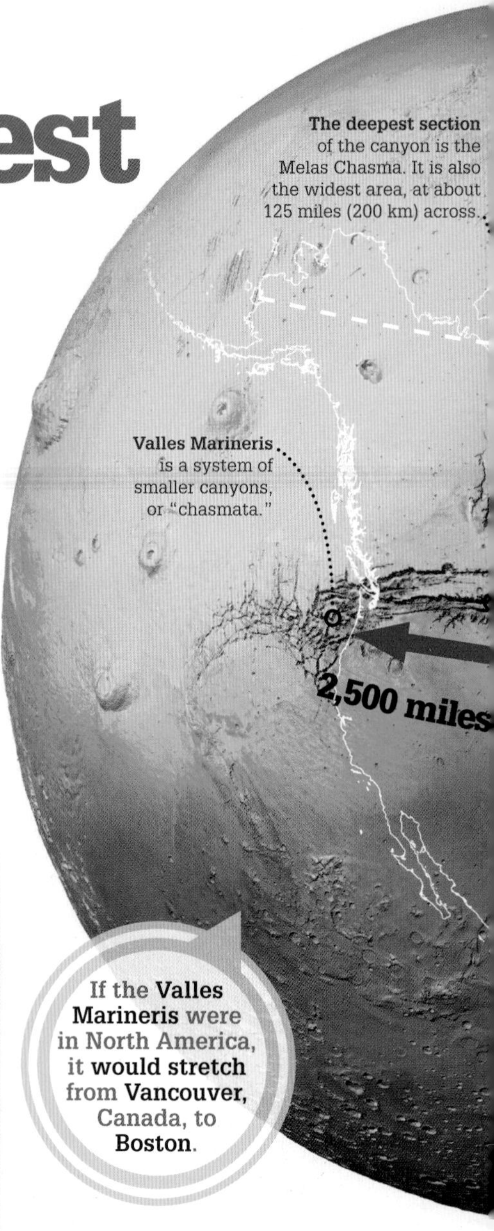

The deepest section of the canyon is the Melas Chasma. It is also the widest area, at about 125 miles (200 km) across.

Valles Marineris is a system of smaller canyons, or "chasmata."

2,500 miles

GRAND CANYON SKYWALK

The Grand Canyon Skywalk is a transparent viewing platfom. Visitors can see through the walkway to the bottom of the canyon 4,000 ft (1,200 m) below.

If the **Valles Marineris** were in North America, it **would stretch** from **Vancouver, Canada, to Boston**.

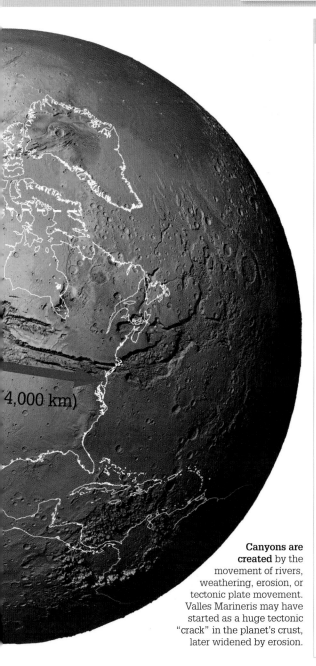

(4,000 km)

Canyons are
created by the
movement of rivers,
weathering, erosion, or
tectonic plate movement.
Valles Marineris may have
started as a huge tectonic
"crack" in the planet's crust,
later widened by erosion.

FAST FACTS

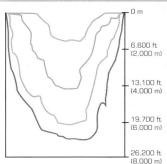

0 m

6,600 ft
(2,000 m)

13,100 ft
(4,000 m)

19,700 ft
(6,000 m)

26,200 ft
(8,000 m)

Valles Marineris (Mars)
22,965 ft (7,000 m)

Yarlung Tsangpo (Tibet, China)
19,685 ft (6,009 m)

Colca Canyon (Peru)
13,650 ft (4,160 m)

Grand Canyon (US)
5,249 ft (1,600 m)

The deepest known canyons on
Earth are the Yarlung Tsangpo and
the Kali Gandaki (in Nepal).

Yarlung Tsangpo (Tibet, China)
308 miles (496 km)

Grand Canyon (US)
277 miles (445 km)

Hell's Canyon (US)
125 miles (201 km)

Fish River Canyon (Namibia)
100 miles (160 km)

The longest canyon on Earth,
the Yarlung Tsangpo, is also the
world's biggest canyon. It was
cut through Tibet by the Yarlung
Tsangpo River, which becomes the
Brahmaputra River when it later
flows through India.

Solar system data

How long would it take a plane traveling at 560 mph (900 kph) to **reach each planet** from the Sun?

THE SIZE
OF THE SOLAR SYSTEM is equal to

100,000
times the distance from the Sun to the Earth.
Traveling at 186,282 miles per second (299,792 km per second), sunlight takes

8¼ minutes
to reach Earth from the Sun, and **555.5 days** to reach the edge of the solar system.

COMETS
The nucleus of a comet can range in size from
300 ft to 25 miles
(100 m to 40 km)

Comets formed at the same time as the rest of solar system, around

4.5
billion years ago. Like the planets, comets orbit the Sun.

When a comet gets near the Sun, its nucleus begins to melt, forming a **tail** of gas and dust that can

stre tch
for **millions of miles**.

A **LONG** DAY
Because Mercury spins very slowly and orbits so close to the Sun, its day (measuring 176 Earth days), is actually

longer
than its year, which lasts for 87.87 Earth days.

DAY LENGTH

A **day** is measured as the **time** it takes for a planet to **spin once on its axis** so that the Sun returns to the same spot in the sky.

Mercury: 176 Earth days
Venus: 117 Earth days
Mars: 24 hr 40 min
Jupiter: 9 hr 56 min
Saturn: 10 hr 33 min
Uranus: 17 hr 14 min
Neptune: 16 hr 6 min

This list measures day length in Earth days, hours, and minutes.

MERCURY 7.4 years

VENUS 13.7 years

EARTH 18.9 years

MARS 28.9 years

JUPITER 98.7 years

180.9 years
SATURN

URANUS 364.1 years

570.5 years
NEPTUNE

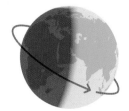

DEEP**PROBES**

11.48
BILLION MILES
(18.47 BILLION KM)

PIONEER 11
April 1973: Launched
December 1974: Jupiter flyby
September 1979: Saturn flyby
November 1995: Final contact received

8
BILLION MILES
(13 BILLION KM)

VOYAGER 1
September 1977: Launched
March 1979: Jupiter flyby
November 1980: Saturn flyby

2.78
BILLION MILES
(4.47 BILLION KM)

NEW HORIZONS
January 2006: Launched
February 2007: Jupiter flyby
July 2015: Pluto flyby

9.43
BILLION MILES
(15.18 BILLION KM)

9.9
BILLION MILES
(16 BILLION KM)

PIONEER 10
March 1972: Launched
First spacecraft to fly through asteroid belt, past Jupiter and through the orbit of Neptune

VOYAGER 2
August 1977: Launched
July 1979: Jupiter flyby
August 1981: Saturn flyby
January 1986: Uranus flyby
August 1989: Neptune flyby

2.5 3.5 5 6 7.5 8.5 10 11

DISTANCE FROM EARTH IN BILLIONS OF MILES

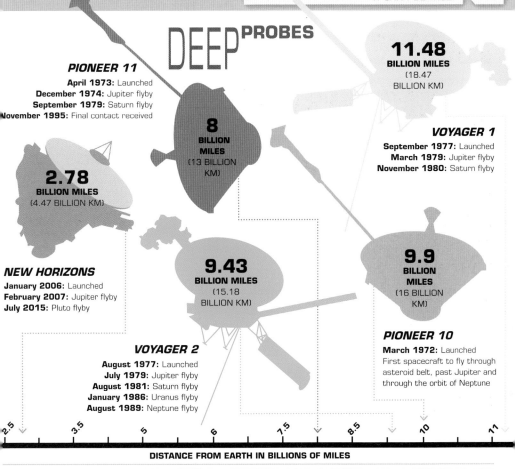

DWARF **PLANETS**

In addition to the eight large planets, the solar system is also home to a number of smaller objects known as **dwarf planets**. The biggest discovered so far are:

Pluto: radius
738 miles (1,187 km)

Eris: radius
723 miles (1,164 km)

2007 OR10: radius
477 miles (769 km)

EX⊙**PLANETS**

Ours is not the only solar system. Other stars are also orbited by large satellites known as **exoplanets**.

The exoplanet **HAT-p-32b** is 1,044 light-years from Earth and orbits a Sunlike star. Its **radius** is

twice that of Jupiter.
However, its **mass** is slightly

less than that of Jupiter.

The exoplanet **KOI-55.01**, 3,850 light-years from Earth, is **11 times**

denser

than Earth. It orbits its star, which is one-fifth the size of the Sun, every 5.8 hours—the **shortest orbit** of any known planet.

How **big** is the **biggest star?**

Hypergiant stars can be **hundreds of times** wider than the **Sun**. The **largest known star** is called **UY Scuti**, whose diameter is nearly **1.5 billion miles** (2.4 billion km).

UY Scuti's diameter is about **1,700 times bigger** than the Sun's.

FAST FACTS

If it were in the center of our solar system, UY Scuti would engulf all the inner, rocky planets, including Earth. It would even swallow Jupiter, so the innermost surviving planet would be Saturn! When our own Sun begins to die in 5 billion years, it will swell to become a red giant, growing beyond the present orbit of Earth.

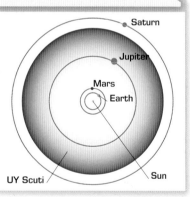

Saturn

Jupiter

Mars

Earth

UY Scuti

Sun

Aldebaran is a red giant star 67 light-years away and 44 times wider than the Sun.

Arcturus is a red giant 37 light-years away and 25 times wider than the Sun. It is the fourth-brightest star in the night sky.

When compared with giant, supergiant, and hypergiant stars, our own Sun appears tiny.

Sun

When large red giants die, their cores may collapse under their great gravity, then may explode with incredible force. These explosions are called supernovas, and they blow a star's matter into space as a cloud of dust and gas called a nebula. This one is the Crab Nebula, and it comes from a star that exploded like this in 1054 CE.

UY Scuti is a red hypergiant about 9,500 light-years away. It is 1,700 times wider than the Sun, but only 7–10 times heavier. Its outer layers are very thin—1,000 times thinner than Earth's atmosphere. UY Scuti is burning very brightly, producing about 340,000 times as much light as the Sun. The force of its burning is pushing its thin outer layers out into space.

Rigel is a blue-white supergiant 860 light-years away and around 75 times wider than the Sun. In spite of its distance from Earth, it is so luminous that it is still one of the brightest stars in our sky.

Neutron stars are among the most extreme places in the universe. Their temperature is more than 1.8 million °F (1 million °C) and some spin hundreds of times a second. Gravity on their surface is around 200 billion times stronger than it is on Earth.

A neutron star is the core of a giant star that has collapsed under its own gravity. The collapse squeezes the neutron star's matter into a minute space.

Earth Neutron star

Neutron stars shrink so much when they collapse that they pack a mass greater than the Sun into a sphere less than 12 miles (20 km) in diameter—about the size of a city. A neutron star's diameter is 600 times smaller than the Earth's.

Neutron stars appear a dim blue-white color. Because they are so hot, they give off little visible light. Instead of light, they shine with more powerful X-rays.

What is the heaviest stuff in the universe?

The **matter** in a **neutron star** is so dense that a piece the size of **sugar cube** weighs the same as all the **humans** on **Earth**.

PULSING STAR

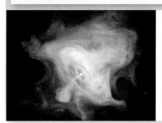

In the center of this whirling disk of hot matter is a neutron star blasting out a beam of radiation and a plume of hot gas. Thirty times every second, the beam points toward Earth, giving viewers a pulse of light.

A pinhead has a volume of around 1 cu mm. The matter in a neutron star is so dense that a pinhead-sized piece would weigh 1.1 million tons (1 million metric tons).

Pinhead-sized piece of neutron star material

A pinhead-sized blob of matter from a neutron star is as heavy as three Empire State Buildings.

The Empire State Building weighs 365,000 tons (331,000 metric tons), so three would weigh 1,095,000 tons (993,000 metric tons).

How **fast** is **light?**

It may seem to move instantly, but **light** takes time to get from place to place. In space, **light travels** at **671 million mph** (1,080,000,000 kph), or **186,282 miles** (299,792 km) in **1 second**.

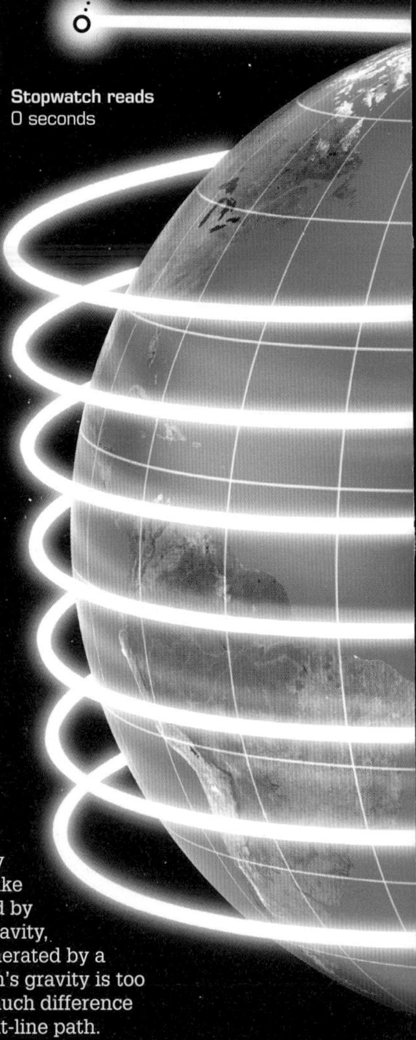

An imaginary light beam begins its journey

Stopwatch reads 0 seconds

FAST FACTS

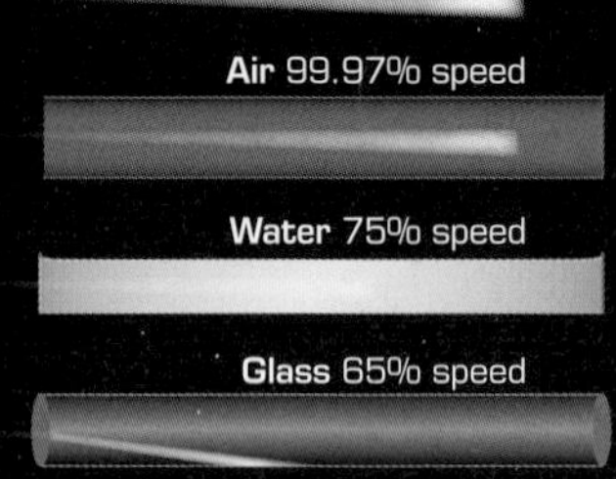

Vacuum 100% speed

Air 99.97% speed

Water 75% speed

Glass 65% speed

Light travels at a constant speed in a vacuum, but it slows down when there are particles in the way. In air, it travels at 99.97 percent of its speed in a vacuum, in water 75 percent, and in glass about 65 percent.

This picture shows light bending, but in reality, light only curves sharply like this when pulled by really intense gravity, such as that generated by a black hole. Earth's gravity is too weak to make much difference to light's straight-line path.

In just **1 second**, a beam of **light** would travel around **Earth** 7.5 times.

LUNAR LASER

A laser beam, traveling at the speed of light, takes 1.28 seconds to reach the Moon. From this, we can precisely measure the distance from the Earth to the Moon: 238,854 miles (384,399 km).

The light beam completes its 1-second journey more than 18,000 times quicker than the fastest-ever spacecraft launched—the *New Horizons* probe, which reached (36,373 mph/ 58,536 kph) as it left the Earth's atmosphere in 2006.

`00:01`

Stopwatch reads 1 second

How cold is space?

Temperatures in **outer space** can reach extremes of hot and cold, but the **average temperature**, far from any star, is -454.8°F (-270.4°C).

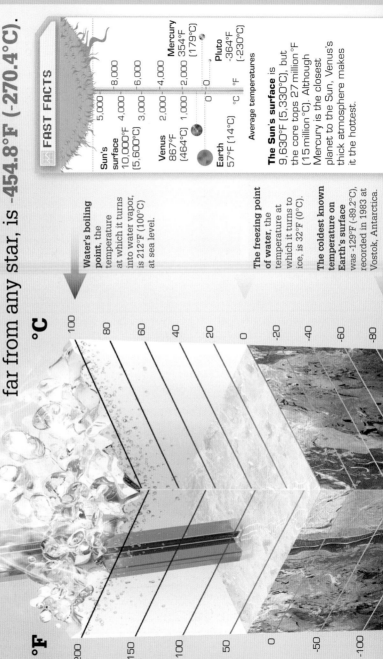

FAST FACTS

Sun's surface
10,000°F
(5,600°C)

5,000	
4,000	8,000
3,000	6,000
2,000	4,000
1,000	2,000
0	0
°C	°F

Venus
867°F
(464°C)

Mercury
354°F
(179°C)

Earth
57°F (14°C)

Pluto
-364°F
(-230°C)

Average temperatures

The Sun's surface is 9,630°F (5,330°C), but the core tops 27 million °F (15 million °C). Although Mercury is the closest planet to the Sun, Venus's thick atmosphere makes it the hottest.

Water's boiling point, the temperature at which it turns into water vapor, is 212°F (100°C) at sea level.

The freezing point of water, the temperature at which it turns to ice, is 32°F (0°C).

The coldest known temperature on Earth's surface was -129°F (-89.2°C), recorded in 1983 at Vostok, Antarctica.

°C
100
80
60
40
20
0
-20
-40
-60
-80

°F
200
150
100
50
0
-50
-100

The lowest temperature recorded in Earth's atmosphere was -225°F (-143°C), in a region called the mesopause, 50 miles (80 km) above the ground.

The coldest temperature in our solar system yet measured by people is -412.6°F (-247°C), in the permanently shadowed craters of the Moon.

The average temperature in space, shown by the blue line, is -454.8°F (-270.4°C). It is so cold because most of space is far from our Sun or any other stars.

Absolute zero, the coldest possible temperature, at which particles stop moving, is -459.67°F (-273.15°C). Nothing can be colder than this.

COLDER THAN SPACE

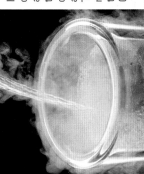

In a lab, scientists can create conditions even colder than any naturally occurring temperature. They have come within a billionth of a degree of absolute zero. They routinely condense nitrogen (the main gas in the atmosphere) into a liquid (left) at -320°F (-196°C).

-140
-160
-180
-200
-220
-240
-260
-273

-200
-250
-300
-350
-400
-450
-459

Space is on average 326.2°F (181.2°C) colder than the coldest temperature on Earth.

How **big** is the **universe?**

The universe is unimaginably vast. Distances are so huge that scientists measure them in **light-years**—the distance that light travels in one year.

The Milky Way, a disk-shaped spiral galaxy, contains the solar system. This galaxy is about 100,000 light-years across. One light-year is 5,879 billion miles (9,461 billion km).

The Sun is about 93 million miles (150 million km) from planet Earth.

FAST FACTS

ONE YEAR

J F M A
M J J A
S O N D

31

The universe is 13.77 billion years old. Humans have not been around for that long. If the universe were just a year old, *Homo sapiens* (humans) would have only emerged at 11:52 p.m. on New Year's Eve.

Our home, Earth, is a small planet measuring about 7,918 miles (12,742 km) across.

From top to bottom, South America stretches about 4,660 miles (7,500 km).

The solar system contains the Sun and the objects traveling around it, which include Earth, seven other planets, and many asteroids.

The orbit of Uranus, the solar system's second most distant planet, lies on average 1.78 billion miles (2.87 billion km) from the Sun.

THE MILKY WAY

Although disk-shaped, the Milky Way appears in our skies as a bright band. That's because Earth (and all stars visible without a telescope) sits within the disk.

The Andromeda galaxy is a large galaxy in the Local Group, a cluster of more than 50 galaxies.

The Local Group of galaxies takes up an area of space that is about 10 million light-years across. The Milky Way is a tiny part of the Local Group.

A supermassive black hole is thought to sit in the middle of the Milky Way. It contains as much mass as 4 million Suns.

The edge of the observable universe is 13.7 billion light-years away.

This image taken by the Hubble Telescope shows galaxies up to 13.7 billion light-years away. However, the universe has expanded since light left these galaxies, so they are now even farther away.

The red dots are the most distant galaxies that we can see.

Universe data

INSIDE A STAR

THE PHOTOSPHERE · · · ·
The part of the Sun
we see from Earth

Stars, such as our Sun,
come in many different
types and **sizes**, but
all work in largely the
same way. At their

c**O**re

atomic collisions take
place that create **huge
amounts of energy**.
This **energy** is then
transferred through
the star to its surface
and **out into space**.

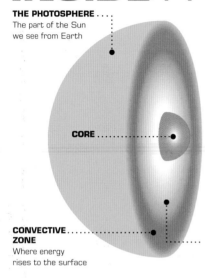

CORE · · · · · · · · · · · · · · ·

CONVECTIVE · · · · · · · · · · · · · ·
ZONE
Where energy
rises to the surface

RADIATIVE ZONE
Where energy shines
outward in the form of light

GALAXIES

There are four main types of galaxy:

SPIRAL

ELLIPTICAL

LENTICULAR

IRREGULAR

OLD
TIMER
The universe is believed to be **13.8** billion years old.

STAR
LIFE

How a star **ends its life** depends on its size and mass.
When an average Sunlike star begins to run out of fuel, it e**xpands**

**AVERAGE SUN-
LIKE STAR** → **RED GIANT** → **PLANETARY NEBULA**

MASSIVE STAR → **RED SUPERGIANT** → **SUPERNOVA**

to become a cooler, fainter star
known as a **red giant**. It eventually
sheds its outer layers, forming a
cloud of material called a **planetary
nebula**. More massive stars become
red supergiants, which eventually
tear themselves apart in gigantic
explosions known as **supernovas**.

THE SUN IN
5 BILLION
YEARS' TIME

······· THE SUN TODAY

BIG **SUNS** AND BIG
BANGS

When the **Sun dies**, in around **5 billion years' time**, it will expand to around 100 times its current width.

The most **massive** stars burn ferociously quickly and die out in just a few million years. But smaller stars, known as **red dwarfs**, can glow weakly for trillions of years. The massive star **Eta Carinae**, located 8,000 light-years from Earth, is due to **explode** as a supernova soon. When it does, it could be the

brightest

object in the sky after the Sun—bright enough to read by at night.

MILKY WAY

Our galaxy, the **Milky Way**, is a spiral around **100,000 light-years** across. It is believed to contain more than **200 billion stars**.

The nearest major galaxy to us, the **Andromeda galaxy**, is about 2.5 million light-years away. It is **260,000 light-years** across—more than twice the size of the Milky Way—and contains around **400 billion stars**.

TRAVELING AT
LIGHT SPEED

The **speed of light** is the fastest speed there is—**186,282 miles per second** (299,797 km per second). But the universe is so vast that, even traveling at this great speed, it can take a long time to travel around.

EARTH

MOON	**1.3** SECONDS	
MARS	**4** MINUTES	
JUPITER	**35** MINUTES	
NEPTUNE	**4** HOURS	
VOYAGER	**17** HOURS	
ALPHA CENTAURI (NEAREST STAR SYSTEM)	**4** YEARS	
ANDROMEDA (NEAREST MAJOR GALAXY)	**2.5** MILLION YEARS	

SECONDS

MINUTES

LIGHT-SPEED TRAVEL LINE

HOURS

YEARS

EDGE OF UNIVERSE

45.7
BILLION YEARS

Which is the biggest continent?

At **17,207,994 sq miles (44,568,500 sq km), Asia is** the **biggest** of the world's seven large landmasses, or **continents.**

Australasia has an area of 3,291,903 sq miles (8,525,989 sq km), and includes Australia, New Zealand, New Guinea, and some of the islands in between.

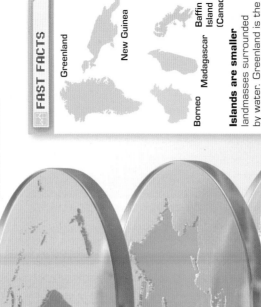

Europe has an area of 3,840,944 sq miles (9,948,000 sq km) and covers only 7 percent of the land surface and is only slightly bigger than Canada.

Antarctica covers an area of 5,405,430 sq miles (14,000,000 sq km). This landmass is almost entirely covered in ice.

A continent is usually a large mass of land that is separated from another by water. In fact, five of the seven continents are joined. Europe and Asia are sometimes considered as a single continent, Eurasia.

Asia covers about 30 percent of Earth's land surface.

South America has an area of 6,879,954 sq miles (17,819,000 sq km). This continent stretches from just above the Equator down to the Antarctic.

North America covers 9,449,078 sq miles (24,473,000 sq km). Greenland is part of this continent, although it belongs to Denmark.

Africa has an area of 11,608,161 sq miles (30,065,000 sq km). It covers an area more than three times bigger than the US.

Asia is a huge continent, and is home to about 60 percent of the world's population.

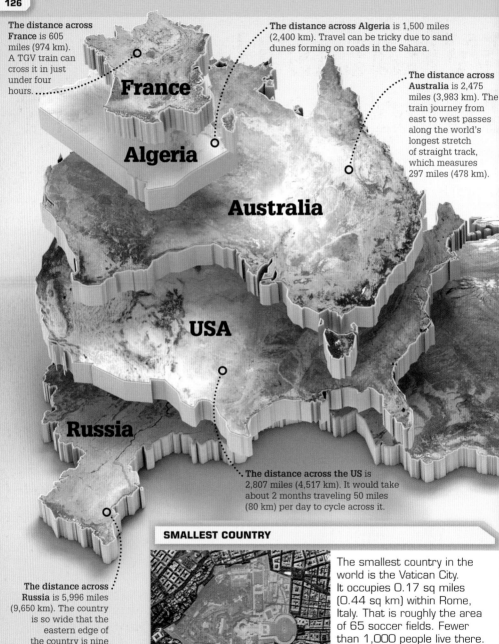

The distance across France is 605 miles (974 km). A TGV train can cross it in just under four hours.

The distance across Algeria is 1,500 miles (2,400 km). Travel can be tricky due to sand dunes forming on roads in the Sahara.

The distance across Australia is 2,475 miles (3,983 km). The train journey from east to west passes along the world's longest stretch of straight track, which measures 297 miles (478 km).

The distance across the US is 2,807 miles (4,517 km). It would take about 2 months traveling 50 miles (80 km) per day to cycle across it.

The distance across Russia is 5,996 miles (9,650 km). The country is so wide that the eastern edge of the country is nine hours ahead of the west.

France

Algeria

Australia

USA

Russia

SMALLEST COUNTRY

The smallest country in the world is the Vatican City. It occupies 0.17 sq miles (0.44 sq km) within Rome, Italy. That is roughly the area of 65 soccer fields. Fewer than 1,000 people live there.

What is the biggest country?

Russia stretches across **two continents** and covers **11.5 percent** of the **Earth's land surface.**

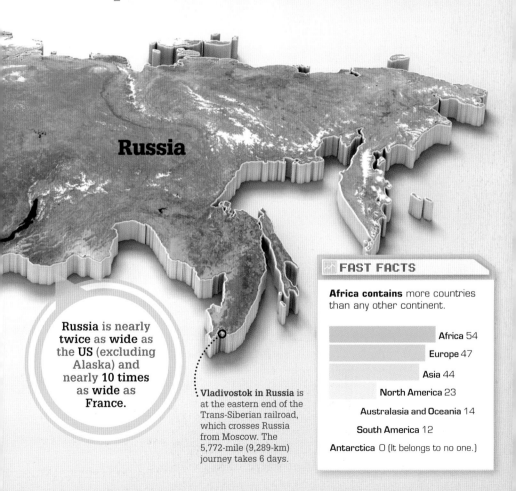

Russia

Russia is nearly twice as wide as the US (excluding Alaska) and nearly 10 times as wide as France.

Vladivostok in Russia is at the eastern end of the Trans-Siberian railroad, which crosses Russia from Moscow. The 5,772-mile (9,289-km) journey takes 6 days.

FAST FACTS

Africa contains more countries than any other continent.

Africa 54

Europe 47

Asia 44

North America 23

Australasia and Oceania 14

South America 12

Antarctica 0 (It belongs to no one.)

How **big** is the largest lake?

The water in **all five** of the North American Great Lakes combined **would not fill Lake Baikal.**

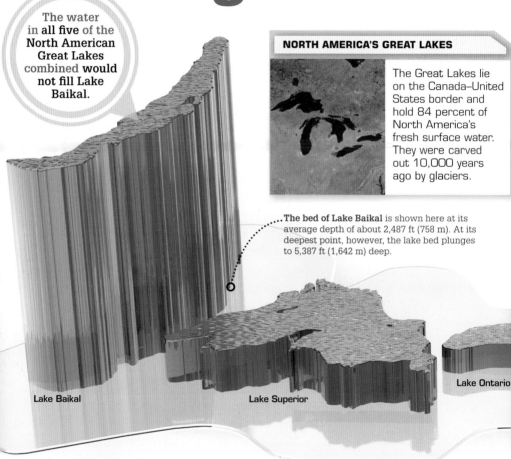

NORTH AMERICA'S GREAT LAKES

The Great Lakes lie on the Canada–United States border and hold 84 percent of North America's fresh surface water. They were carved out 10,000 years ago by glaciers.

The bed of Lake Baikal is shown here at its average depth of about 2,487 ft (758 m). At its deepest point, however, the lake bed plunges to 5,387 ft (1,642 m) deep.

Lake Baikal

Lake Superior

Lake Ontario

Lake Baikal contains roughly 20 percent of the world's unfrozen fresh surface water.

Lake Superior contains just over half the amount of water of Lake Baikal and is on average 482 ft (147 m) deep. It is the largest of the Great Lakes in terms of area, depth, and volume of water.

Lake Ontario is 282 ft (86 m) deep on average and Lake Baikal would fill it 15 times.

The **largest freshwater lake** in the world by volume is **Lake Baikal**, in Siberia. It contains around **6,238,500 billion gallons** (23,615,000 billion liters) of water.

FAST FACTS

Lake Baikal

Caspian Sea

The Caspian Sea, between Asia and Europe, is 12 times larger than Lake Baikal in area and contains three times as much water. It is salty and is all that remains of an ancient ocean. Experts think of it as an inland sea, rather than a lake.

Lake Superior

Ligeia Mare

Lake Michigan

Lake Huron

Saturn's moon, Titan, has several huge lakes made of liquid methane. Ligeia Mare is similar in size to one of the Great Lakes. Kraken Mare is even bigger, at around the size of the Caspian Sea.

Together, the Great Lakes cover an area more than seven times greater than that of Lake Baikal. But Lake Baikal holds more water because it is so deep. In fact, it's the deepest lake on Earth, and also the oldest. It was created some 25 million years ago, when Earth's crust pulled apart to create a deep valley, which filled with water.

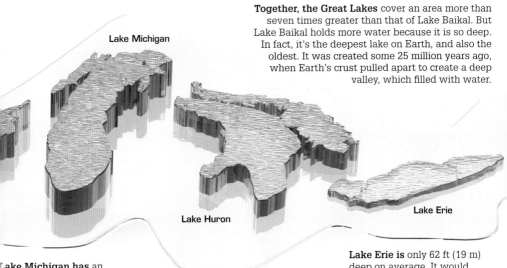

Lake Michigan

Lake Huron

Lake Erie

Lake Michigan has an average depth of 279 ft (85 m) and contains one-fifth the amount of water in Lake Baikal.

Lake Huron has an average depth of 194 ft (59 m) and one-seventh of the amount of water in Lake Baikal.

Lake Erie is only 62 ft (19 m) deep on average. It would take nearly 50 lakes this size to fill Lake Baikal.

What is the biggest river?

Along much of its length, the Amazon is 1–6 miles (1.6–10 km) wide in the dry season. In the rainy season, however, some parts expand to 30 miles (48 km) or more.

Although not as **long** as the **Nile**, the **Amazon** carries **far more water**. It empties **58 million gallons** (219 million liters) into the ocean every second—that's **one fifth** of all the **world's river water flow**.

FAST FACTS

The Amazon Basin is the area drained by the Amazon River. It is almost as big as Australia and is the largest river basin in the world. It covers 40 percent of South America, and all of it recieves heavy yearly rainfall, which swells the river with water.

The Pará River joins the Amazon at its mouth, broadening its estuary still farther.

The Amazon spreads out when it reaches the Atlantic Ocean and merges with the mouth of another wide river, the Pará. This image shows the region around this mouth or estuary—sometimes called "The Mouths of the Amazon."

Pará River

FLOODED RAIN FOREST

More than 1,100 tributaries feed directly into the Amazon, 15 of which are themselves more than 620 miles (1,000 km) long.

In the yearly rainy season, the Amazon River rises over 30 ft (9 m) and floods about 90,000 sq miles (240,000 sq km) of surrounding forest.

The Amazon Rain Forest, the world's largest rain forest, surrounds the river. It covers much of Brazil and parts of eight other countries.

Amazon River

London to Paris 214 miles (344 km)

The Amazon flows with such force that it sends a plume of fresh water about 250 miles (400 km) into the Atlantic. It floats on the ocean, so freshwater can be found on the surface even far out of sight of land.

The **mouth** of the Amazon is nearly **as wide as** the distance from **London** to **Paris.**

How **high** is the **tallest waterfall?**

The **tallest waterfall** in the world, **Angel Falls** in Venezuela is **3,212 ft** (979 m) **in height**. Known locally as **Kerepakupai Merú**, it found fame when US pilot **Jimmy Angel** discovered it in 1933.

Vinnufossen, Norway 2,837 ft (865 m)

Sutherland Falls, New Zealand 1,903 ft (580 m)

Surtherland Falls drops down the almost sheer side of a fjord—a valley carved by a glacier and flooded by the sea.

Victoria Falls, Zambia/Zimbabwe 354 ft (108 m)

Niagara Falls, US/Canada 167 ft (51 m)

The spray can be seen from 30 miles (48 km) away.

VICTORIA FALLS

Victoria Falls forms the largest continuous sheet of falling water in the world, at 1.1 miles (1.7 km) wide and 355 ft (108 m) tall.

Angel Falls,
Venezuela
3,212 ft (979 m)

FAST FACTS

Niagara Falls

Olympic
swimming pool

Niagara Falls, on the US–Canadian border, is the world's largest waterfall in terms of water flow. In just 1 second, 740,000 gallons (2.8 million liters) of water gush over the falls—enough to fill an Olympic-sized swimming pool.

In 1901, Ann Taylor became the first person to go over Niagara Falls in a barrel and survive to tell the tale. Of the 14 other people who have intentionally gone over the falls since, five did not survive the experience.

Angel Falls is formed by water tumbling down the side of one of the "tepuis," Venezuela's vertical-sided mountains. Here, it is pictured next to some of the world's other tall and famous waterfalls.

The Empire State Building measures 1,453 ft (443 m) tall.

Angel
Falls is
**more than
twice as tall**
as New York's
**Empire State
Building.**

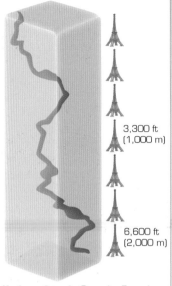

3,300 ft
(1,000 m)

6,600 ft
(2,000 m)

Krubera Cave in Georgia, Eurasia, is the world's deepest at 7,208 ft (2,197 m)—nearly as deep as seven Eiffel Towers.

An underground river runs through the first 1.5 miles (2.5 km) of the 5.5-mile (9-km) cave. There are thought to be more than 150 chambers in total.

How **big** is the **biggest** cave?

Deep in the **Vietnamese jungle** lies the **Hang Son Doong** cave—the **biggest** in the **world**. In places it is more than **650 ft** (200 m) **deep**.

Each of the sinkholes on the surface is up to 330 ft (100 m) across.

Hang Son Doong cave was not discovered until 1991 because it is hidden by thick jungle. The cave formed between 2 and 5 million years ago, when underground river water eroded away the limestone rock. In places where the rock was weak, the ceiling collapsed into giant sinkholes.

Six Towers of Pisa would fit in the **deepest shaft** if stacked one top of the other.

ROCK PILLARS

Stalagmites in the cave, like the "Hand of Dog" shown here, are so big that they make the man standing in the middle look tiny.

The two main chambers within the cave system have 100-ft (30-m) trees growing inside because the roofs fell in and let in enough light for plants to grow.

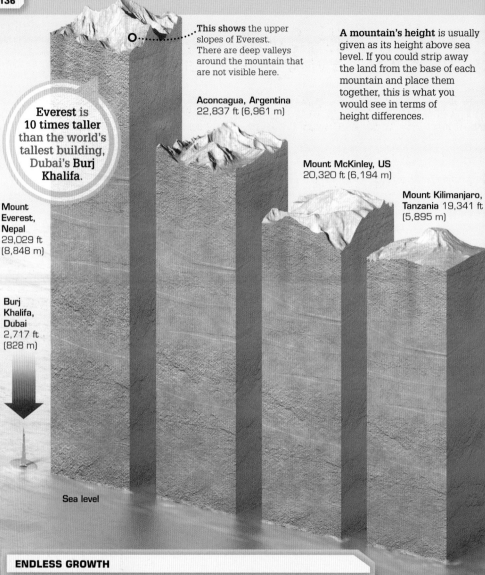

This shows the upper slopes of Everest. There are deep valleys around the mountain that are not visible here.

A mountain's height is usually given as its height above sea level. If you could strip away the land from the base of each mountain and place them together, this is what you would see in terms of height differences.

Aconcagua, Argentina 22,837 ft (6,961 m)

Mount McKinley, US 20,320 ft (6,194 m)

Mount Kilimanjaro, Tanzania 19,341 ft (5,895 m)

Everest is 10 times taller than the world's tallest building, Dubai's **Burj Khalifa**.

Mount Everest, Nepal 29,029 ft (8,848 m)

Burj Khalifa, Dubai 2,717 ft (828 m)

Sea level

ENDLESS GROWTH

Mount Everest was formed by two tectonic plates (sections of the Earth's crust) colliding. The two plates are still pushing together, so the mountain is growing by about ¼ in (5 mm) every year.

How high is Mount Everest?

The peak of **Mount Everest,** the **highest mountain** in the world, is **29,029 ft (8,848 m)** above sea level.

Mount Elbrus, Russia
18,510 ft (5,642 m)

Vinson Massif, Antarctica
16,077 ft (4,900 m)

Mount Wilhelm, Papua New Guinea
14,793 ft (4,509 m)

These seven mountains are known as the "Seven Summits"; each is the highest mountain on its continent. Reaching the top of all of them has become a mountaineering challenge.

FAST FACTS

Olympus Mons

Mauna Kea   Everest

Everest is not the Earth's tallest mountain. Measured from its base on the ocean floor, Mauna Kea, Hawaii, is taller. However, both are dwarfed by Olympus Mons on Mars, which is 14 miles (22 km) high.

Highest bird flight
Rüppell's vulture, at
33,000 ft (10,000 m)

Highest city
La Rinconada, Peru, at
16,700 ft (5,100 m)

Highest ski resort
Chacaltaya, Bolivia,
at 17,789 ft (5,422 m)

Highest ground resident
Himalayan jumping
spider, at 22,000 ft
(6,700 m)

Sea level

A small jumping spider on Everest is thought to be the Earth's highest animal ground resident. In Africa, Rüppell's vulture can fly even higher.

FAST FACTS

The Australian, Arabian, and Sahara deserts are hot deserts in the tropics. The biggest is the Sahara in Africa, which is as big as the US. The Kalahari and Gobi lie farther from the equator and can be cool or even very cold.

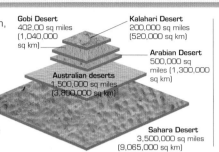

Gobi Desert
402,00 sq miles
(1,040,000 sq km)

Kalahari Desert
200,000 sq miles
(520,000 sq km)

Arabian Desert
500,000 sq miles (1,300,000 sq km)

Australian deserts
1,500,000 sq miles
(3,800,000 sq km)

Sahara Desert
3,500,000 sq miles
(9,065,000 sq km)

The biggest erg, or sand sea, is the Rub' al Khali in the Arabian Desert. At 250,000 sq miles (650,000 sq km), it covers an area bigger than France.

France

How **tall** are sand dunes?

Camel trains were the best method of transportation in the Sahara for many centuries and are still sometimes used to carry goods across the desert.

Tall dunes often reach **1,500 ft** (460 m) in height, but occasionally, dunes **can** even **grow** to **4,000 ft** (1,200 m).

MARTIAN SAND DUNES

Near Mars's north pole is a field of dunes covered with frozen pink carbon dioxide in winter. In spring, dark sand trickles down the slopes as the carbon dioxide melts.

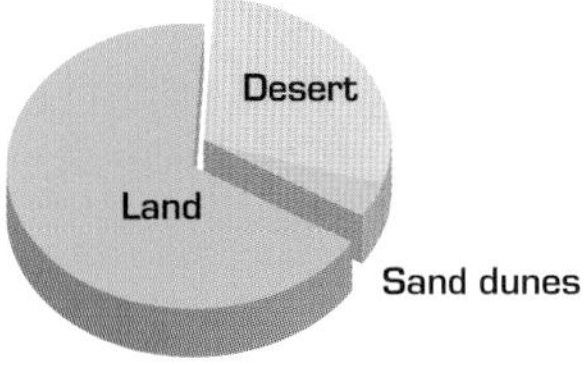

One third of the Earth's land surface is desert, but only 10 percent of the desert is sand dunes. The rest is rock, soil, and sheets of sand.

Desert

Land

Sand dunes

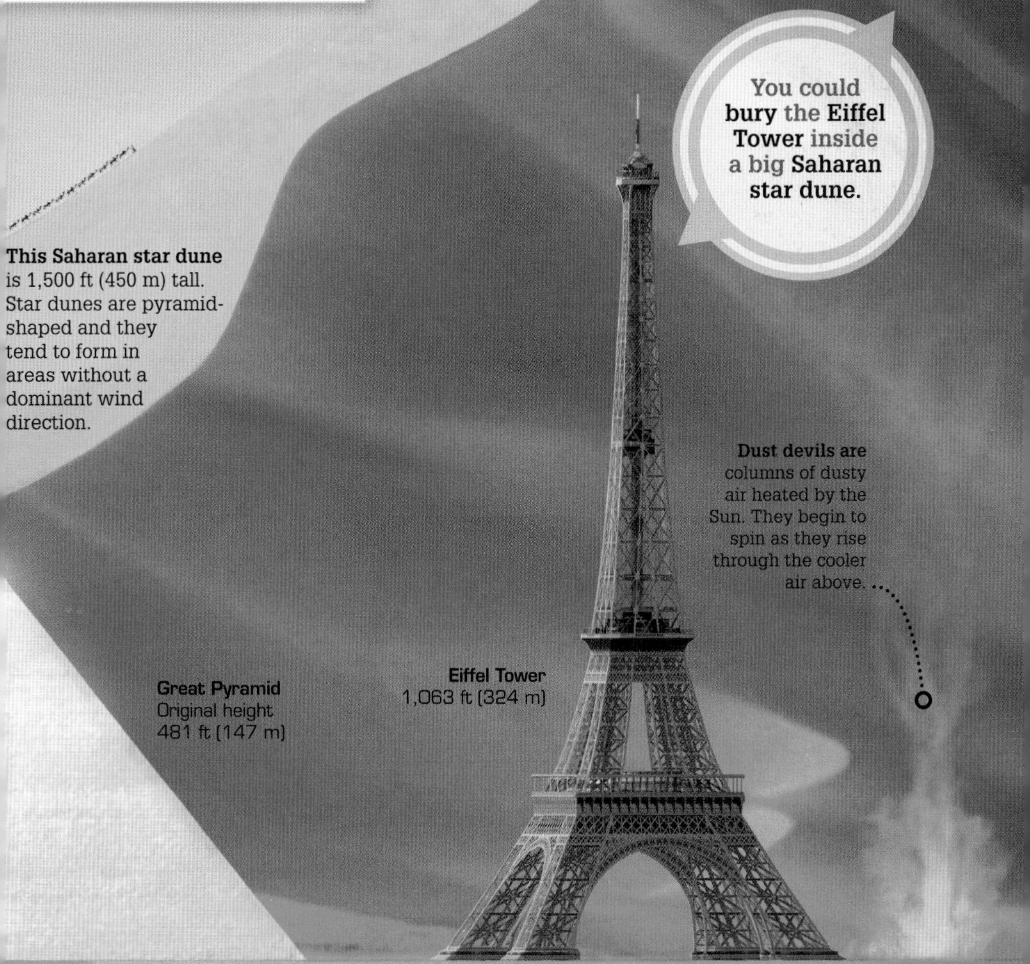

The peak is sculpted by winds blowing from many directions, piling sand up into the center.

Saharan trader with camel loaded with goods

You could **bury the Eiffel Tower inside** a big **Saharan star dune.**

This Saharan star dune is 1,500 ft (450 m) tall. Star dunes are pyramid-shaped and they tend to form in areas without a dominant wind direction.

Dust devils are columns of dusty air heated by the Sun. They begin to spin as they rise through the cooler air above.

Great Pyramid
Original height
481 ft (147 m)

Eiffel Tower
1,063 ft (324 m)

How **powerful** was the **Krakatoa volcano?**

In **1883**, Krakatoa, a volcano in **Indonesia**, erupted with a force of about **200 megatons** of **TNT** explosive, or **several nuclear bombs**.

ASH CLOUD LIGHTNING

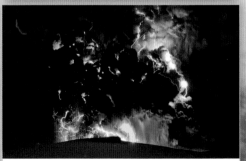

The electrical charge in the ash cloud from a volcanic eruption can cause lightning, as in the 2010 Eyjafjallajökull eruption in Iceland.

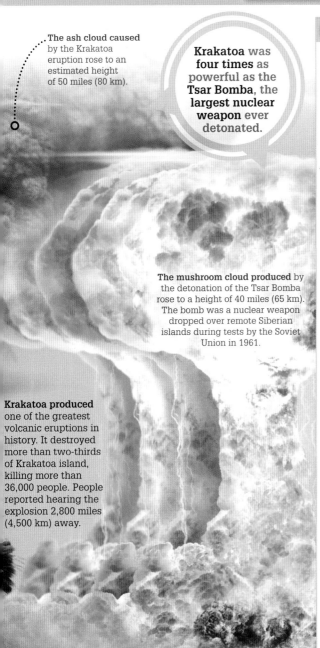

The ash cloud caused by the Krakatoa eruption rose to an estimated height of 50 miles (80 km).

Krakatoa was **four times** as **powerful** as the **Tsar Bomba**, the largest nuclear **weapon** ever detonated.

The mushroom cloud produced by the detonation of the Tsar Bomba rose to a height of 40 miles (65 km). The bomb was a nuclear weapon dropped over remote Siberian islands during tests by the Soviet Union in 1961.

Krakatoa produced one of the greatest volcanic eruptions in history. It destroyed more than two-thirds of Krakatoa island, killing more than 36,000 people. People reported hearing the explosion 2,800 miles (4,500 km) away.

FAST FACTS

9 years	1,390 ft (424 m)	
1 year	1,102 ft (336 m)	Empire State Building
7 days	500 ft (150 m)	

A volcano in Parícutin, Mexico, suddenly erupted in 1943 from a cornfield. It grew 500 ft (150 m) in one week and continued to erupt and grow for another nine years.

Mt St. Helen's 0.25 cu miles (1 cu km)

Krakatoa 4 cu miles (18 cu km)

Yellowstone 600 cu miles (2,500 cu km)

The Yellowstone supervolcano, 2.1 million years ago, produced 135 times more ash than Krakatoa and 2,500 times more than Mount St. Helen's.

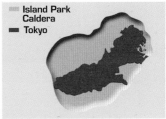

▨ Island Park Caldera
■ Tokyo

Yellowstone's Island Park Caldera, an enormous volcanic crater, could fit a city of 13 million people, such as Tokyo, inside it.

What's the **largest crater** on **Earth?**

Asteroid and **comet** impacts make **craters** on **Earth** just like they do on the Moon. The **largest** one is the **Vredefort crater** in South Africa, which is over **186 miles** (300 km) **wide**.

You could fit **250 Barringer** craters into **Vredefort.**

Barringer crater is a well-preserved impact crater in Arizona. Its shape is so clear because it is only 50,000 years old.

Asteroids and comets have battered Earth over the course of its life, but we can see only a few clear craters on Earth's surface today. This is because most craters are worn down or buried under younger rock.

FAST FACTS

Herschel crater central peak
21,300 ft
(6,500 m)

Mt. Everest
29,029 ft
(8,848 m)

Saturn's moon Mimas is marked by a huge crater, named Herschel, with a central peak made by the shock wave of the impact. The peak is almost as tall as Mount Everest.

The Borealis Basin on Mars is thought to be the biggest known land feature caused by an impact. If it is, it must have been the result of a blow from an object the size of Pluto. The basin covers most of the northern half of Mars, and is nearly five times the size of the US.

US

Borealis Basin

Barringer crater is only ³/₄ mile (1.2 km) in diameter.

Chicxulub crater in Mexico is 110 miles (180 km) wide. It was formed 65 million years ago by the impact of an object 6 miles (10 km) across hitting Earth. The destruction it caused is blamed for the death of the dinosaurs. The crater is now buried and half of it is hidden on the seabed.

BIGGEST METEORITE

Vredefort crater was made around 2 billion years ago. In all that time, it has been eroded by wind, rain, and rivers, and bent and distorted by movements in the Earth's crust.

When an object falls from space and survives the impact, it is known as a meteorite. The Hoba meteorite in Namibia is the biggest ever found and weighs more than 66 tonnes (60 metric tons).

How **big** are the **biggest crystals?**

Crystals of **selenite** discovered in a cave in Mexico measure up to **37 ft 5 in (11.4 m) long.**

With temperatures in the cave of 118 °F (48 °C) and 98 percent humidity, people have to wear protective suits to explore the amazing crystals formations.

FAST FACTS

The longest Naica crystal found so far, Crystal Cin, is around the length of a bus and weighs about the same as 8 African elephants!

Crystal Cin

Length 37 ft 5 in (11.4 m)

Single decker bus

The oldest crystal in the cave dates back 600,000 years—about the time when *Homo heidelbergensis*, the ancestors of modern humans, first appeared.

Present day

600,000 years ago

These vast selenite crystals are in the Cave of Crystals, which lies 985 ft (300 m) below ground in a mine at Naica, northern Mexico. Selenite is a form of the mineral gypsum. The crystals began to grow because of water boiling in this underground chamber. The water actually boiled for about 500,000 years, the heat solidifying the crystals in the water.

DESERT ROSE

Fingal's Cave, off the coast of Scotland, is unique. It is formed from hexagonal pillars of basalt rock more than 65 ft (20 m) tall. They formed when an ancient lava flow cooled and cracked.

The **largest crystals** in the cave are more **than six times taller than** a **person.**

How **much** water is there?

The world contains **332 million cu miles** (1.3 billion cu km) of **water** in its oceans, rivers, lakes, groundwater, and clouds, and—as **ice**—in its glaciers and ice caps.

Scooped up, **the world's water** would form **a ball just 860 miles (1,384 km) wide.**

ICE CAPS AND GLACIERS

Only 2.5 percent of the world's water is fresh, and most freshwater is locked up in glaciers and ice caps. Less than 1 percent of the Earth's water is liquid and fresh.

This globe shows the ocean basins with all their water removed. Nearly 97 percent of the world's water is in oceans. The next biggest store of water is the ice caps and glaciers, with 1.75 percent.

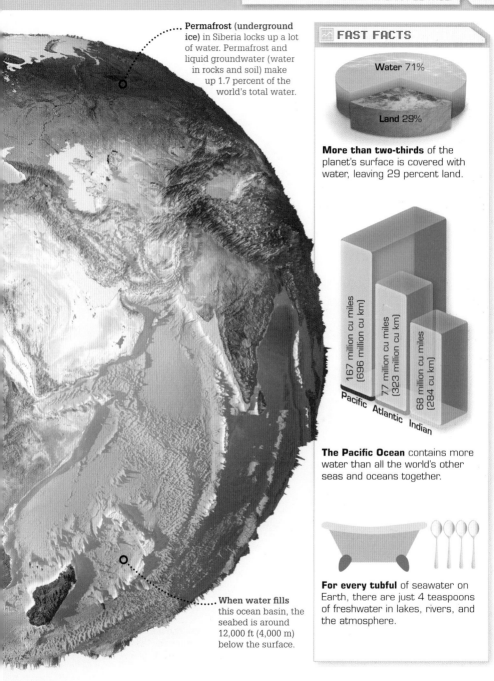

Permafrost (underground ice) in Siberia locks up a lot of water. Permafrost and liquid groundwater (water in rocks and soil) make up 1.7 percent of the world's total water.

When water fills this ocean basin, the seabed is around 12,000 ft (4,000 m) below the surface.

FAST FACTS

Water 71%

Land 29%

More than two-thirds of the planet's surface is covered with water, leaving 29 percent land.

167 million cu miles (696 million cu km)

77 million cu miles (323 million cu km)

68 million cu miles (284 cu km)

Pacific   Atlantic   Indian

The Pacific Ocean contains more water than all the world's other seas and oceans together.

For every tubful of seawater on Earth, there are just 4 teaspoons of freshwater in lakes, rivers, and the atmosphere.

How **deep** is the **ocean?**

Continental shelves are the shallow regions fringing deep oceans. They are actually part of the continental landmass. A shelf may extend hundreds of miles from the coast.

The **average depth** of the ocean is 14,000 ft (4,300 m), but the **deepest point** is **36,200 ft** (11,030 m) below sea level at **Challenger Deep** in the Pacific Ocean.

BARRELEYE

This barreleye, or spookfish, is one of the many peculiar creatures that inhabit the dark ocean depths. The barreleye lives 2,000–2,600 ft (600–800 m) under water and has unique tube-shaped eyes inside a transparent head.

The Empire State Building measures 1,250 ft (381 m) to the top of its roof.

It would take **29 stacked Empire State Buildings to** reach the bottom of **Challenger Deep**.

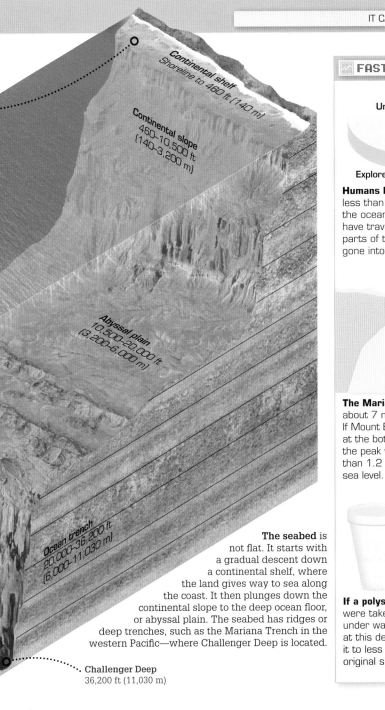

Continental shelf
Shoreline to 460 ft (140 m)

Continental slope
460–10,500 ft
(140–3,200 m)

Abyssal plain
10,500–20,000 ft
(3,200–6,000 m)

Ocean trench
20,000–36,200 ft
(6,000–11,030 m)

The seabed is not flat. It starts with a gradual descent down a continental shelf, where the land gives way to sea along the coast. It then plunges down the continental slope to the deep ocean floor, or abyssal plain. The seabed has ridges or deep trenches, such as the Mariana Trench in the western Pacific—where Challenger Deep is located.

Challenger Deep
36,200 ft (11,030 m)

FAST FACTS

Unexplored ocean

Explored ocean

Humans have explored less than 10 percent of the ocean. Fewer people have traveled to the deepest parts of the ocean than have gone into outer space.

Mount
Everest

Mariana
Trench

The Mariana Trench is about 7 miles (11 km) deep. If Mount Everest were put at the bottom of the trench, the peak would still be more than 1.2 miles (2 km) below sea level.

Cup before
dive

Cup after
dive

If a polystyrene cup were taken 2 miles (3 km) under water, the pressure at this depth would squeeze it to less than half of its original size.

How **tall** was the **biggest wave** ever **surfed?**

In 2013, American professional big-wave surfer **Garrett McNamara** surfed a **wave** that was **78 ft** (23.8 m) **tall** off the coast of Nazaré, Portugal.

FAST FACTS

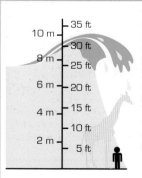

Tsunamis tend to be less than 33 ft (10 m) tall, but because there is a lot of water following behind them, they cause a flood that reaches far inland. They are caused by earthquakes on the sea bed, land slips, and asteroid strikes.

Highest tsunami
1,720 ft (520 m)

Highest ocean waves
115 ft (35 m)

Highest surfed wave
78 ft (23.8 m)

The biggest wave ever known occurred in Lituya Bay, Alaska, when a slab of rock slipped into the bay and caused a huge tsunami. Giant ocean waves also form far out at sea, caused by high winds and strong currents.

Foaming breakers rise up almost vertically before curling over to form a tube. The surfer tries to stay inside the tube and, if possible, reach the end of it before the wave collapses.

A **78-ft (23.8 m) wave** is the **height** of more than **13 people** standing on top of each other.

Surfboards come in a variety of sizes. This championship board is 7 ft (2.1 m) long.

TSUNAMI DAMAGE

Tsunamis are so powerful that anything in their way is flattened and swept away. Even large ships can be carried inland, leaving them stranded miles from the shore.

Record waves occur off Nazaré because it faces the huge swells caused by distant Atlantic storms. An undersea canyon then funnels the wave energy of the swells onto a short stretch of the coast, piling the waters high.

How **big** was the **biggest iceberg?**

The **biggest-ever** iceberg began its life when it broke free from an ice shelf off **Antarctica** in 1956. It was **208 miles** (335 km) **long** and **60 miles** (100 km) **wide.**

Antwerp

Brussels

Ghent

Bruges

B E L G

Flanders

The biggest iceberg was not really shaped like Belgium. It was longer and thinner, but its area of 12,000 sq miles (31,000 sq km) was slightly larger than Belgium's. It was larger even than iceberg B-15—the Jamaica-sized iceberg that broke off Antarctica's Ross Ice Shelf in 2000.

HIDDEN DEPTHS

Icebergs float low in the water, with around 90 percent of their height hidden beneath the waves. The ice below the water melts faster than that above it, so that an iceberg may suddenly roll over with a great crash that can be heard for miles.

The **biggest-ever iceberg** covered an **area larger** than that of **Belgium**.

Belgium covers an area of 11,787 sq miles (30,528 sq km), which is about the same size as Maryland.

Liege

U M

harleroi

Ardennes

The height of this iceberg is exaggerated in this picture. It would have stood no more than 500 ft (150 m) above the sea's surface.

Glacier

Snail

Glaciers are rivers of ice that move very slowly, averaging only 12 in (30 cm) a day. A fast snail can zip across this distance in 2¼ minutes.

Volume of ice today

Volume of ice during the Ice Age

In the last ice age, ice covered more than 30 percent of the planet. Nearly 60 percent of it has melted since then, leaving us with ice only on mountaintops and in the ice caps at the poles.

Tallest iceberg
550 ft (168 m)

Great Pyramid
482 ft (147 m)

The tallest iceberg was sighted near Greenland in 1957. Standing even higher above sea level than the Great Pyramid, the iceberg may have extended another 4,900 ft (1,500 m) below the surface.

What if all the ice melted?

Ten percent of the **world's land** is covered by thick **glaciers** and **ice sheets**. If it all melted, the **sea level** would rise by up to **230 ft** (70 m). Many **major world cities** would be **covered** by the **ocean**.

SHRINKING GLACIERS

Glaciers are great rivers of slowly flowing ice. The ice builds up over many years from fallen snow. Glaciers can begin on any high ground where the snow does not thaw completely in spring. In parts of the Arctic, glaciers reach down to the sea, but most are shrinking. Between 1941 and 2004, the Muir Glacier in Alaska (above) retreated more than 7 miles (12 km) and the sea filled its valley.

Low-lying cities by the coast would be devastated by big sea level rises. New York City would be almost completely swallowed by the ocean, along with the bases of its famous landmarks.

The first 18 floors of the Empire State Building would be flooded if sea level rose by 230 ft (70 m).

If the world's ice melted, the Statue of Liberty would stand waist-deep in water.

Current coastline

Coastline after flooding

If all the ice melted, the coastlines of many countries would dramatically change. Britain and Ireland would turn into a group of smaller islands. Low-lying Bangladesh and the Netherlands would almost disappear.

The ice over Antarctica is extremely thick, averaging 6,000 ft (1,830 m)—nearly as deep as six Eiffel Towers. In some places it is more than twice as deep, at 15,670 ft (4,776 m)

The Statue of Liberty's pedestal is 154 ft (47 m) high.

The base of the statue's pedestal is only about 20 ft (6 m) above current sea level.

Earth data

L O N G E S T **RIVERS**

RIVER	CONTINENT	LENGTH
NILE	AFRICA	**4,145 MILES** (6,670 KM)
AMAZON	SOUTH AMERICA	**4,000 MILES** (6,404 KM)
YANGTZE	ASIA	**3,693 MILES** (6,378 KM)
MISSISSIPPI-MISSOURI	NORTH AMERICA	**3,741 MILES** (6,021 KM)
YENISEI-ANGARA	ASIA	**3,442 MILES** (5,540 KM)

FLOW RATE

The world's **longest** river is the **Nile**, but the **Amazon** is by far the **largest**. At its mouth in the Atlantic Ocean, it **carries more water** than the next four rivers combined.

CHANGING CONTINENTS

Earth's crust is divided into **giant** slabs of rock called **tectonic plates**. These plates are moving constantly, but very slowly. Around **200 million years ago**, all the continents were joined into one giant landmass called **Pangea**. The movement of the tectonic plates gradually **broke the continents apart** to form the Earth we know today.

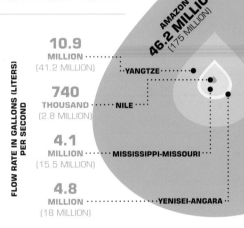

FLOW RATE IN GALLONS (LITERS) PER SECOND

10.9 MILLION (41.2 MILLION) ···· **YANGTZE** ···

740 THOUSAND (2.8 MILLION) ···· **NILE** ···

4.1 MILLION (15.5 MILLION) ···· **MISSISSIPPI-MISSOURI** ···

4.8 MILLION (18 MILLION) ···· **YENISEI-ANGARA** ···

AMAZON 46.2 MILLION (175 MILLION)

THE **BIG** ONES

There are **14 mountains** over **26,250 ft** (8,000 m) high. All are found in **Asia** in the region where the Indian subcontinent is pushing into the Asian continent. In 1986, **Reinhold Messner** became the **first mountaineer to climb all 14 peaks**.

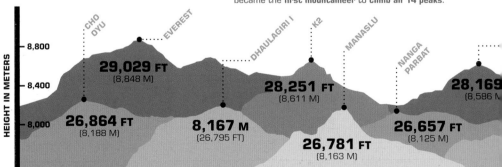

HEIGHT IN METERS

- 8,800
- 8,400
- 8,000

CHO OYU — **26,864 FT** (8,188 M)

EVEREST — **29,029 FT** (8,848 M)

DHAULAGIRI I — **8,167 M** (26,795 FT)

K2 — **28,251 FT** (8,611 M)

MANASLU — **26,781 FT** (8,163 M)

NANGA PARBAT — **26,657 FT** (8,125 M)

28,169 (8,586 M)

INSIDE **EARTH**

Our planet is divided into several different **layers**, which get **hotter** the **deeper** you go. The **crust**, where we live, makes up just **0.4%** of Earth's mass.

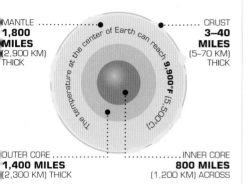

MANTLE ....
1,800 MILES
(2,900 KM) THICK

The temperature at the center of Earth can reach **9,900°F (5,500°C)**

CRUST ....
3–40 MILES
(5–70 KM) THICK

OUTER CORE ....
1,400 MILES
(2,300 KM) THICK

INNER CORE ....
800 MILES
(1,200 KM) ACROSS

MOST POWERFUL ⊚**EARTHQUAKES** ⊚

Where	When	Magnitude	Death toll
Chile	22.05.1960	9.5	4,485
Prince William Sound, Alaska	28.03.1964	9.2	128
Indian Ocean	26.12.2004	9.1	230,000
Kamchatka, Soviet Union	04.11.1952	9.0	0 (+ 6 cows)

5 OF THE **LARGEST** LAVA FLOWS

This image shows how much **lava** each volcanic eruption produced and how many years ago (YA) or millions of years ago (MYA) they took place.

LONG VALLEY
CALIFORNIA, US
144 CU MILES
(600 CU KM),
760,000 YA

MESA FALLS
YELLOWSTONE, US
67 CU MILES
(280 CU KM),
1.3 MYA

LAVA CREEK
YELLOWSTONE, US
240 CU MILES
(1,000 CU KM),
640,000 YA

TOBA
SUMATRA, INDONESIA
670 CU MILES
(2,800 CU KM),
74,000 YA

HUCKLEBERRY RIDGE
YELLOWSTONE, US
590 CU MILES
(2,450 CU KM),
2.1 MYA

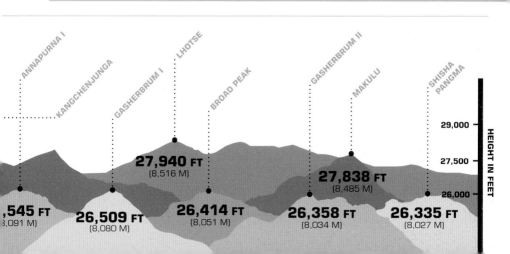

ANNAPURNA I

KANGCHENJUNGA

GASHERBRUM I

LHOTSE

BROAD PEAK

GASHERBRUM II

MAKULU

SHISHA PANGMA

HEIGHT IN FEET

29,000

27,500

26,000

,545 FT
,091 M)

26,509 FT
(8,080 M)

27,940 FT
(8,516 M)

26,414 FT
(8,051 M)

27,838 FT
(8,485 M)

26,358 FT
(8,034 M)

26,335 FT
(8,027 M)

Where is the snowiest place on Earth?

The **greatest snowfall** over one year was **95 ft** (29.86 m) in **Mount Baker Ski Area**, Washington, measured in the **1998–1999** season.

Mount Baker's record snowfall would bury over half the Leaning Tower of Pisa.

EXTREME SNOW

Japan's sightseeing road, the Tateyama Kurobe Alpine Route, is closed all winter. It opens in spring, when diggers cut through 66 ft (20 m) of snow to the road below.

The Leaning Tower of Pisa is 183 ft 4 in (55.9 m) from the ground on its higher side.

This 100-ft (30-m) pile of snow is much less dense than water. To compare it to a rainfall total, experts would melt it down in a snow gauge, which would produce just 8 ft (2.5 m) of water.

The most snowfall in one month was in Tamarac, California, where 37 ft 5 in (11.4 m) of snow fell in March 1911.

New York City receives an average of 2 ft 5 in (68 cm) of snow every year.

FAST FACTS

Compared to snowfall records, extremes of rainfall are far higher in terms of total amount of water.

72 in (1.825 m)

Foc-Foc

The highest-ever rainfall in 24 hours took place in January 1966 in Foc-Foc, on the island of Réunion, where 6 ft (1.825 m) of rain fell.

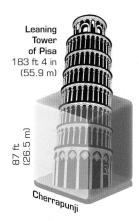

Leaning Tower of Pisa 183 ft 4 in (55.9 m)

87 ft (26.5 m)

Cherrapunji

Cherrapunji, India, saw the most rainfall in one year in 1860–1861, when 87 ft (26.5 m) of rain fell— enough to flood almost half the Leaning Tower of Pisa.

How big was the largest hailstone?

The **largest hailstone** ever known fell in **Vivian, South Dakota**, in a storm on **July 23, 2010**. It was **8 in (20 cm)** across.

DIVIDED IN TWO

This hailstone cut in half shows the layers of ice that form hail. Hailstones grow because winds in storm clouds throw them upward again and again. Each time, water freezes on to them, building up another layer of ice.

Giant hailstones like this form in clouds with very powerful updrafts, such as those in intense thunderstorms and tornadoes. When giant hail is finally heavy enough to fall to the ground, it can dent cars, smash windshields, flatten crops, and injure living things.

The South Dakota hailstone was about **three times the width** of a tennis ball.

FAST FACTS

Hail most often forms in giant thunderclouds, which are also the source of lightning.

Cloud top
40,000 ft (12,000 m)

Mount Everest
29,029 ft (8,848 m)

Cloud base
6,600 ft (2,000 m)

Thunderclouds, technically known as cumulonimbus, are the tallest kind of clouds. They are sometimes more than 40,000 ft (12,000 m) high—half again as high as the highest mountain. They are column-shaped with a wide, flat top.

A bolt of lightning can have a temperature of around 54,000°F (30,000°C)—more than five times hotter than the surface of the Sun, which is the hottest object in our solar system by several thousand degrees.

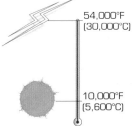

54,000°F
(30,000°C)

10,000°F
(5,600°C)

The lumps that covered the hailstone are the result of smaller hailstones colliding with each other and sticking together. Each lump is a former smaller hailstone with layers of ice added on top.

Record hailstone
8 in (20 cm) across,
2 lb 3 oz (1 kg) in weight

Tennis ball
2¾ in (6.7 cm) across

W ather dat

HOT

The **hottest** temperature ever recorded at ground level in the shade was in **Death Valley, California**, in 1913—a scorching

134°F
(56.6°C).

AND COLD

The **coldest** temperature ever recorded at ground level was at **Vostok, Antarctica**, in 1983. It was a bone-chilling

-129°F (-89.2°C).

CLOUD COVER

High-level above 20,000 ft (6,000 m)
- ⌐ CIRRUS
- ∠ CIRROCUMULUS
- ∠ CIRROSTRATUS

Mid-level 6,500–20,000 ft (2,000–6,000 m)
- ⫽ ALTOSTRATUS   ∽ ALTOCUMULUS
- ⫽ NIMBOSTRATUS

Low-level 6,500 ft (0–2,000 m)
- ∨ STRATOCUMULUS   △ CUMULUS   ⌐ CUMULONIMBUS

THE ATMOSPHERE

Surrounding the planet is a **layer of gases** called the atmosphere. The Earth's atmosphere contains five separate layers.

EXOSPHERE 430–500 MILES (690–800 KM)

THERMOSPHERE 53–430 MILES (85–690 KM)

MESOSPHERE 31–53 MILES (50–85 KM)

STRATOSPHERE 7.5–31 MILES (12–50 KM)

TROPOSPHERE 0–7.5 MILES (0–12 KM)

RAINY DAYS

The **wettest** place on Earth is Mawsynram in northeast India with average annual rainfall of

467 in
(11,870 mm) per year.

The place with the **most rainy days** each year is Mt. Waialeale, Kauai, Hawaii, with **350** rainy days a year. On average it is dry just one day a month.

The longest continuous rainfall lasted **247 days**, from August 27, 1993, to April 30, 1994, in Kaneohe Ranch, Oahu, Hawaii.

WINDY DAYS

The Beaufort scale lists the effects of increasing wind speeds.

BEAUFORT NUMBER	WIND SPEED	WIND EFFECT ON LAND
0	0	Smoke rises vertically
1	1–2 mph (1–3 kph)	Smoke drifts gently
2	3–7 mph (4–11 kph)	Leaves rustle
3	8–12 mph (12–19 kph)	Twigs move
4	13–18 mph (20–29 kph)	Small branches move
5	19–24 mph (30–39 kph)	Small trees sway
6	25–31 mph (40–50 kph)	Umbrellas hard to use
7	32–38 mph (51–61 kph)	Whole trees sway
8	39–46 mph (62–74 kph)	Difficulty walking
9	47–54 mph (75–87 kph)	Roofs damaged
10	55–63 mph (88–101 kph)	Trees blown down
11	64–74 mph (102–119 kph)	Houses damaged
12	over 74 mph (119 kph)	Buildings destroyed

TWISTERS

300

At ground level, tornadoes have the *fastest winds*. The most powerful recorded had wind speeds of 300 mph (500 kph) or more. Tornadoes can also move at speeds of up to 70 mph (110 kph)—far too fast for anyone to outrun.

HURRICANE DAMAGE

Hurricanes are categorized according to their speed and destructiveness using the Saffir-Simpson scale.

CATEGORY	WIND SPEED	EFFECTS	
1	**74–95 mph** (120–153 kph)	Minor building damage; branches snapped	
2	**96–110 mph** (154–177 kph)	Some roof, door, and window damage	
3	**111–130 mph** (178–208 kph)	Roof tiles dislodged; large trees uprooted	
4	**131–155 mph** (209–251 kph)	Roofs blown off; major coastal flooding	
5	**over 155 mph** (over 252 kph)	Buildings destroyed; catastrophic flooding	

BOLTS FROM THE BLUE

Lightning strikes somewhere on Earth

100 times

a second. It strikes the Empire State Building roughly

100 times

a year.

What was the biggest natural disaster ?

The **disease** known as the **Black Death**, which swept the world in the 14th century, **killed** up to **75 million people**.

The Rose Bowl sports stadium, Pasadena, California, USA, has an official capacity of about 91,000 people.

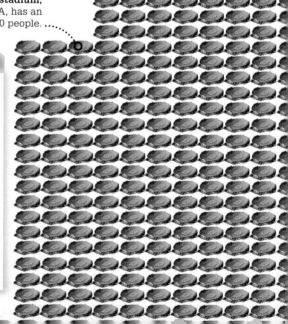

SPANISH FLU

In 1918, after World War I, there was a global outbreak of the disease "Spanish Flu." Spread by the mass movement of troops, it killed over 50 million people—more than the war itself. Diseases on a global scale are called pandemics.

The Black Death, or plague, was caused by bacteria carried by fleas on rats. It began in Central Asia but spread quickly, as rats boarded merchant ships, taking the disease with them. The plague reached Europe in 1346, where it killed at least 30 percent of the people.

The number of **people killed by the Black Death** would fill 827 Rose Bowl stadiums.

FAST FACTS

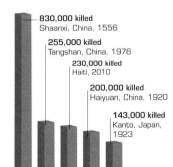

Tohoku earthquake and tsunami, Japan, 2011 $235 billion

Hurricane Katrina, USA, 2005 $165 billion

Yangtze floods, China, 1998 $55 billion

Drought, USA, 1988 $45 billion

The economic cost of natural disasters today can run to billions of dollars. Earthquakes can be particularly costly because they cause severe damage to houses and factories and key transportation links such as roads.

830,000 killed
Shaanxi, China, 1556

255,000 killed
Tangshan, China, 1976

230,000 killed
Haiti, 2010

200,000 killed
Haiyuan, China, 1920

143,000 killed
Kanto, Japan, 1923

Earthquakes often claim thousands of lives in built-up areas. In addition to knocking down buildings, they can also cause fires, due to damaged electricity cables and gas pipes.

How **many people** are there in **China?**

The **population** of **China**, including Taiwan, is about **1.4 billion**. In around 2022, **India** is likely to displace China as the world's most populous country.

Australia is the world's sixth-largest country, after Russia, Canada, China, the US, and Brazil.

Austral

China

CHINESE COMMUNITIES

One in every five people on Earth is Chinese. Most major cities outside of China have large Chinese communities, making Chinese culture an important influence across the world.

There are as many people in China today as there were in the whole world around 150 years ago!

The area of China is only slightly greater than that of the US, and Australia is not far behind. But China's population is more than four times bigger than the US's and nearly 60 times larger than that of Australia. Here, the three countries are shown in proportion to their populations.

China has a population almost 60 times larger than that of **Australia**.

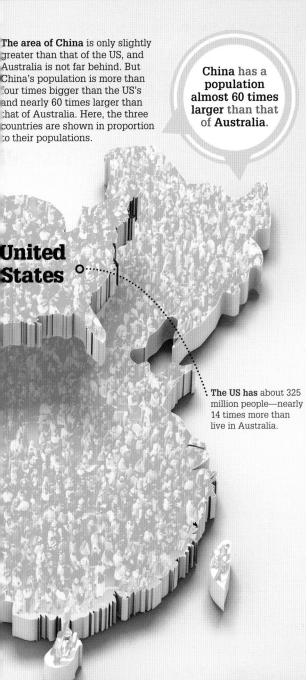

United States

The US has about 325 million people—nearly 14 times more than live in Australia.

FAST FACTS

Australia
Population of about 24 million
Density of 9 people per sq mile

Sri Lanka
Population of about 21 million
Density of 900 people per sq mile

Australia and Sri Lanka have roughly similar-sized populations, but Australia is about 120 times larger. If Australia were as densely populated as Sri Lanka, it would be home to nearly 2.5 billion people!

Manila, Philippines

London, UK

Court area
2,808 sq ft
(261 sq m)

Some cities are more crowded than others. If Manila and London were divided into tennis courts, Manila would have nine people on each court and London only one.

How **fast** is the **population** of the world **growing**?

Around **360,000 babies** are **born each day** and about **160,000 people die**. So overall, the world's population **grows by 200,000 people** every **day** of the year.

AGING WORLD

The world's population is getting older. Better health care means that more babies are surviving, and so people are having fewer children. It also enables older people to live longer.

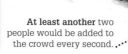

At least another two people would be added to the crowd every second.

FAST FACTS

The human population is growing faster in some places than in others. Using a graph called a population pyramid, we can see which countries have fast-growing populations.

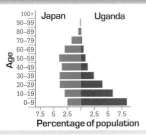

Japan   Uganda

Age: 100+, 90–99, 80–89, 70–79, 60–69, 50–59, 40–49, 30–39, 20–29, 10–19, 0–9

7.5 5 2.5   2.5 5 7.5
Percentage of population

Japan's narrow-based, bulging pyramid shows an older population, with relatively few young people. The birth rate is low and the population is falling.

Uganda's sloping pyramid shows the country has a high birth rate, many children but few older people, and a fast-growing population.

This crowd of **8,000 people** shows how much **Earth's population** increases **every** single **hour.**

In just one hour, the world's population grows by more than 8,000 people. That's the same as 23 plane-loads of passengers arriving on the planet every 60 minutes. Over one day, there would be enough new inhabitants of Earth to fill London's Olympic Stadium 2.5 times.

How many people live on Earth?

Our planet is home to **7.4 billion people**. If everyone stood next to each other, we could all fit into a **square** with **each side** measuring **21.8 miles** (35.11 km).

Kaua'i island covers an area of 554 sq miles (1,435 km²), with room for five people to stand in every square yard.

Everyone in the world could fit into the **Hawaiian island** of **Kaua'i**.

ASIAN POPULATION

More people live in Asia than in the rest of the world combined—about 4.4 billion people, or 60 percent of the population. China and India each have more than 1 billion residents.

The total area required to fit the entire global population is 476 sq miles (1,233 km²), which is slightly smaller than the Hawaiian island of Kaua'i in the Pacific Ocean.

Kaua'i

Hawaii's chain of six major islands includes Kaua'i, the oldest and most northerly island.

Hawaii

7,400,000,000 people

FAST FACTS

People around the world vary in height. The tallest live in the Netherlands, where the average man is 6 ft 1 in (184.8 cm) tall, while the shortest people are from Indonesia, with an average male standing 5 ft 2 in (157.5 cm) tall.

More people now live in cities than ever before. In 1960 most people lived in the countryside, with only 34 percent inhabiting urban areas. By 2014 about 54 percent of people lived in urban areas.

Netherlands
6 ft 1 in
(184.8 cm)

Indonesia
5 ft 2 in
(157.5 cm)

1960

2014

How **long** have **people** been on **Earth?**

Our species, *Homo sapiens*, emerged about **200,000 years ago**, but our *Homo* **ancestors** first appeared more than **2.4 million years ago** (mya). This is only **1.5 percent** of the time that **dinosaurs roamed Earth**.

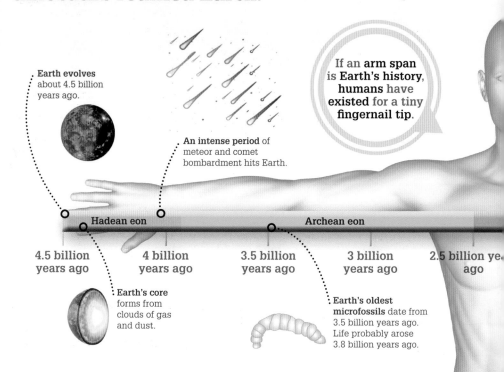

Earth evolves about 4.5 billion years ago.

An intense period of meteor and comet bombardment hits Earth.

If an **arm span** is **Earth's history, humans have existed** for a tiny fingernail tip.

Hadean eon

Archean eon

4.5 billion years ago

4 billion years ago

3.5 billion years ago

3 billion years ago

2.5 billion years ago

Earth's core forms from clouds of gas and dust.

Earth's oldest microfossils date from 3.5 billion years ago. Life probably arose 3.8 billion years ago.

Scientists predict Earth could support life for another 1.75 billion years (two-fifths of another human arm span). It's thought the planet will survive for a further 3–5 billion years before it will collapse and be absorbed by the Sun.

Humans may die out / Earth may die out

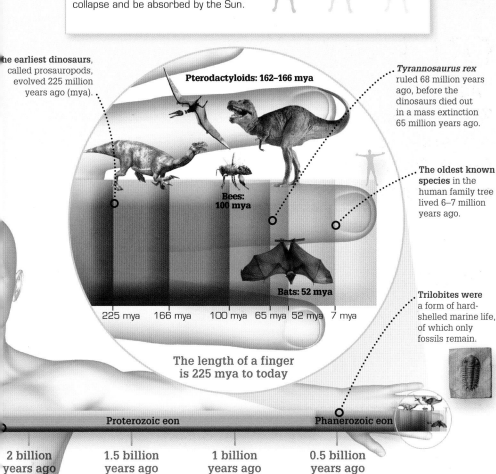

The earliest dinosaurs, called prosauropods, evolved 225 million years ago (mya).

Pterodactyloids: 162–166 mya

Tyrannosaurus rex ruled 68 million years ago, before the dinosaurs died out in a mass extinction 65 million years ago.

The oldest known species in the human family tree lived 6–7 million years ago.

Bees: 100 mya

Bats: 52 mya

225 mya   166 mya   100 mya   65 mya 52 mya   7 mya

Trilobites were a form of hard-shelled marine life, of which only fossils remain.

The length of a finger is 225 mya to today

Proterozoic eon   Phanerozoic eon

2 billion years ago   **1.5 billion years ago**   **1 billion years ago**   **0.5 billion years ago**

The first eukaryotes— living cells with a nucleus—begin to form.

Humans have existed for a short time when compared to the history of Earth. Spread your arms out to represent the history of our planet (4.5 billion years). The very tip of a fingernail equates to all of *Homo* history.

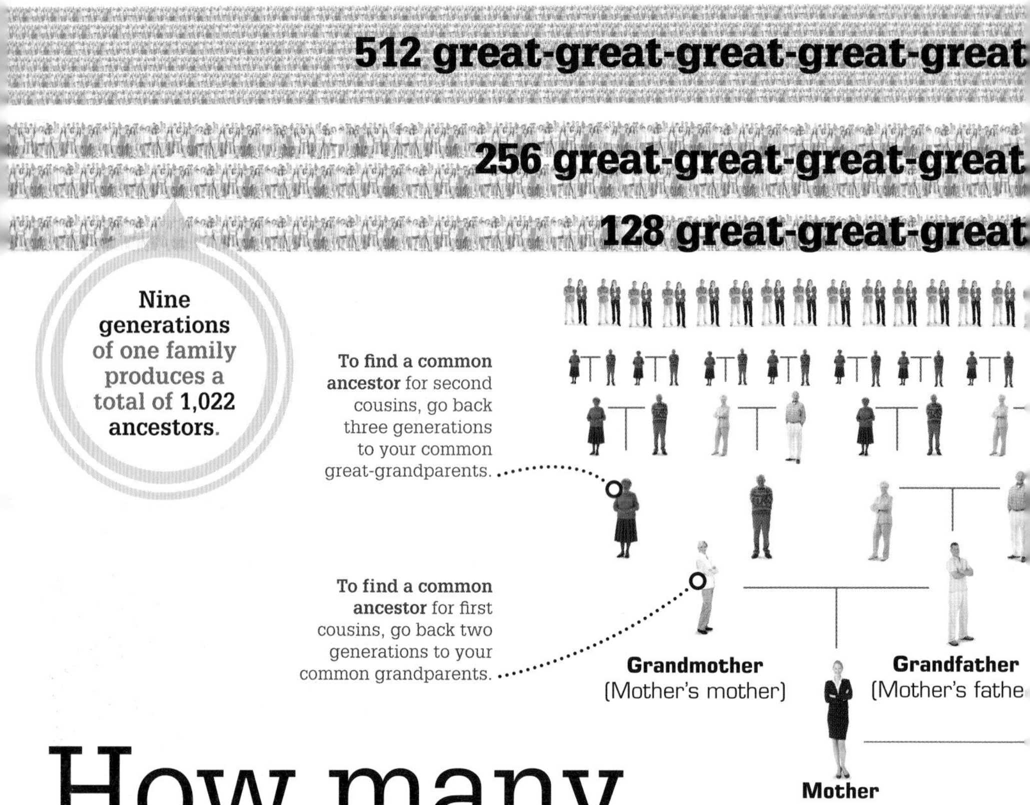

512 great-great-great-great-great

256 great-great-great-great

128 great-great-great

Nine generations of one family produces a total of **1,022** ancestors.

To find a common **ancestor** for second cousins, go back three generations to your common great-grandparents.

To find a common **ancestor** for first cousins, go back two generations to your common grandparents.

Grandmother
(Mother's mother)

Grandfather
(Mother's fathe

Mother

How many
ancestors
do we have?

Your **family tree** starts with you today, but involves many thousands of other people making up **generations** of family **history**. Going back just **two centuries** gives you **1,022** ancestors.

great-great-grandparents

great-great-grandparents

great-great-grandparents

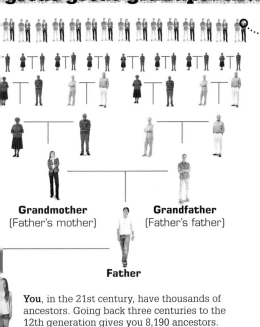

.... Six generations back, you have 64 great-great-great-great-grandparents, who lived in the mid-19th century.

Grandmother
(Father's mother)

Grandfather
(Father's father)

Father

You, in the 21st century, have thousands of ancestors. Going back three centuries to the 12th generation gives you 8,190 ancestors. One generation is usually 20–25 years.

HEREDITARY GENES

People inherit family features—such as eye color—from both sides of their family. Some traits may skip a generation, giving a grandchild the same color eyes as her grandmother, but not her mother.

FAST FACTS

The current world population is nearly 7.4 billion people. This is 7 percent of the 107 billion people who have ever lived.

■ **Current population** 7.4 billion people

■ **Total population** 107 billion people

Genghis Khan, Mongol leader in the 13th century, had many children. Today 8 percent of men in 16 Asian countries have genes suggesting they descended from him.

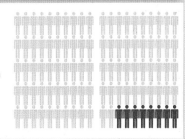

How **far** does a person **walk** in a **lifetime?**

The average person takes at least **5,000 steps** every day. Over a lifetime of 70 years, this adds up to a distance of more than **64,000 miles** (103,000 km).

Studies have shown that people of different nations walk different distances each day depending on their location and lifestyle.

It takes roughly 2,000 steps to cover a distance of 1 mile (1,240 steps over 1 km). Walking 5,000 steps a day covers 2.5 miles (4 km), but most people actually take more steps.

Average number of steps taken per day

12,000		
10,000		
8,000		Australia, Switzerland
6,000		Japan
4,000	USA	UK, Germany
2,000		

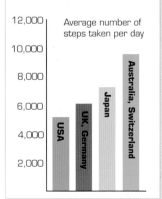

THE WANDERER

The world's longest circumnavigation on foot was by Canadian Jean Béliveau. Starting in 2000, he walked through 64 countries in 11 years, covering 46,000 miles (75,000 km) and wearing out 54 pairs of shoes.

The equator is an imaginary line around Earth's center. At 24,902 miles (40,075 km) long, it would take almost 50 million steps to walk the length of it.

In **70 years**, the average person will walk **2.5 times** around Earth's equator.

Earth is not a perfect sphere— it is slightly squashed at the poles and bulges around the middle.

Time data

HAPPY BIRTHDAY

▶ In a group of 23 people, there's more than a **50 percent** chance (actually 50.73 percent) that two of them share a birthday.

▶ With a group of 57 people, there's a **99.01 percent** probability, and for 70 people the probability is **99.92 percent.**

TIME IS MONEY

If you earned $1 every second, it would take 12 days to become a **millionaire,** but you would need 31 years to become a billionaire.

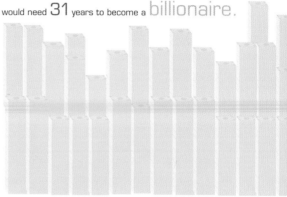

TIME IS RELATIVE

Einstein said that time changes depending on where you are (roughly speaking): the closer you are to the center of Earth, the slower time passes. If you were at the top of

Mount Everest,

a year would be 15 microseconds (millionths of a second) **shorter** than if you were at sea level.

Meanwhile, the shortest measure of time you can have is **Planck time**.
This is the time it takes for light to travel in a vacuum for a distance of 1 Planck length. This is the same as:

**0.000,000,000,000,000,000,000,000,000,
000,000,000,000,000,000,054** seconds.

TIME ZONES

If everyone in the **world** set their **clocks** to noon, it would be **daytime** in some parts of the world and **nighttime** in others. To avoid this problem, **Earth** is divided into a number of **time zones**.

 There are **39 different time zones** in use. Most are set whole hours ahead or behind GMT (Greenwich Mean Time). Some, however, are **30** or **45 minutes** different.

 Greenwich, in London, UK, was chosen as the location of standard time because it lies at **0° longitude** on the world map.

 Time zones meet at the **North** and **South Poles**. By walking around the poles, you can travel through **all** of the time zones in a few seconds.

 India straddles **two** time zones, but has chosen a time halfway between them **(GMT + 5 h 30 m)** so that the whole country can use one time.

Time zones run along **lines of longitude**, but **bend** to include entire countries or states into one zone.

The Greenwich Meridian is an imaginary line that runs along **0° longitude**.

If you stood where the borders of Finland, Norway, and Russia meet, you can be in **three time zones at once!**

Russia has **11 time zones**—the most of any country.

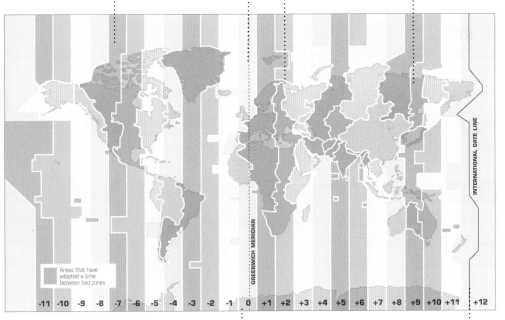

Areas that have adopted a time between two zones

-11 -10 -9 -8 -7 -6 -5 -4 -3 -2 -1 0 +1 +2 +3 +4 +5 +6 +7 +8 +9 +10 +11 +12

GREENWICH MERIDIAN

INTERNATIONAL DATE LINE

Each **time zone** is measured in hours ahead of or behind **GMT**. When it's **noon** in London, it's **1 p.m.** in most of Europe.

The **International Date Line** is an imaginary line at 180° longitude. Countries **east** of the line are one day **ahead** of those on the **west** of it.

In 1990 Malaysian strong man Ramasamy Letchemanah used his hair to pull a Boeing 737 aircraft in Kuala Lumpur 56 ft (17 m), setting a new world record. His abilities were passed on to his daughter, who pulled a truck with her hair in 2002.

STICKY SITUATIONS

One head of hair pulled a 37 ton (34 metric tons) aircraft for a record-breaking 56 ft (17 m).

In some countries, hairdressers and pet groomers donate cut hair to help clean up oil spills at sea. Leaked oil clings to these hairy mats (above), just like oil coats your hair when it's on your head.

7 METER

8 METER

10 METER

11 METER

How strong is hair?

A **head** of **human hair** is strong enough to lift **13 tons** (12 metric tons). Just a small bunch of **100 hairs** can support **22 lb** (10 kg).

...The Boeing 737 passenger aircraft weighed 37 tons (34 metric tons).

Letchemanah's hair was dressed in two braids to attach them to the aircraft.

Nicknamed **"Mighty Man,"** Letchemanah went on to pull a double-decker bus in 1999.

FAST FACTS

Hair grows up to ½ in (1.25 cm) a month, or 6 in (15 cm) a year. Studies show Asian hair grows fastest, while African hair grows at nearer 4 in (10 cm) a year and Caucasian hair at 5 in (13 cm) a year.

It takes 2 years for hair to reach shoulder-length (10 in/25 cm)

It takes 7 years for hair to reach waist-length (34 in/85 cm)

12 METER | 13 METER | 14 METER | 15 METER | 16 METER | 17 METER

How much power does your brain have?

Your brain has more than **80 billion neurons,** or nerve cells. When you're awake, these can generate **0.085 watts of electricity.**

Your brain generates enough **electricity to power an LED lightbulb.**

An average brain is about the size of a cauliflower. It is 75 percent water and has the texture of soft cheese.

The adult brain weighs about 3 lb (1.3 kg), which is only about two percent of the body's total weight—yet it uses 20 percent of the oxygen and 20 percent of the glucose in the blood.

Each groove on the brain's surface is called a sulcus, which means "furrow" in Latin. The ridged area around each sulcus is called a gyrus, which means "circle."

Electricity produced by the brain cannot be harnessed and used as a power supply. Rather, electrical signals carry messages within the brain and to the body. Billions of neurons act as messengers, carrying chemical and electrical signals between brain and body.

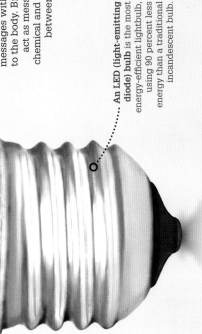

An LED (light-emitting diode) bulb is the most energy-efficient lightbulb, using 90 percent less energy than a traditional incandescent bulb.

BRAIN DRAIN

Some creatures do not have a brain. Sponges have no brain or nervous system. They do not need to move: food comes to them, filtered from the water that is drawn into their bodies.

FAST FACTS

A human brain is about 6½ in (16.7 cm) long and 5½ in (14 cm) wide. If all the wrinkles were stretched out, the surface area would cover 2¾ sq ft (2,500 cm²)—about the area of two of these books, opened.

Brain size varies in the animal kingdom. Generally, the bigger the animal's body, the larger the brain—although elephants have small brains in relation to their body size. The heaviest brain belongs to the sperm whale, around six times heavier than the average adult human brain; and a whopping 130,000 times the weight of the smallest mammal brain, which is that of the Etruscan shrew.

Elephant
10½ lb (4.8 kg)

Sperm whale
17 lb (7.8 kg)

Adult human
3 lb (1.3 kg)

Etruscan shrew
0.002 oz (0.06 g)

How much saliva do you produce in a day?

The average person produces between ½ and 1½ quarts (0.5–1.5 liters) of saliva a day, adding up to around **115 gallons** (436 liters) a year.

A human can produce enough **spit every day** to fill a 1½ quart (1.5 liter) **bottle.**

Saliva helps you dissolve substances in food in your mouth so they can come into contact with your taste buds, which detect tastes.

SALIVA!

SWIFT SALIVA

Many birds in the swift family use saliva to glue together nest materials. Some species make their nests from only saliva, which hardens in the air. These nests are used by people to make the delicacy bird's nest soup.

Saliva is produced by salivary glands. The three major pairs of salivary glands are located on the inside of each cheek, at the bottom of the mouth, and under the jaw at the front of the mouth.

Human saliva is 98 percent water, which helps to keep your mouth and teeth clean.

Helps to taste food!

Assists in keeping teeth clean!

1½ quarts
Contains water, electrolytes, enzymes, mucus, and bacteria-killing substances

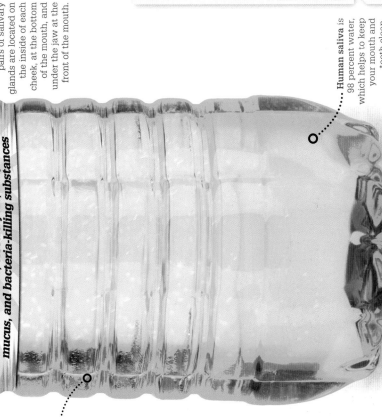

The main purpose of saliva is to aid the body's digestive process. Food is moistened, making it easier to swallow, and broken down by substances called enzymes. Saliva is also a natural painkiller and mouth cleaner.

Most saliva is produced during the day, which is why people can wake up with dry mouths in the morning.

FAST FACTS

In a lifetime, a person creates enough saliva to fill between 1 and 2 small swimming pools.

Every time you cough, about 3,000 droplets of saliva are released from the mouth at speeds of up to 50 mph (80 kph).

How much oxygen is in your body?

There are **25 different elements** in your body. **Oxygen** is by far the most abundant, at **65 percent** of your **body mass**. Adding **nitrogen, hydrogen,** and **carbon** accounts for **96 percent** of your mass.

All these elements are essential for life to exist. Elements are substances made from one type of atom: for example, oxygen is made of oxygen atoms. An atom is the smallest, most basic particle that cannot be broken down further. Atoms often bond with each other to produce molecules, such as water. Each water molecule contains two hydrogen atoms and one oxygen atom.

Oxygen

This colorless gas allows your body cells to obtain the energy from food that keeps them alive.

Nitrogen

A small amount of nitrogen is needed to make complex molecules such as proteins and DNA.

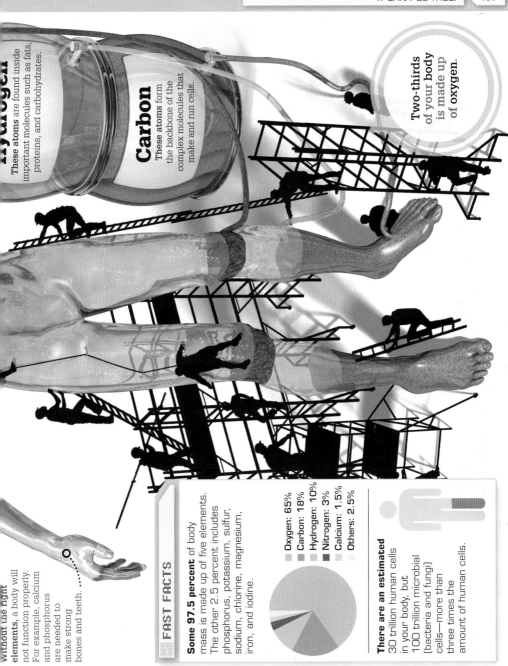

Hydrogen

These atoms are found inside important molecules such as fats, proteins, and carbohydrates.

Carbon

These atoms form the backbone of the complex molecules that make and run cells.

> Two-thirds of your body is made up of oxygen.

without the right elements, a body will not function properly. For example, calcium and phosphorus are needed to make strong bones and teeth.

FAST FACTS

Some 97.5 percent of body mass is made up of five elements. The other 2.5 percent includes phosphorus, potassium, sulfur, sodium, chlorine, magnesium, iron, and iodine.

- Oxygen: 65%
- Carbon: 18%
- Hydrogen: 10%
- Nitrogen: 3%
- Calcium: 1.5%
- Others: 2.5%

There are an estimated 30 trillion human cells in your body, but 100 trillion microbial (bacteria and fungi) cells—more than three times the amount of human cells.

How much do your feet sweat?

There are about **250,000 sweat glands** in your feet, producing at least **1 cup (250 ml)** of sweat **every day**.

Feet produce about **one glassful** of **sweat** a day.

Smelly feet is the result of body odor, which occurs when sweat mixes with bacteria on the skin.

Sweat contains tiny amounts of minerals and metals, including sodium, potassium, calcium, magnesium, zinc, copper, iron, chromium, nickel, and lead.

FAST FACTS

People's bodies produce different amounts of sweat depending on how hard they work and how hot it is.

Average: 1 quart (1 liter) per day

Moderate exercise: 6 quarts (6 liters) per day

Lots of exercise: 15 quarts (15 liters) per day

Sweat is produced in glands in the skin. A tube carries the sweat to the surface, where it is released through a pore.

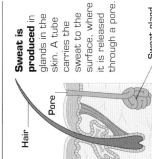

Hair

Pore

Sweat gland

The average adult has 2–4 million sweat glands on most areas of the skin. These glands help the body regulate its temperature to 98.6 °F (37 °C).

Sweat is salty water, which the body produces to control temperature. When the body is hot, sweat evaporates from the surface of the skin to cool it down. This evaporation, and the fact that your clothes absorb sweat, is why you don't always feel wet when you sweat.

STRESSED OUT

People sweat when they are feeling nervous or are in stressful situations. Emotional sweating occurs on the forehead, armpits, palms of hands, and soles of feet.

How **tiny** is a **virus?**

Rhinoviruses are the **tiny** chemical packages that cause the common **cold**. They measure **30 nanometers** (nm) across, which is **30 billionths** of **3 ft** (1 m).

pinhead magnified **190 times**

The pin and viruses are shown here at 190 times magnification.

SPEEDY SNEEZE

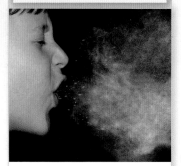

A single sneeze produces more than 40,000 droplets of moisture that may contain millions of viruses and bacteria. These exit the nose at up to 80 mph (130 kph) and can travel up to 33 ft (10 m).

Around 2,267,250,000 rhinoviruses can fit on the head of a pin.

A pinhead measures 0.06 in (1.5 mm) in diameter.

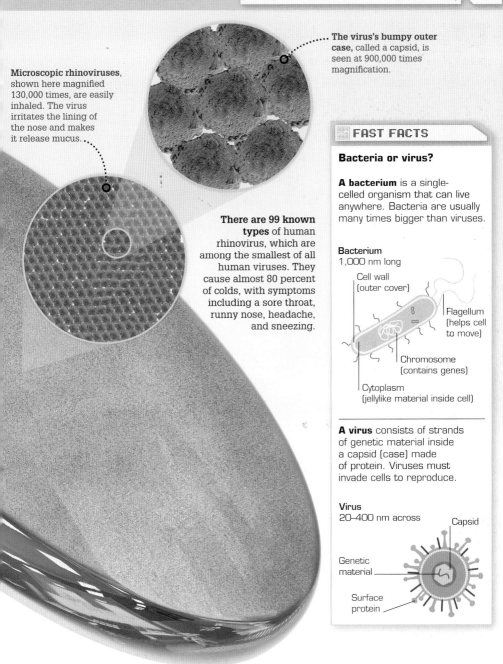

The virus's bumpy outer case, called a capsid, is seen at 900,000 times magnification.

Microscopic rhinoviruses, shown here magnified 130,000 times, are easily inhaled. The virus irritates the lining of the nose and makes it release mucus.

There are 99 known types of human rhinovirus, which are among the smallest of all human viruses. They cause almost 80 percent of colds, with symptoms including a sore throat, runny nose, headache, and sneezing.

FAST FACTS

Bacteria or virus?

A **bacterium** is a single-celled organism that can live anywhere. Bacteria are usually many times bigger than viruses.

Bacterium
1,000 nm long

Cell wall
(outer cover)

Flagellum
(helps cell
to move)

Chromosome
(contains genes)

Cytoplasm
(jellylike material inside cell)

A **virus** consists of strands of genetic material inside a capsid (case) made of protein. Viruses must invade cells to reproduce.

Virus
20–400 nm across

Capsid

Genetic
material

Surface
protein

Body data

SKIN STATISTICS

Your skin is the **largest**, heaviest organ of your body. The average adult has **22 sq ft (2 m²)** of skin, which is enough to cover a doorway. • An adult's skin can weigh more than **20 lb** (9 kg)—the same as four house bricks. • The cells that make up your skin die and fall off. We lose **30,000–40,000** dead skin cells every hour. This adds up to **105 lb** (47 kg) over a lifetime. • Your skin's upper layer is replaced every 4 weeks.

IN ONE YEAR, THE AVERAGE PERSON...

- grows **6 in** (15 cm) of **H A I R**.
- creates **26 gallons** (100 liters) of **tears**.
- sweats **71 gallons** (270 liters) of **SWEAT**.
- produces **159 gallons** (600 liters) of URINE and **360 lb** (160 kg) of **poop**.

D N A

Each cell in your body contains instructions (called **genes**) that determine how the cell works and what your body looks like. The genes are carried on structures called **chromosomes**, which are made from **deoxyribonucleic acid**, or DNA.

Humans share **98 percent** of our DNA with chimps. We also share **50 percent** with bananas!

BACTERIA   BANANA   MOUSE   CHIMP   HUMAN

0%   18%   50%   85%   98%   100%

FEELING FINE

▶ Your sense of touch is incredible, with your fingers able to feel objects as small as **13 nanometers** (about one-fifth of the thickness of a hair).

WHAT NERVE!

▶ **Nerves transmit impulses** (send signals) around your body to keep it moving and working. The signals travel *to and from* the **brain along the spinal cord**.

▶ The average speed of **nerve impulses** traveling to and from the brain is **165–200 ft** (50–60 meters) per second, which works out to **112–134 mph** (180–216 kph).

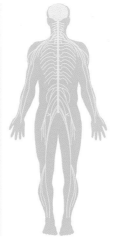

Stretched out

...e DNA from **one cell nucleus** would be about 6 ft (1.8 m) long, ...hich is the height of an average man.

All the DNA found in your body's cells would create a chain more than **10 billion miles (16 billion km) long.** It could reach to Pluto and back when Earth and Pluto are at their farthest apart!

HAIR *RAISING*

...n average...

blonds have **130,000** hairs on their head.

brunettes have **110,000** hairs on their head.

redheads have **90,000** hairs on their head.

▶ Hair is made of **keratin**, the same protein found in animal hooves and claws.

Hair is made up of:

50 percent carbon,

21 percent oxygen,

17 percent nitrogen,

6 percent hydrogen,

and 5 percent sulfur.

How much **rice** is **eaten** in a **year?**

As an average across the world, each person eats **150 lb** (68 kg) of **rice** a **year**. That gives a total amount of **481,210,000 tons** (436,546,368 metric tons) eaten across the world.

The amount of **rice** eaten **globally** is the same weight as **84 Great Pyramids**.

Almost half of the global population eat rice regularly. Farmers in Asia produce about 90 percent of the world's rice, with China and India producing more than half of the total amount grown.

Rice is the biggest staple food for much of the world, particularly in Asia, where rice consumption is highest.

Rice comes in 40,000 varieties. Most is eaten in the region in which it is grown.

FLOODED FIELDS

Rice is grown in wet paddy fields. These are affected by climate change, and damage from droughts and floods may cut rice production by 50 percent by 2050.

More than 2.3 million blocks of stone were used in the construction of the Great Pyramid in Giza, Egypt. The largest blocks weigh 0 tons (63 metric tons) each.

The Great Pyramid weighs about 5.7 tons (5.2 million metric tons).

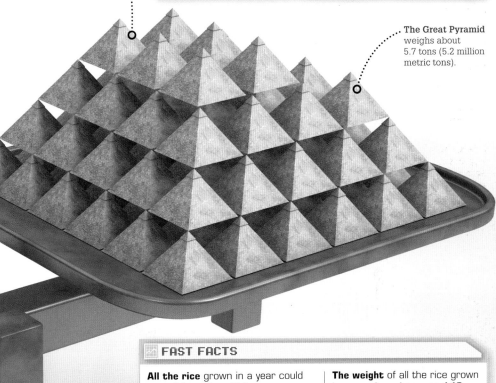

FAST FACTS

All the rice grown in a year could cover Mongolia, which has an area of 0.6 million sq miles (1.6 million km²).

The weight of all the rice grown in a year is as heavy as 142 Great Pyramids.

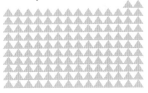

What's the hottest chili pepper?

The **Carolina Reaper** holds the record for the hottest chili, hitting 1,569,300 on the **Scoville scale**. This measures how hot a chili is in Scoville Heat Units (**SHU**).

FAST FACTS

A chili is the fruit of a plant that protects the seeds. The placenta is the hottest part of the pepper because it contains the most capsaicin—the chemical that makes them spicy. The endocarp also has high levels of capsaicin.

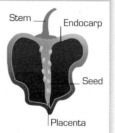

Stem

Endocarp

Seed

Placenta

In 1912 American pharmacist Wilbur Scoville devised the Scoville scale to measure how many times a chili would have to be diluted in sugar water before its heat could not be felt. This was originally judged only by an individual's taste, which was highly inaccurate. Today the scale is measured scientifically, with pure capsaicin at 16 million SHU.

Tabasco peppers are hot, but they are watered down to make tabasco sauce, which has a rating of 2,500–5,000 SHU.

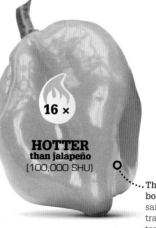

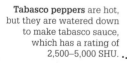

16 ×

HOTTER than jalapeño (100,000 SHU)

JALAPEÑO pepper

(2,500–10,000 SHU)

6 ×

HOTTER than jalapeño (30,000–50,000 SHU)

The Scotch bonnet chili is said to resemble a traditional Scottish tam o'shanter hat.

Although the **Carolina Reaper's** world record is logged at an average 1,569,300 SHU, there are claims that the hottest peaked at 2,200,000 SHU.

296 ×

HOTTER
than jalapeño
(1,500,000–
2,200,000 SHU)

140 ×

HOTTER
than jalapeño
(55,000 SHU)

The **ghost pepper** shows that the stronger the chili, the more wrinkly the exterior.

The **official hottest Carolina Reaper** was 230 times times hotter than a **jalapeño pepper.**

How many **apples** do we **grow?**

More than **88 million tons** (80 million metric tons) of apples are grown around the world **each year.** Because an apple weighs about **5.3 oz** (150 g), that works out to **44,900,000,000** apples every **month.**

SQUARE APPLES

The packaging problems of round fruit can be solved by making them square. In Korea, some apples are grown in plastic molds so they take on a square shape.

All the apples grown in a **month** would fill **the** Colosseum six times over.

There are thought to be 7,500 varieties of apple grown across the world. The fruit originated in central Asia thousands of years ago.

The Colosseum in Rome, Italy, was built in 80 CE for sporting events. It seated 50,000–87,000 spectators.

The 538,800,000,000 apples grown globally in a year are enough for each person on Earth to have 73.8 apples a year.

All the apples grown in a year would cover 910 sq miles (2,380 km²)—larger than the entire island of Mauritius in the Indian Ocean.

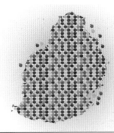

This chart shows how much fruit was grown in a year, by weight. The most popular fruit grown in the world is the banana.

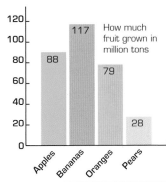

How much fruit grown in million tons

Apples	Bananas	Oranges	Pears
88	117	79	28

How much **sugar** is in our **food?**

Sugar is **added** to most of the **packaged** foods we eat and can make up **one-third** of the content. Eating too much sugar leads to **health problems**, such as tooth decay, obesity, and diabetes.

Ketchup is almost one-quarter sugar, making it a high-sugar food. It is low in fat and contains vitamins A and C, but should still be eaten sparingly.

Ketchup
16 oz (460 g)

30% SUGAR

Cereal bar
1.3 oz (35 g)

23% SUGAR

One can of regular **soda** contains **9 teaspoonfuls of sugar.**

One sugar cube is 0.14 oz (4 g) of sugar, which is a teaspoonful. Just 0.03 oz (1 g) of sugar has four calories, making 16 calories in every cube.

Strawberry yogurt
4 oz (120 g)

16% SUGAR

Soda
12 fl oz (330 ml)

10.6% SUGAR

▦ FAST FACTS

About 188 million tons (180 million metric tons) of raw sugar is processed in a year, mainly from sugar cane and sugar beet. It includes minor sugar sources, such as the sap of sugar palm trees.

272,120,586 tons (247,382,351 metric tons)

1,023,000 tons (930,000 metric tons)

208,802,718 tons (1,898,206,534 metric tons)

■ Sugar cane   ■ Sugar beet   ■ Minor sources

Sugar cane, type of grass, 10–15 percent sucrose (compound that makes sugar)

Sugar maple sap, 1.6–2 percent sucrose

Sugar beet, root crop, 13–18 percent sucrose

Orange juice
18 fl oz (500 ml)

The World Health Organization recommends the daily allowance of "free sugar" (sugar added to food) for a healthy adult is a maximum of 1.7 oz (50 g), or 12 teaspoons. This equates to no more than 10 percent of an adult's 2,000-calorie daily diet. For children, the allowance is less.

Flavored water
9 fl oz (250 ml)

Tomato soup
14 oz (400 g)

8.3% SUGAR

8% SUGAR

5% SUGAR

Which **food** has the most **vitamin C?**

Oranges are known as a source of **vitamin C,** but other **fruit** and **vegetables** contain much more. **Yellow peppers** are the **richest source** of all.

Vitamin C helps to repair bones, blood, and other body tissues. It also keeps gums healthy, helps the body absorb iron from food, protects against bruises, and heals cuts.

One orange could supply a nine-year-old plus a five-year-old with their recommended daily allowance (RDA) of vitamin C.

One yellow pepper contains almost **five times** as much **vitamin C** as an **orange**.

PEPPERS PAST

Peppers are native to Central and South America and have been eaten since ancient times. Christopher Columbus named the pungent fruit after the hot spice pepper; he is thought to have brought them to Europe.

69.7 mg
Vitamin C

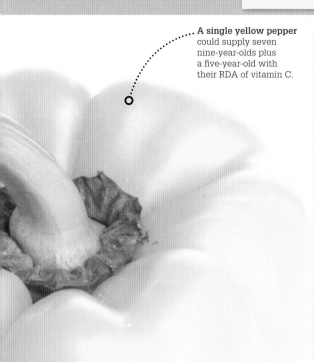

A single yellow pepper could supply seven nine-year-olds plus a five-year-old with their RDA of vitamin C.

341.3 mg
Vitamin C

The color of a pepper changes as it ripens, starting green, then turning yellow, and through orange to red. The level of vitamin C the pepper contains changes as it changes color, increasing from 120 mg (green) to 341.3 mg (yellow), then decreasing to 190 mg (red).

Recommended daily allowances (RDA) of vitamin C differ around the world, and recommended amounts also increase with age. This chart shows the US RDA.

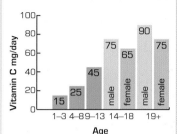

Vitamin C mg/day

					90	
15	25	45	75	65		75
			male	female	male	female
1–3	4–8	9–13	14–18		19+	

Age

The human body cannot make or store vitamin C, so, to stay healthy, your diet must include regular amounts. Below shows how much you need to eat of certain foods to get 60 mg of vitamin C.

30 black currants

6 strawberries

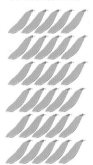

30 snow peas

85% of an orange

How much **milk** do we **consume?**

About **885 million tons** (805 million metric tons) of milk is produced each year. People don't just **drink** it: milk is used to make dairy products, including **cheese**, **butter**, and **yogurt**.

All mammals are brought up drinking milk—but humans are the only species that regularly drinks the milk of a different animal.

Each tanker has a capacity of 8,360 gallons (38,000 liters).

FAST FACTS

On average, one cow produces 6–8 gallons (27–36 liters) of milk each day, which is enough to fill 144 glasses.

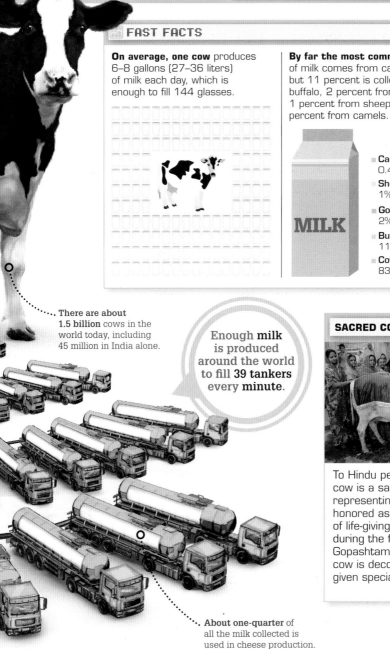

By far the most common type of milk comes from cattle (83 percent), but 11 percent is collected from buffalo, 2 percent from goats, 1 percent from sheep, and 0.4 percent from camels.

MILK

- Camel milk 0.4%
- Sheep milk 1%
- Goat's milk 2%
- Buffalo milk 11%
- Cow's milk 83%

There are about 1.5 billion cows in the world today, including 45 million in India alone.

Enough **milk** is produced around the world to fill **39 tankers** every **minute**.

SACRED COWS

To Hindu people, the cow is a sacred symbol representing all life. It is honored as the provider of life-giving milk, especially during the festival of Gopashtama, when the cow is decorated and given special food.

About one-quarter of all the milk collected is used in cheese production.

Food and drink data

HOW MUCH FOOD?

All the people in the world **eat** a total of **5,658 tons** (5,144 metric tons) of food **every minute**. It would take **23 supertankers** to carry the world's food for one day. We also waste 2,719 tons (2,472 metric tons) of food **each minute**, so another **11 supertankers** would be needed to carry the world's food waste every day.

 Waste

 Eaten food

TIME FOR TEA

 PRODUCTION

There are around **1,500 types** of tea. • Tea was first brewed in China around 5,000 years ago. • More than **5½ million tons** (5 million metric tons) of tea are produced in a year—enough for a daily cup for everyone on Earth.

Tea is the world's most widely drunk beverage after water. • People in Turkey drink the most tea: **7 lb** (3.16 kg) per person each year, which works out to more than **three cups** every day. • Blocks of tea were used as currency in Siberia until **200** years ago.

 CONSUMPTION

of the **eggs** laid in the world are laid in **China**—that's around **495.75 billion per year.**

 %

 7

 3

Some **4 billion eggs** are laid every day. These could make an omelet **24.3 sq miles (63 km²)** in area, which is around **15 times** the size of **Disneyland, Paris**.

CHOCOLATE TREATS

- Around **4½ million tons** (4 million metric tons) of cocoa beans are produced every year • That's **12,056 tons** (10,960 metric tons) a day.
- It takes **400 cocoa beans** to make **1 lb** of chocolate (880 for 1 kg) • Two-thirds of the world's cocoa beans are grown in **Africa**, with the **Ivory Coast**, the world's leading producer, harvesting **2 million tons** (1.8 million metric tons) a year. • Europe doesn't grow any cocoa, but eight of the top ten chocolate-consuming countries are European. • Swiss people eat the most chocolate: **20 lb** (9 kg), or **180 bars** per person per year.

MORE THAN **YOUR FIVE A DAY**

The longest carrot ever grown was **20.5 ft** (6.25 m)—more than three times the height of a man.

The heaviest cabbage grown weighed **138¼ lb** (62.7 kg)—the same as two children.

The heaviest lemon grown weighed **11 lb 10 oz** (5.26 kg)—about the weight of a small dog.

The heaviest pumpkin grown weighed **2,624.6 lb** (1,190.5 kg)—as much as a large walrus.

The heaviest tomato grown weighed **8 lb 6½ oz** (3.81 kg)—as much as a house cat.

How **big** was the *Titanic*?

At almost **883 ft** (270 m) **long**, the ill-fated *Titanic* was the **largest liner** of its day, yet it would be dwarfed by **modern cruise ships**, such as *Harmony of the Seas*.

It took two years to build the *Titanic*, which was claimed to be the safest ship ever and carried just 20 lifeboats for the 2,200 people on board. In April 1912, on its maiden voyage from the UK to New York, the *Titanic* collided with an iceberg and sank. More than 1,500 people died.

FOUR FUNNELS

The *Titanic* was built in Belfast, Northern Ireland, and is shown above on its way from the shipyard to Southampton, England. The ship had four funnels, but only three worked. The fourth was added because the builder thought it looked better.

Harmony of the Seas is nearly **five times** greater in **volume** than the *Titanic*.

FAST FACTS

Titanic

length 1,188 ft (362 m)
Harmony of the Seas

length 882 ft (269 m)

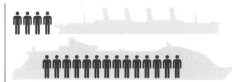

Modern cruiseliner *Harmony of the Seas* is almost 328 ft (100 m) longer than the *Titanic*, while its beam (width) is 217 ft (66 m) compared to the *Titanic's* 92 ft (28 m).

Harmony of the Seas can carry 3½ times more people than the *Titanic* did. The *Titanic* had 2,200 passengers and crew; *Harmony of the Seas* has 5,479 passengers and 2,100 crew.

The biggest cruise ship on the ocean, *Harmony of the Seas* has 16 decks and more than 2,700 rooms on board.

The doomed luxury liner *Titanic* had 10 decks and 840 rooms. There were also 20 lifeboats, used by the 705 survivors.

What's the world's biggest truck?

The **BelAZ 75710** is a huge **dump truck**, used for mining. It measures **67 ft** (20.6 m) **long**, **26 ft** (8 m) **high**, and **32 ft** (10 m) **wide**.

The BelAZ can travel at 40 mph (64 kph)—as fast as a zebra can run, but slower than a standard-size LGV (large goods vehicle). Powering the monster-size truck takes 553 gallons of diesel fuel per 100 miles (1,300 liters per 100 km).

FAST FACTS

The BelAZ 75710 could just about squeeze inside a tennis court.

249 ft (76 m)

13 miles (21 km)

If the BelAZ and a car were both given 1 gallon (4 liters) of fuel, the car would be able to travel 281 times farther than the truck.

African elephants are the largest land animals, weighing up to 5½ tons (5 metric tons).

The truck weighs 400 tons (360 metric tons), but it can carry more than it weighs, taking on 500 tons (450 metric tons).

The **BelAZ 75710** could carry **90** fully grown **African elephants**.

Eight wheels are arranged in pairs to support the weighty truck.

75710

958

WEENY WHEELS

The Peel P50 is one of the world's smallest cars. The three-wheeled microcar is 53 in (134 cm) long, 39 in (99 cm) wide, and 39½ in (100 cm) tall. It was manufactured on the Isle of Man, UK, in the 1960s.

FJ61 NAA

Relative size of a human and an African elephant compared to the truck

How many **cars** are in the **world?**

Globally there are an estimated **1.2 billion cars**, which works out to about **one car** for every **six people**. Parked together, they would fill an area of **9,637 sq miles** (24,960 km²).

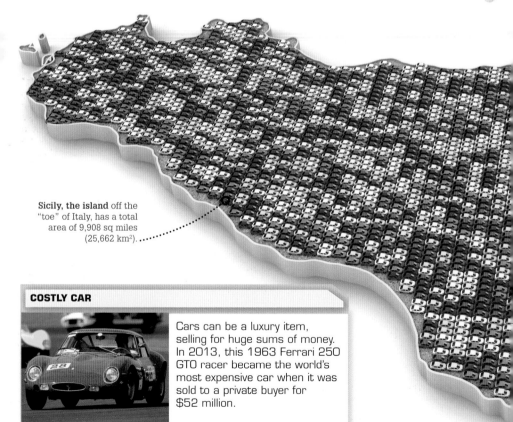

Sicily, the island off the "toe" of Italy, has a total area of 9,908 sq miles (25,662 km²).

COSTLY CAR

Cars can be a luxury item, selling for huge sums of money. In 2013, this 1963 Ferrari 250 GTO racer became the world's most expensive car when it was sold to a private buyer for $52 million.

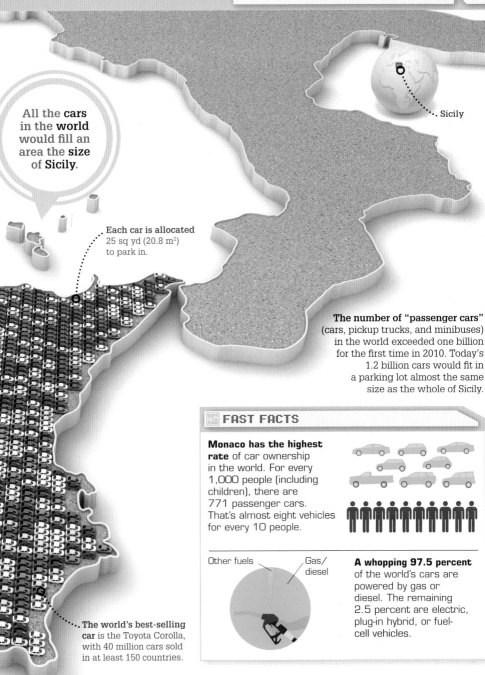

All the **cars** in the **world** would fill an area the **size** of **Sicily**.

Each car is allocated 25 sq yd (20.8 m²) to park in.

Sicily

The number of "passenger cars" (cars, pickup trucks, and minibuses) in the world exceeded one billion for the first time in 2010. Today's 1.2 billion cars would fit in a parking lot almost the same size as the whole of Sicily.

FAST FACTS

Monaco has the highest rate of car ownership in the world. For every 1,000 people (including children), there are 771 passenger cars. That's almost eight vehicles for every 10 people.

Other fuels

Gas/ diesel

A whopping 97.5 percent of the world's cars are powered by gas or diesel. The remaining 2.5 percent are electric, plug-in hybrid, or fuel-cell vehicles.

The world's best-selling car is the Toyota Corolla, with 40 million cars sold in at least 150 countries.

How **big** is the **biggest plane?**

The **largest** and **heaviest** airplane to take flight is the Ukrainian cargo jet **Antonov An-225**. Built to carry the Soviet space shuttle *Buran*, its maximum takeoff weight is **1.32 million lb** (600,000 kg) and it is **275 ft** (84 m) long.

The nose flips up to allow loading from the front.

INTERNATIONAL CARGO TRANSPORTER

ANTONOV 225

There are 32 tires on the plane, 20 of which are steerable.

More than six million classic and new MINIs have been sold since the car was first produced in 1959.

FAST FACTS

The An-225 is the longest plane, but another has a bigger wingspan—the Hughes H-4 Spruce Goose, a World War II military prototype.

An-225 290 ft
(88.4 m)

Hughes H-4 320 ft
(97.5 m)

To be level with the tailfin of the An-225, a person must look from a fifth-story window.

Tailfin 59½ ft
(18.1 m)

PIGGYBACK PLANE

Anything that cannot fit inside the An-225 goes on its back. It can take objects up to 33 ft (10 m) wide and 230 ft (70 m) long. The *Buran* space shuttle was just 119 ft (36.37 m) long.

There are six engines (three on each side), taking the aircraft to a top speed of 500 mph (800 kph).

The twin tailfin was designed to allow for the plane to carry external loads. ....O

UR-00000

22 MINI cars could **line up nose to tail alongside an An-225.**

There is only one An-225—a second was partly built and remains in storage. The aircraft is nicknamed Mriya, which is Ukrainian for "dream." At the time of the An-225's first flight in 1988, it was 50 percent larger than any other aircraft.

How **big** is the **biggest** submarine?

Russia's **Typhoon-Class** is the largest submarine ever built. It measures **574 ft** (175 m) long, **70 ft** (23 m) wide, and weighs **29,000 tons** (26,500 metric tons). The Typhoon is designed for **size**, **speed**, and **deep dives**.

Only six Typhoon-Class submarines were built, and just one remains in operation today. These nuclear-powered ballistic missile submarines were developed in the 1970s for the Russian Navy, but were phased out at the end of the Soviet Union's Cold War with the West.

Two large nuclear reactors inside the Typhoon submarine provide the power.

In Russia, Typhoon-Class is called Project 941 Akula Class, and is nicknamed "Shark."

The **Typhoon-Class** is the same **length** as 350 children stood shoulder-to-shoulder.

FAST FACTS

A Typhoon-Class submarine can reach a maximum depth of 1,300 ft (400 m). This is deeper than the height of the Eiffel Tower in Paris, France.

Each Typhoon submarine carried a crew of 150 on board, which would fill up three buses.

Typhoon is almost half the length of the *TI Oceania*—one of the longest supertankers in the sea today.

TI Oceania
1,246 ft (380 m)

Typhoon
574 ft (175 m)

Typhoon can stay submerged for at least 120 days. The only restriction is the crew must bring in new food supplies after that time.

The maximum speed underwater is 30 mph (50 kph), which is the same as a blue whale over a short distance.

DREBBLE'S DREAM

Dutch designer Cornelius Drebble built the first navigable submarine in 1620. Based on a rowboat, it had a watertight hatch, four oars, and a rudder.

FAST FACTS

Laid out flat, the balloon fabric for the Red Bull Stratos mission would cover 40 acres (161,874 m²)—about the size of 22 soccer fields.

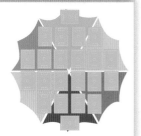

Uninflated, the Red Bull Stratos balloon weighed 3,708 lb (1,682 kg)—the same as 12 giant pandas.

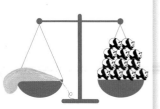

The balloon was made of very thin strips of high-performance plastic film.

The largest **hot-air balloon** was **taller** than the Elizabeth Tower (known as **Big Ben).**

How **big** is the **largest** hot-air balloon?

The Red Bull Stratos hot-air balloon was **334 ft** (102 m) **tall**. It carried Austrian skydiver Felix Baumgartner **24 miles** (39 km) into the atmosphere so he could freefall and **parachute** back to Earth.

READY FOR LAUNCH

At launch, the Red Bull Stratos balloon was as tall as a 55-story building. As the balloon climbed higher in the sky, the helium gas expanded to fill the balloon slowly, giving it an almost perfectly round shape.

Hot-air balloons are the oldest form of human flight, comprising a balloon (called an envelope), burners, and a basket.

Houses of Parliament, London, UK

he alloon bric was so elicate that it uld never be sed again.

Average-size hot-air balloon

What's the longest subway in the world?

ENGLAND

Adding together all 18 lines of the subway in **Seoul**, South Korea, gives a distance of **614 miles** (987.5 km)—long enough to cross several countries!

This **map** shows how far you could travel on the five longest underground systems if they all started in Paris, France. All routes are direct, as the crow flies, and crossing water if necessary.

Beijing Subway 327 miles (527 km)

China's capital city subway could reach from Paris to central England.

London Underground 250 miles (402 km)

Paris, FRANC

The world's oldest underground system, found in the UK, could run from Paris to La Rochelle on France's coast.

FAST FACTS

Underground networks can have hundreds of stations. The runaway winner is the New York City Subway, with more than 100 more stations than its closest challenger.

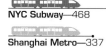

NYC Subway—468

Shanghai Metro—337

Beijing Subway—319

Seoul Subway—311 (lines 1–9 only)

Paris Metro—303

At 33.5 miles (53.85 km) long, Japan's Seikan Tunnel is the world's longest undersea rail tunnel, with 40 percent 330 ft (100 m) below the seabed.

Hokkaido Island

Tsugaru Strait

Honshu Island

Yoshioka-Kaitei undersea station

Tappi-Kaitei undersea station

New York Subway
232 miles (373 km)

The world's longest subway (including all 18 lines, some of which travel beyond Seoul) could just reach inside Poland.

America's busiest subway could take you to Rotterdam in the Netherlands.

NETHERLANDS

BELGIUM

LUXEMBOURG

POLAND

Seoul Metropolitan Subway
614 miles (987.5 km)

GERMANY

CZECH REPUBLIC

Seoul's subway could stretch from **Paris** to **Poland**.

SWITZERLAND

AUSTRIA

Shanghai Metro
340 miles (548 km)

The subway system for China's biggest city could break into northern Italy.

ITALY

TIGHT SQUEEZE

Japan's capital is home to the world's busiest underground. The Tokyo Subway carries more than 3 billion people a year, with white-gloved train-pushers squeezing them onto already packed carriages.

How many **shipwrecks** are there?

Shipwrecks are not confined to the open seas. Sunk in 1885, *Sweepstakes* lies just 20 ft (6 m) underwater in Big Tub Harbor, on the edge of Lake Huron in Canada.

There are more than **160,000 shipwrecks** whose positions have been mapped in the world's oceans.

It is likely the total number of wrecks, from warships to liners, runs into millions. By comparison, there are about 50,420 merchant ships (ships that transport cargo or passengers) currently sailing the oceans.

Viking ship

Phoenician bireme

HMS Sussex (1694)

FAST FACTS

The deepest shipwreck found is a German World War II vessel in the South Atlantic Ocean. At 18,904 ft (5,762 m) down, it lies almost as deep as Mount Kilimanjaro is tall.

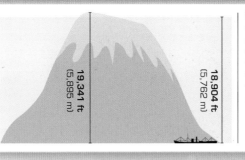

19,341 ft (5,895 m)

18,904 ft (5,762 m)

Shipwrecks contain an estimated $60 billion of treasure, which works out as $8 for every person in the world.

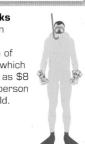

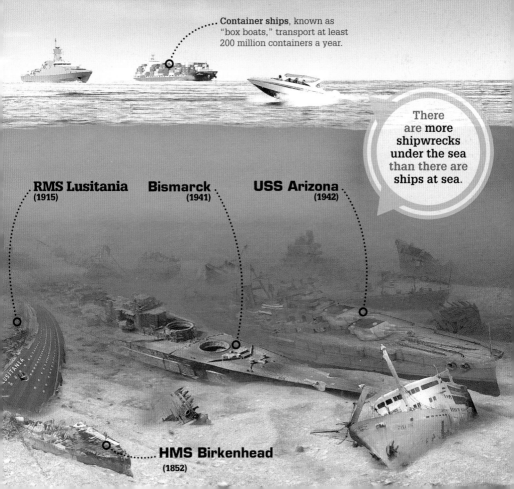

Container ships, known as "box boats," transport at least 200 million containers a year.

There are **more shipwrecks under the sea than there are ships at sea.**

RMS Lusitania
(1915)

Bismarck
(1941)

USS Arizona
(1942)

LUSITANIA

HMS Birkenhead
(1852)

Buildings data

The world's **first residential block** to have independently rotating floors was completed in 2001 and is located in **Curitiba, Paraná, Brazil**. It has 11 floors that can each rotate clockwise or counterclockwise, and it takes 1 hour for these to rotate the full **360 degrees**.

SKYSCRAPER CITIES

HONG KONG
316 SKYSCRAPERS

NEW YORK CITY
249 SKYSCRAPERS

DUBAI
154 SKYSCRAPERS

A skyscraper is a building taller than *492 ft* (150 m). The taller the tower, the more that can be packed into a city.

TALLEST STRUCTURES

2,625 FT	(800 M)
2,300 FT	(700 M)
1,970 FT	(600 M)
1,640 FT	(500 M)
1,310 FT	(400 M)
985 FT	(300 M)
655 FT	(200 M)
330 FT	(100 M)

TALLEST BUILDING: *BURJ KHALIFA, DUBAI 2,716 FT (828 M)*

The **Burj Khalifa** in Dubai is the world's tallest building, but there are many other tall structures around the world that hold their own titles.

GOING UNDERGROUND

Aquarius Reef Base, Florida Keys, USA; **62 ft** (19 m) deep

DEEPEST UNDERWATER LAB

DEEPEST FOUNDATIONS

Petronas Towers, Kuala Lumpur; deepest pile is **374 ft** (114 m) deep. The Towers rise 1,483 ft (451.9 m) above ground.

DEEPEST HOTEL ROOM

The Mine Suite, Sala, Sweden; **508 ft** (155 m) underground

DEEPEST UNDERGROUND LAB

It's not just the foundations of buildings that can be found underground, or underwater: there are some entire buildings down there!

China Jinping Underground Laboratory, Sichaun, China; **7,874 ft** (2,400 m) deep

TALLEST TOWER: *TOKYO SKYTREE, JAPAN* 2,080 FT (634 M)

TALLEST OBELISK: *THE WASHINGTON MONUMENT,* **USA** 554 FT 7 IN (169.05 M)

TALLEST ARCH: *THE GATEWAY ARCH,* **MISSOURI, USA** 630 FT (192 M)

TALLEST LIGHTHOUSE: *JEDDAH LIGHT,* **SAUDI ARABIA** 436 FT (133 M)

Spring Temple Buddha,
Henan, China
682 ft (208 m)

FAST FACTS

India's Statue of Unity will be the world's tallest statue when completed. At 597 ft (182 m), it will be three times the height of Italy's Leaning Tower of Pisa.

The largest of the Easter Island Moai statues stands 33 ft (10 m) high, while the heaviest weighs 95 tons (86 metric tons)—the same as seven school buses.

Spring **Temple Buddha** is more than **twice as tall as** the **Statue of Liberty**.

Laykyun Setkyar Standing Buddha, Burma (Myanmar) 423¼ ft (129 m)

This statue depicting the Vairocana Buddha is made from 238 lb (108 kg) of gold, 3,600 tons (3,300 metric tons) of copper, and 17,500 tons (15,000 metric tons) of steel.

The world's largest statues often pay tribute to a god, leader, or other influential figure, with the size of the sculpture and the materials used emphasizing the person's significance. The heights given here include bases.

How **tall** is the **tallest statue**?

The **Spring Temple Buddha** or Zhongyuan Buddha is the world's **tallest** statue, with the Buddha and lotus base reaching **418¾ ft** (127.64 m) tall. With extra bases added since, the structure now stands at **682 ft** (208 m).

The Statue of Liberty was a gift from France to the US in 1886. Visitors must climb 354 stairs to reach the crown.

TERRA-COTTA ARMY

Discovered in 1974, China's terra-cotta army is a collection of more than 8,000 life-size terra-cotta statues, each with individual facial features. They are part of Emperor Qin Shi Huang's burial complex.

Statue of Liberty, New York
305 ft (93 m)

This is the tallest statue including a horse. It is made from 270 tons (245 metric tons) of stainless steel.

Genghis Khan Equestrian Monument, Mongolia
131 ft (40 m)

Christ the Redeemer, Rio de Janeiro, Brazil
124¾ ft (38 m)

The **Sphinx** is the largest monolith statue in the world (created from a single piece of rock).

The Great Sphinx of Giza, Egypt
63½ ft (20.22 m)

Average human
6 ft (1.8 m)

What's the **fastest ball** in **sports?**

The **official world record** goes to a **golf ball**, which was hit at a **driving range** (golf practice area) in Orlando, Florida, in January 2013.

175 mph
(281 kph)

Tennis balls have a rubber center full of pressurized air and are covered in wool or nylon. About 300 million tennis balls are produced every year.

163 mph
(263 kph)

Squash balls are rubber with a hollow center. These small, speedy balls bounce off the walls and floor of a squash court.

202 mph
(325 kph)

A **Lamborghini Huracán** can go from 0 to 60 mph (0 to 100 kph) in 3.2 seconds, but couldn't beat a golf ball for speed.

The speed of a golf ball is measured immediately after the golf club hits the ball. The speed is the result of how fast the golf club is swung and how hard it hits the ball. The faster the ball speed, the farther the ball travels. Increasing speed by just 1 mph (1.6 kph) can add up to 2 yards (1.8 m) to the distance.

Golf balls were once basic balls crafted from wood. Today they are rubber balls covered with dimpled resin, designed to carry them higher and farther on the golf course.

217 mph (349 kph)

188 mph (302 kph)

Pelota balls have a wooden core surrounded by layers of latex (a natural rubber) and covered in goat skin. Set in 1979, the previous record for fastest ball was a pelota ball.

At **217 mph (349 kph),** the **golf ball is faster** than a **Lamborghini**.

📊 FAST FACTS

Badminton birdie
306 mph (493 kph)

Soccer ball
130 mph (210 kph)

Hockey ball
114 mph (183 kph)

Baseball
108 mph (174 kph)

Cricket
100 mph (161 kph)

Table tennis
70 mph (112 kph)

A birdie is a flying cone of feathers or plastic, and so, strictly speaking, not a ball. However, one birdie blew all the balls out of the park when a player smashed it at more than 300 mph (500 kph) in 2013.

The Golden Gate Bridge in California stretches 8,981 ft (2,737 m) across the Golden Gate strait, connecting San Francisco to Marin County.

A standard pencil is 7½ in (19 cm) long, with the average diameter measuring about ¼ in (7 mm). The traditional wooden casing was invented in the mid 16th-century: before then, graphite was wrapped in string or sheepskin.

📊 FAST FACTS

A pencil lasts 62 times longer than a pen. You would need 62 pens to draw a line the same length as one pencil can.

More than 14 billion pencils are used every year around the world. Laid end to end, these could circle the globe 60 times.

How **far** could a **pencil** draw?

It is estimated that a **typical pencil** has enough **graphite** to draw a line **35 miles** (56 km) long, but no one has actually tested this!

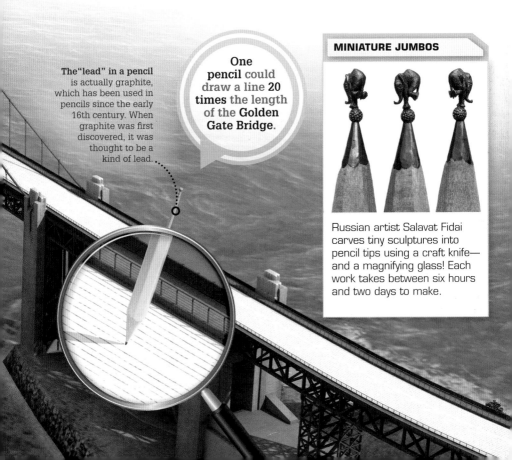

The "lead" in a pencil is actually graphite, which has been used in pencils since the early 16th century. When graphite was first discovered, it was thought to be a kind of lead.

One pencil could draw a line **20 times** the length of the **Golden Gate Bridge**.

MINIATURE JUMBOS

Russian artist Salavat Fidai carves tiny sculptures into pencil tips using a craft knife—and a magnifying glass! Each work takes between six hours and two days to make.

What's the most extreme roller coaster?

The most **forceful roller coaster** is **"Tower of Terror"** at Gold Reef City in Johannesburg, South Africa. At the bottom of the ride's **huge drop**, people experience a G-force of **6.3 g**.

SPACE SHUTTLE
3 g

During a space shuttle launch, an astronaut experiences a maximum force of 3 g.

FIGHTER PLANE
8–9 g

Fighter pilots are trained to withstand a maximum of 9 g. They wear "g-suits" to stop blood from sinking to their legs and

Tower of Terror riders experience twice the G-force of a space shuttle launch.

ROLLERCOASTER
6.3 g

The rollercoaster features a vertical drop of 154 ft (47 m) from the top of an authentic

F1 CAR
2–6 g

Formula 1 drivers usually experience 2 g while accelerating, 5 g while braking, and 4–6 g turning corners.

As well as the G-forces, riders also experience a short period of weightlessness.

HUMAN STANDING ON EARTH
1 g

For the last 50 ft (15 m) of the drop, riders descend into a dark tunnel.

FAST FACTS

Rollercoasters generate negative G-force at the top of hills, making you briefly rise out of your seat. During a drop, you experience 0 g.

At the bottom of a dip, you experience positive G-force. This multiplies the force of gravity and pushes you into the chair.

G-force is the apparent "pull" or "push" that an object feels as a result of acceleration. A force of 1 g is equal to the force of gravity. The peak G-force on most rollercoasters is about 4 g. At about 9 g, most humans black out as blood struggles to reach the brain.

How many solar panels could power the world?

SOLAR-POWERED WINGS

NASA's Helios Prototype was a solar powered, remote-controlled, unmanned aircraft. It holds the record for the highest non-rocket powered flight, reaching 96,863 ft (29,524 m). It crashed into the Pacific in 2003.

Spain (shown in orange) has an area of 195,364 sq miles (505,992 km²), so the amount of solar panels needed would have to extend into Portugal (shown in green) as well. ....

Solar panels absorb the light from the Sun's rays and convert it into electricity or heating. Today, solar panels are not very efficient: only around 15 percent of the sunlight that hits the panel gets turned into electricity you can use. In future, as solar panels improve, fewer panels will be needed to generate the same amount of power.

If the **whole world** were powered by **solar panels**, the amount needed would cover an enormous area of **206,282 sq miles** (534,268 km²).

Solar panels to power the **world** would cover an area **bigger than Spain**.

The solar panels would provide the estimated 213,707,423,840,000 kWh (kilowatt-hours) of electricity, needed to run the world's machinery, technology, transportation, homes, and more.

FAST FACTS

Most of the world's power comes from non-renewable fossil fuels such as coal, oil, and gas. Less than one-fifth of power comes from renewable alternatives, including solar power.

- Fossil fuels 78.3%
- Traditional biomass 9%
- Nuclear power 2.6%
- Biomass/geothermal/solar heat 4.1%
- Hydropower 3.9%
- Wind 1.3%
- Biofuels 0.8%

Internet data

VIDEO VS. YOUTUBE

The first-ever commercial *video tape recorder*, which was made in 1956, was the size of a **piano!** Videos could hold around *4 hours* of material, the same amount that is now uploaded to **YouTube** every *0.6 seconds*.

WHO'S OUT THERE?

Almost **two-thirds** (61.5 percent) of internet traffic is not generated by humans, but is **unwanted** spam or junk automatically sent by **bots** and **malware**.

PERCENTAGE DIFFERENCE

The **percentage of people** who are online varies widely across different countries: from **Iceland,** with 100 percent of its population having access to the internet, to **Eritrea,** with a mere 1.1 percent online.

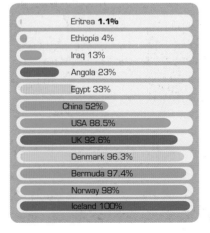

Eritrea **1.1%**
Ethiopia 4%
Iraq 13%
Angola 23%
Egypt 33%
China 52%
USA 88.5%
UK 92.6%
Denmark 96.3%
Bermuda 97.4%
Norway 98%
Iceland 100%

GOOGLE IT

A single *Google* query uses **1,000 computers** to retrieve an answer in **0.2 seconds**. **Around 15 percent** of the searches *Google* gets each day have never been *Googled* before.

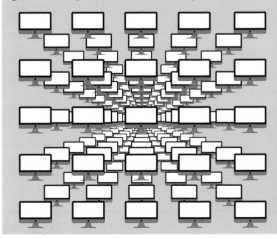

INTERNET **USERS**

Use of the internet has boomed in the last **20 years**. In December 1995, **0.4 percent** of the world's population used the Net; by December 2015, this had zoomed up to an estimated **46.4 percent**.

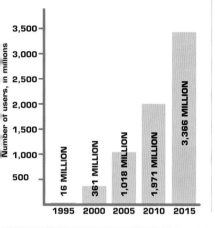

Number of users, in millions

- 16 MILLION — 1995
- 361 MILLION — 2000
- 1,018 MILLION — 2005
- 1,971 MILLION — 2010
- 3,366 MILLION — 2015

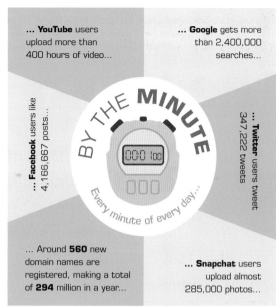

... **YouTube** users upload more than 400 hours of video...

... **Google** gets more than 2,400,000 searches...

BY THE MINUTE

Every minute of every day...

... **Facebook** users like 4,166,667 posts...

... **Twitter** users tweet 347,222 tweets

... Around **560** new domain names are registered, making a total of **294** million in a year...

... **Snapchat** users upload almost 285,000 photos...

UNDER THE SEA

Around **99 percent** of the world's internet traffic travels via **undersea cables**. There are more than **613,009 miles** (986,543 km) of submarine communication cables— enough to reach the Moon **2.5 times**!

If a website were a country...

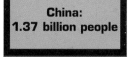

Facebook: 1.6 billion people

China: 1.37 billion people

... *Facebook* would have a **higher population** than the world's **actual most** populous country, **China**.

FACEBOOK **COUNTRY**

Which **film cost** the **most** to make?

The **cinematic boom** of the 21st century has made **big budget** movies with spectacular **special effects** now the norm. At **$398 million**, *Pirates of the Caribbean: On Stranger Tides* is the costliest film to date.

Three of the **10** most expensive movies are *Pirates of the Caribbean*, with costs of over **$1 billion**.

$264 million

$267 million

$272 million

$276 million

$280 million

Pirates of the Caribbean: Dead Man's Chest (2006)

Waterworld (1995)

John Carter (2012)

Harry Potter and the Half-Blood Prince (2009)

Avengers: Age of Ultron (201..)

📈 FAST FACTS

The most expensive "back-to-back" production (set of movies) was *The Hobbit* trilogy (2012–14), which cost $745 million. This is larger than some countries' GDP (gross domestic product; how much all their goods and services are worth in a year).

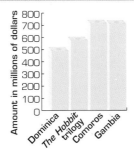

Amount in millions of dollars
800, 700, 600, 500, 400, 300, 200, 100, 0

Dominica · The Hobbit trilogy · Comoros · Gambia

Some movie stars are paid huge sums of money. The highest-paid actor in 2015 earned almost one-third more than the highest-paid actress—a difference of $30 million.

Robert Downey Jr.
$80 million

Jennifer Lawrence
$52 million

These are the top 10 most costly films ever made, and eight of them were made in the 21st century. The amounts have been adjusted in line with inflation so all the movies can be judged on equal value.

$282 million

$294 million

$295 million

$342 million

$398 million

Tangled (2010)	*Spider-Man 3* (2007)	*Titanic* (1997)	*Pirates of the Caribbean: At World's End* (2007)	*Pirates of the Caribbean: On Stranger Tides* (2011)

How big is the
biggest screen?

The world's **largest permanent projection screen** can be seen at **Hengqin Ocean Kingdom** theme park in **China**.

With an area of more than 17,000 sq ft (1,580 m²), the screen sits in a theater as big as five IMAX theaters and has 1,000 hi-tech seats.

FAST FACTS

The largest true TV screen is "Big Hoss" at the Texas Motor Speedway in Fort Worth. At 218 x 94½ ft (66.4 x 22.8 m), it is longer than a Boeing 767 and taller than a 7-story building.

The "Viva Vision" LED display board in Las Vegas has 12.5 million LED lamps and is 1,500 ft (457 m) long—as long as 4½ soccer fields.

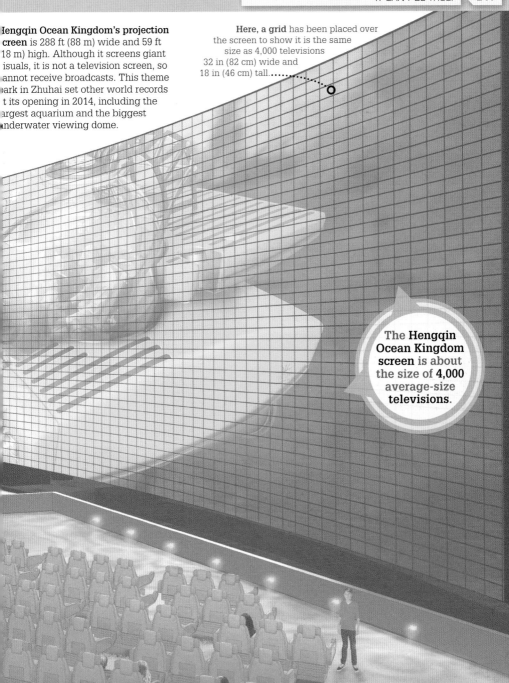

Hengqin Ocean Kingdom's projection screen is 288 ft (88 m) wide and 59 ft (18 m) high. Although it screens giant visuals, it is not a television screen, so cannot receive broadcasts. This theme park in Zhuhai set other world records at its opening in 2014, including the largest aquarium and the biggest underwater viewing dome.

Here, a grid has been placed over the screen to show it is the same size as 4,000 televisions 32 in (82 cm) wide and 18 in (46 cm) tall.

The **Hengqin Ocean Kingdom screen** is about the size of **4,000 average-size televisions**.

How small is the smallest camera?

The **smallest** camera in the world is smaller than a **grain of sand**, at just **0.039 in** (1 mm) wide. The **microcamera** is used to see inside people's bodies during operations.

The **medical microcamera** has a resolution of 45,000 pixels, which is about one-twentieth of a megapixel.

The **smallest camera** is **375 times smaller** than a mobile phone's **SIM** card.

FAST FACTS

The first photograph was taken in 1814. Today, the number of photographs taken every two minutes is the same as the number of pictures taken by the whole world in the 1800s.

1800s:
A few million

1960s:
3 billion a year

2000:
86 billion

2012:
More than 380 billion

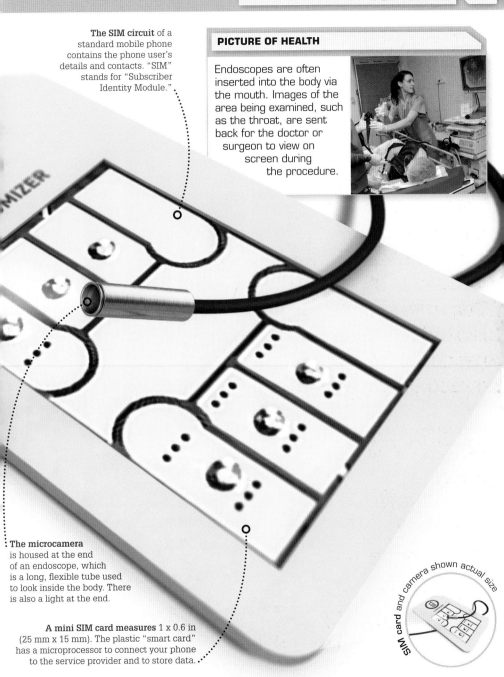

The SIM circuit of a standard mobile phone contains the phone user's details and contacts. "SIM" stands for "Subscriber Identity Module."

PICTURE OF HEALTH

Endoscopes are often inserted into the body via the mouth. Images of the area being examined, such as the throat, are sent back for the doctor or surgeon to view on screen during the procedure.

The microcamera is housed at the end of an endoscope, which is a long, flexible tube used to look inside the body. There is also a light at the end.

A mini SIM card measures 1 x 0.6 in (25 mm x 15 mm). The plastic "smart card" has a microprocessor to connect your phone to the service provider and to store data.

SIM card and camera shown actual size

CHINESE SUPERPOWER

Today, one of the most powerful computers is China's Tianhe 2 ("Milky Way 2"), with a 1,375-tebibyte (1.4 million gigabyte) memory. It can perform 100,000 times as many tasks as there are stars in the Milky Way every second.

Weighty ENIAC featured 40 panels and filled a room with its vast size. To perform each new task, its plugs and switches had to be moved (reprogrammed) by hand.

At the time, ENIAC was an efficient machine, working 1,440 times faster than a person on a calculator

20 YEARS

How **powerful** were the **first** computers?

Launched in **1946**, **ENIAC** (Electronic Numerical Integrator and Computer) was one of the **earliest** computers. It could perform up to **357 calculations** in **one second**.

ENIAC would take more than **20 years** to perform the same tasks as an **iPad** can in **1 second**.

... An iPad can perform 22 billion operations in a single second.

Computers have decreased in size, but increased in capability. Miniature computers are built into phones, cars, cameras, and all sorts of other devices. These are light, easy to operate, and able to perform a huge range of useful functions at incredibly fast speeds.

FAST FACTS

ENIAC was not the first computer: that was Colossus, used from 1943 by British code-breakers during World War II. Despite its name, Colossus was smaller than ENIAC. While ENIAC filled a room 30 ft x 50 ft (9 m x 15 m), Colossus was less than one-ninth of that size.

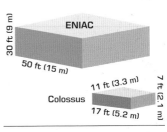

30 ft (9 m)

ENIAC

50 ft (15 m)

11 ft (3.3 m)

Colossus

17 ft (5.2 m)

7 ft (2.1 m)

ENIAC weighed 30 tons (27 metric tons), which was heavier than five elephants. Colossus was less than 1.1 tons (1 metric ton).

How much paper does it take to print the world wide web?

The **world wide web** is the network of all the world's websites. Calculations suggest **136 billion sheets** of **letter-size paper** would be needed to print it all out.

If the A4 printouts of the world wide web were piled up, the stack would be taller than Earth.

Stack of paper:
8,450 miles
(13,600 km)

Height of Earth:
7,900 miles
(12,713 km)

PAPER RECYCLING

Making recycled sheets from used paper uses 40 percent less energy than making new paper from trees. Going paperless is the most tree-efficient of all!

To make 136 billion sheets of letter-size paper, you would need around 16 million trees. The average tree provides around 8,500 sheets of paper.

The information on the world wide web is divided into "visible" and "deep" webs. The visible web is the pages accessible by search engines such as Google and Yahoo, and it makes up less than 1 percent of content online. The other 99 percent is the deep web—trillions of pages of databases, intranets, and other communications not available on the usual search engines.

FAST FACTS

When the world wide web was launched in 1991, there was just one website. Today there are about 1 billion websites.

Year	Number of websites
2000	17,087,182
2001	29,254,370
2002	38,760,373
2003	40,912,332
2004	51,611,646
2005	64,780,617
2006	85,507,314
2007	121,892,559
2008	172,338,726
2009	238,027,855
2010	206,956,723
2011	346,004,403
2012	697,089,489
2013	672,985,183
2014	968,882,453

How **heavy** is the **internet?**

The **internet** runs on **electricity**, and the **electrons** involved are virtually **weightless**. Estimates suggest that the internet's **trillions** of active electrons weigh only **2 oz** (50–60 g).

SUBATOMIC PARTICLES

This apricot is about 2 in (5 cm) across.

Atoms are made up of tiny particles called protons, neutrons, and electrons. Each atom has a nucleus (center) made up of protons and neutrons, while electrons spin around the nucleus.

A USB ("Universal Serial Bus") is used to plug electronic devices into a computer or a power socket.

The **internet weighs about** as much as an **apricot**.

FAST FACTS

Some experts estimate the weight of all the data on the internet (including photographs, emails, and social media messages) totals the same weight as a grain of sand.

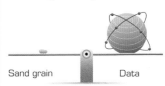

Sand grain   Data

Internet speed, or bandwidth, is measured in megabits per second (Mbps). Technically, 4 Mbps is not four times faster than 1 Mbps. Bandwidth is like a highway: 1 Mpbs means there is one lane of traffic, and 4 Mpbs means there are four lanes that the same amount of traffic can use. It all moves at the same speed, but more arrives at the same time.

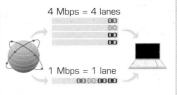

4 Mbps = 4 lanes

1 Mbps = 1 lane

An electron is a mind-blowingly miniscule particle of electricity with minimal mass. Though the content of the internet is vast, the electrons that run it have almost no mass, which is why the total internet weighs so little.

An apricot has the same mass as the electrons that carry the internet's 5 million terabytes of online information.

What's the largest diamond?

The **Cullinan** is the **largest uncut diamond** ever found. At just over **4 in** (10.5 cm) across at its widest, it is about the **size** of a **man's fist**.

The Cullinan was bought for the equivalent of nearly **31 gold bars**.

FAST FACTS

The Cullinan was cut into nine large diamonds and 96 smaller polished stones.

The uncut diamond weighed 3,106 carats. One carat is 0.007 oz (0.2 g), so the diamond weighed 21.9 oz (621.35 g)—about as much as a kitten.

Each gold bar has a value of $800,000 (£560,000), which is a high price. If the price dropped to $500,000 (£350,000), it would take nearly 50 bars to buy the diamond.

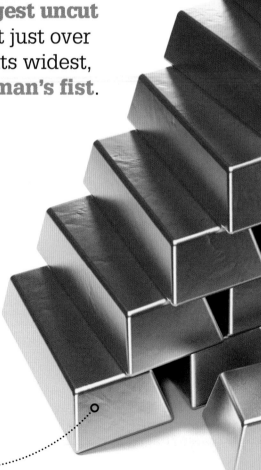

The uncut Cullinan was sold in 1905 for $727,500 (£150,000), which is worth more than $24.6 million (£16 million) in today's money.

TERMITE TREASURE

The richest diamond deposit, at Jwaneng in Botswana, was found thanks to termites. Burrowing into the ground, the insects brought soil to the surface that was tested and revealed minerals linked to diamonds and gold.

The Cullinan diamond was discovered in a diamond mine in Cullinan, South Africa, in the early 20th century. The largest diamond cut from the stone is the Great Star of Africa, which weighs 530 carats (3.7 oz/106 g) and is part of the UK's Crown Jewels.

What's the most **expensive** object ever **built?**

The most expensive man-made object is the **International Space Station**, which is in orbit **240 miles** (390 km) above Earth. Its final cost will be more than **$114 billion** (£80.7 billion).

There are **12 large solar panels** powering the space station.

Most expensive building:
Abraj Al-Bait, Saudi Arabia

Most expensive power plant:
Three Gorges Dam, China

Most expensive hotel:
Marina Bay Sands, Singapore

37 billion dollars

5.5 billion dollars

15 billion dollars

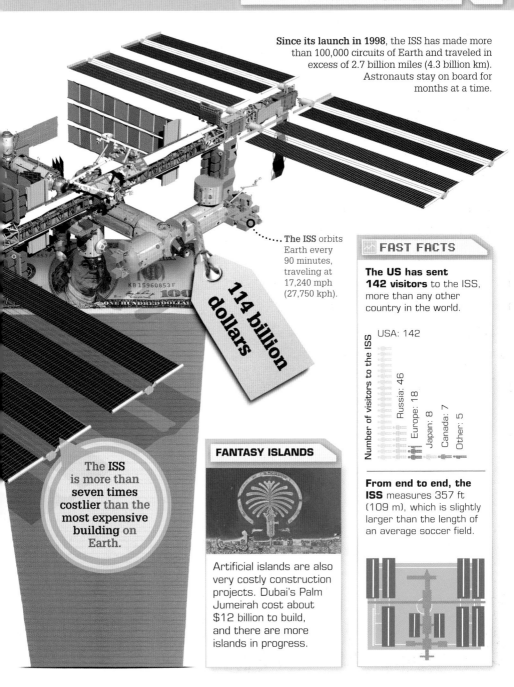

Since its launch in 1998, the ISS has made more than 100,000 circuits of Earth and traveled in excess of 2.7 billion miles (4.3 billion km). Astronauts stay on board for months at a time.

114 billion dollars

The ISS orbits Earth every 90 minutes, traveling at 17,240 mph (27,750 kph).

The ISS is more than seven times costlier than the most expensive building on Earth.

FANTASY ISLANDS

Artificial islands are also very costly construction projects. Dubai's Palm Jumeirah cost about $12 billion to build, and there are more islands in progress.

📊 FAST FACTS

The US has sent 142 visitors to the ISS, more than any other country in the world.

Number of visitors to the ISS

USA: 142
Russia: 46
Europe: 18
Japan: 8
Canada: 7
Other: 5

From end to end, the ISS measures 357 ft (109 m), which is slightly larger than the length of an average soccer field.

Money data

RICHEST RESIDENTS

This chart shows the richest nations measured by **GDP** (gross domestic product; the value of its goods and services) **per person** (if the GDP were shared equally among its population). According to this, the richest place to live is Qatar.

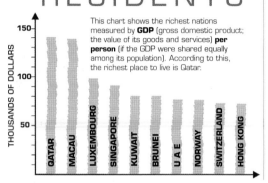

THOUSANDS OF DOLLARS

150—
100—
50—

QATAR · MACAU · LUXEMBOURG · SINGAPORE · KUWAIT · BRUNEI · U A E · NORWAY · SWITZERLAND · HONG KONG

THE RICH GET
RICHER

The richest **62** people in the world (only nine of whom are women) are as wealthy as half of the world's population. In 2010, the same proportion of wealth was in the hands of **388** people.

GLOBAL WEALTH PYRAMID

The global wealth pyramid demonstrates how many people have how much wealth. At the bottom of the pyramid, the majority of the world's population **(69.8 percent)** have the lowest amount of money **(less than $10,000)**.

At the very top of the pyramid, **35 million people** (a tiny **0.7 percent** of the world's population) own more than **$1 million**. In fact, the total amount owned by the **35 million** people is a whopping **$115.9 trillion.**

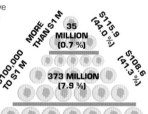
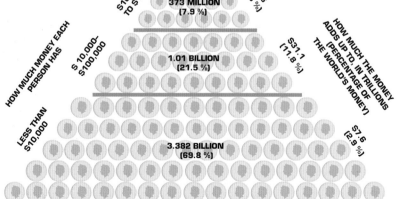

HOW MUCH MONEY EACH PERSON HAS

MORE THAN $1 M — 35 MILLION (0.7 %) — $115.9 (44.0 %)

$100,000 TO $1 M — 373 MILLION (7.9 %) — $108.6 (41.3 %)

$10,000–$100,000 — 1.01 BILLION (21.5 %) — $31.1 (11.8 %)

LESS THAN $10,000 — 3.382 BILLION (69.8 %) — $7.6 (2.9 %)

HOW MUCH THE MONEY ADDS UP TO, IN TRILLIONS (PERCENTAGE OF THE WORLD'S MONEY)

**HOW MANY ADULTS HAVE THIS AMOUNT OF MONEY
(PERCENTAGE OF WORLD POPULATION)**

HOW **MUCH MONEY** IS THERE?

The total value of the world's money is **$81.21 trillion**. This includes **coins**, **banknotes**, and *money registered to bank accounts*. However, the value of all the world's **actual** coins and banknotes is just **$5 trillion**!

$5 trillion   **$81.2 trillion**

PLAYING WITH **MONEY**

The amount of money in a Monopoly game is **$15,140**. That's **40** each of **$1, $5**, and **$10** bills; **50 $20** bills; **30 $50** bills; and **20** each of **$100** and **$500** bills. More than **250 million** games have been sold in **103** countries and **37** languages.

PERSON ON THE MOST **MONEY**

Queen Elizabeth II of the UK holds the record for appearing on more currency than any other person. Her portrait is on the currency of at least **35** different countries.

BIG MONEY

The **biggest** gold coin in the world was made by the **Perth Mint** in **Australia** in 2012. It is **31½ in** (80 cm) aross, **4¾ in** (12 cm) thick, and weighs **1.1 tons** (1 metric ton). Containing **99.99 percent** pure gold, it is the most valuable gold bullion coin in the world.

UNDER THE HAMMER

Most expensive painting:
Picasso's *Women of Algiers*, sold in 2015 for **$179.4 million** (£102.6 million)

Most expensive sculpture:
Giacometti's *Pointing Man*, sold in 2015 for **$141.3 million** (£90.5 million)

Most expensive instrument:
Lady Blunt Stradivarius violin made in 1721, sold online in 2011 for **$15.9 million** (£9.8 million)

EVEN BIGGER MONEY!

Ceremonial money called **Rai** is used on the island of Yap (part of Micronesia). The huge limestone disks are

12 ft (3.6 m) across,
1½ ft (0.5m) **thick,** and
weigh **4.4 tons** (4 metric tons).

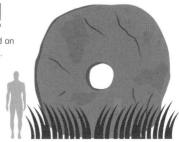

TRUE OR FALSE?

Sometimes it's difficult to separate fact from fiction. Does eating spinach really make you stronger? Was T-rex the biggest dinosaur? Is your body 75% water? Find out more on this myth-busting tour of fascinating facts, with some truth-testing questions along the way. You can check if you got the answers right at the back of the book.

This basilisk lizard really is walking on water—its big feet allow it to skim across the surface for up to 50 ft (15 m). Luckily, if it runs out of steam, it's also an excellent swimmer.

TRUE or FALSE? The body is 75% water

Water is not just the world's best thirst-quencher. It is essential to your life on Earth. More than **75 percent** of a baby's body weight is water. Adult **males are 60 percent** water, while **females are 50 percent**. About **65 percent** of the body's water is in its **40 trillion cells**.

Is it possible to die from drinking too much water?

When the body's water levels fall, the brain's hypothalamus recognizes the drop and triggers the thirst response. Losing 10 percent will leave you seriously ill.

TYPES OF TEARS

There are three types of tears. Basal tears clean and lubricate the eyes. Reflex tears form in response to an irritant, such as an onion or pollen. Emotional tears form to express feelings, and these have a different chemical makeup from basal and reflex tears.

Newborn babies have the highest water content at 75 percent. That's because they have proportionally much more water in their tissue fluid and blood than adults do.

The amount of sweat produced by the body depends on the number of sweat glands—ranging between two and four million per person.

Elderly people have the lowest water content at 45 to 50 percent. As people age, fat tissue replaces lean muscle. Unlike muscle and most other tissues, fat tissue contains just 10 to 15 percent water, explaining older people's lower water content.

The body gains and loses water constantly. Water is taken into the body in food and drinks. Water is lost from the body in four main ways. Every day, an average adult loses about 2.6 pints (1.5 liters) of water in urine, 0.9 pints (0.5 liters) in sweat, 0.7 pints (0.4 liters) breathing out, and 0.2 pints (0.1 liters) in feces (poop). Water loss is constantly adjusted to match water gain in order to maintain a steady water balance inside the body.

muscle is 75 percent water, fat is 10 to 15 percent water, and bone is 22 percent water.

FAST FACTS

THE HUMAN BODY CONTAINS ABOUT 8.8 PINTS (5 LITERS) OF

BLOOD

This accounts for about 7 percent of the body's weight. People have one of four main blood types. These are A, B, AB, and O. Each of these can be either RhD-positive or RhD-negative, so your blood can be one of eight different types.

OUR SALIVARY GLANDS PRODUCE ABOUT 2.6 PINTS (1.5 LITERS) OF SALIVA EVERY DAY

Since saliva is released gradually, we swallow it bit by bit without realizing it. Human saliva is 99 percent water and 1 percent other substances.

TRUE or FALSE? We use only 10% of our brains

Premotor cortex initiates guides, and coordinates actions...

This is a crazy myth from the **19th century**, when scientists had many strange ideas about the human brain. In fact, sensors and scanners reveal that we use **all of our brain,** and most tasks involve **activity in many different areas** at the same time.

BRAIN AT WORK

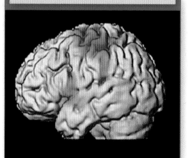

MRI scans can show when parts of the brain are active. The areas in red above indicate activity in the left brain when a right finger is moved. They include parts of the premotor cortex and primary motor cortex, and the cerebellum, which coordinates movement.

Prefrontal cortex is the main area associated with personality, thinking, and awareness...

Broca's area controls speech and the formation of words.

The auditory association cortex links sound signals with memories, emotions, and other senses...

Scientists have mapped areas of the brain responsible for tasks such as seeing hearing, speaking, and movement. But consciousness, memory, and learning do not seem to be related to particular areas—they may involve activity in many parts of the brain at once.

Motor cortex controls coordinated muscle movement.

Somatic sensory cortex analyzes nerve signals from the skin, muscles, and joints.

Sensory association cortex coordinates information from all the senses.

Visual association cortex analyzes visual data to form mental images.

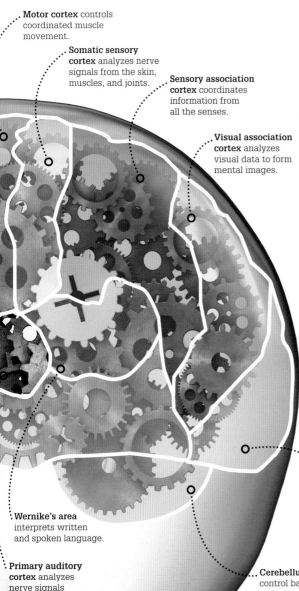

Wernike's area interprets written and spoken language.

Primary auditory cortex analyzes nerve signals from the ears.

Cerebellum helps control balance and movement.

Primary visual cortex receives visual information from the eyes.

FAST FACTS

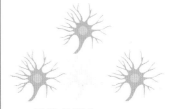

THE BRAIN DOESN'T FEEL PAIN

Headaches are caused by pain-sensitive structures that surround the brain. Brain tissue itself lacks pain receptors, which is why brain surgery can be carried out while patients are awake.

IF A BRAIN CELL DIES, IT MAY BE REPLACED

It was once believed that the brain grew and developed only during childhood and adolescence. Now it is known that human brains are constantly changing in various ways, including replacing some damaged cells.

Are people with larger brains more intelligent?

The brain's left side controls the body's right side

You're a **bundle of nerves**! That's because the brain and spinal cord use billions of **nerve cells** to send instructions around the body. The **brain's left side controls the body's right side**, and vice versa.

Divided by a groove, the brain has two halves—the left and right hemispheres, each responsible for the opposite half of the body.

The left hemisphere controls the right side of the body and oversees language and math skills.

The right hemisphere controls the left side of the body and manages creativity and spatial awareness.

The brain is the control center for the nervous system, responsible for all nerve activity inside the body. The spinal cord receives instructions as signals from the brain to transmit via the nerve cells attached to it. The nerve cells act as messengers, carrying out the

Damage to one side of the brain will affect the opposite side of the body.

The sciatic nerve supplies the hamstring muscles at the back of the thigh. It is the body's thickest and longest nerve.

The ulnar nerve supplies some of the muscles that move the wrist and the fingers.

NEURON NETWORK

The brain contains about 100 billion microscopic nerve cells called neurons, which all have connections with thousands of other neurons. These neurons have "tails" that receive or transmit electrical nerve impulses from or to other neurons. They create and send more messages than all the telephones in the world.

When the tendon below the kneecap is tapped, a sudden kicking movement of the lower leg results. This knee-jerk reflex is used by doctors to test the nervous system.

Branches of the sciatic nerve control muscles in the lower leg and foot.

What percentage of the global population is right-handed?

FAST FACTS

LAID END TO END, ALL THE NEURONS IN THE HUMAN BODY WOULD REACH THE MOON

MOON

Neurons laid end to end

EARTH

Neurons (nerve cells) are microscopic, with each one measuring about 10 microns (1/100th of a mm) wide. However, you have so many, and some are so long, that if they were laid end to end, they would extend for about 236,000 miles (380,000 km).

REFLEX ACTIONS BYPASS THE BRAIN

SIGNAL reaches brain and pain is felt only after hand pulls away

IMPULSES from spinal cord can make arm muscle contract

WITHDRAWAL REFLEX moves hand away

In many reflex actions, nerve signals travel through the spinal cord but not the brain. If you touch something hot, your hand moves away automatically without brain involvement.

TRUE or FALSE? We lose most **body heat** through our **heads**

The head makes up **9 percent** of the body's surface area, and the heat lost from it is **10 percent**. However, the head and chest are **five times as sensitive** to temperature change as the rest of the body. This makes it feel like covering them up does more to stop heat loss.

FREEZING FROSTBITE

Like other body areas, the fingers and toes are kept warm by blood flowing through them. But when they're exposed to freezing conditions, they lose heat rapidly and blood vessels narrow. This stops blood flow, so their tissues die. The resulting damage is called frostbite.

If we get too cold, blood vessels in the skin's dermis narrow to minimize heat loss, and we get goosebumps. ·····

If we start to overheat, blood vessels in the skin's dermis widen to lose heat, and sweat evaporates from the skin's surface to cool the body down.

COLOR CHART

Fahrenheit	Celsius
103.8	39.9
86	30
68	20
50	10
41.5	5.3

Does drinking hot tea really cool you down?

This thermogram records infrared radiation given off through the skin to show what really happens inside the body when the heat is on. The colors represent the full temperature range; white represents the hottest parts and black represents the coolest.

Injured areas would show up red, yellow, or white because of the heat from inflammation and swelling.

A thermogram is used to show different types

☷ FAST FACTS

THE BRAIN REGULATES BODY TEMPERATURE, WORKING TO MAINTAIN A CONSTANT

98.6°F
(37°C)

A part of the brain called the hypothalamus acts as a thermostat for the body. If the body becomes too hot or cold, the hypothalamus will stimulate a response to return it to normal temperature.

CAPILLARIES
ARE SO SMALL THAT
RED BLOOD CELLS HAVE TO TRAVEL
ALONG THEM IN
SINGLE FILE

On average, capillaries are about a tenth of the diameter of a human hair, which makes them only slightly bigger than a red blood cell. The smallest capillaries are so narrow that red blood cells have to squeeze themselves into odd shapes to fit through.

THE **HEART**
BEATS ABOUT
THREE
BILLION TIMES IN AN AVERAGE LIFETIME

Regular aerobic exercise helps keep your heart healthy. During exercise, your heart rate increases to pump extra blood, and the oxygen and fuel it carries, to the muscles that move you.

TRUE or FALSE? If you **swallow** an apple seed, a **tree will grow in your stomach**

Your stomach does not provide a **suitable environment** for a tree to grow. Instead, seeds **pass along** your intestines, and are pushed outside in feces. If a seed survives this journey, it may still **grow into a tree**, using sunlight energy.

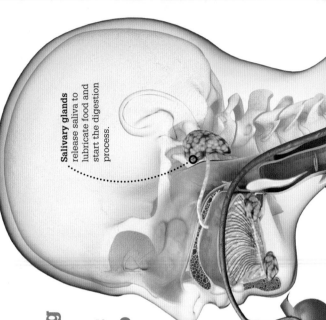

Salivary glands release saliva to lubricate food and start the digestion process.

APPENDIX DEFENSE

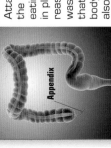

Appendix

Attached to the large intestine, the appendix is used by plant-eating animals to digest cellulose in plants. But for a long time the reason people had appendixes was a mystery. It is now known that this organ helps defend the body from attack by germs, and also stores "friendly" gut bacteria.

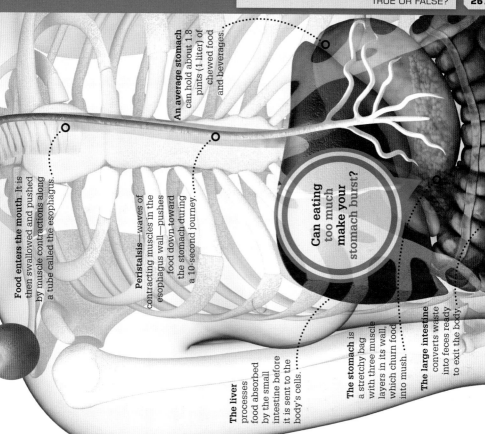

An average stomach can hold about 1.8 pints (1 liter) of chewed food and beverages.

Food enters the mouth. It is then swallowed and pushed by muscle contractions along a tube called the esophagus.

Peristalsis—waves of contracting muscles in the esophagus wall—pushes food down toward the stomach during a 10-second journey.

Can eating too much make your stomach burst?

The liver processes food absorbed by the small intestine before it is sent to the body's cells.

The stomach is a stretchy bag with three muscle layers in its wall, which churn food into mush.

The large intestine converts waste into feces ready to exit the body.

...to develop and thrive. Food travels through the digestive system where it is broken down to release the necessary nutrients. Passing through the small intestine, nutrients are absorbed into the blood and carried, by way of the liver, to body cells that need them. What is left of the food becomes waste in the intestines before it leaves the body, completing the digestive process.

FAST FACTS

THE AVERAGE PERSON EATS THE WEIGHT OF A SPERM WHALE IN A LIFETIME

That's a whopping 40 tons! In Western society, we consume about 3 lb (1.4 kg) of food daily. We also drink about 9,680 gallons (44,000 liters) over the course of our lives, which works out to 2.6 pints (1.5 liters) a day.

STOMACH ACID IS STRONG ENOUGH TO STRIP PAINT

Cells in the stomach lining release hydrochloric acid, which is needed to digest proteins. The stomach lining itself is not affected by this strong acid because other cells produce mucus that coats the lining, forming a physical barrier that prevents the acid from digesting it.

The skull consists of 22 bones, with 21 of them locked together. Only the lower jaw (mandible) can move.

There are 12 pairs of ribs, 10 of which are attached to the sternum (breastbone) by flexible cartilage.

The backbone is a column of 26 bones called vertebrae that are linked by shock-absorbing cartilage disks.

TRUE or FALSE? You are taller in the morning than in the evening

This is not a tall tale—we are bigger in bed. The backbone doesn't have to support our body weight, so the disks between vertebrae are not squashed as in the day. The **long and the short of it** is that we are 0.2 in (0.5 cm) taller in the morning than we are in the evening.

SPONGY CENTER

Bones are a mix of calcium salts and flexible collagen. The outer tissue, called compact bone, is dense and hard. The interior, called spongy bone (pictured), is lightweight but resilient. Resembling honeycomb, it can withstand everyday stresses and strains.

Each hand has 27 bones and multiple movable joints called knuckles.

The pelvic (hip) girdle attaches the legs to the skeleton via the hip joints.

The femur (thighbone) is the longest bone in the human body, running from the pelvic girdle to the knee joint.

About 400 joints connect the bones, which are held together by strong tissue called ligaments.

The skeleton is an intricate wonderland of 206 bones, supporting and shaping the human body. As strong as steel but only one-sixth as heavy, bone makes the skeleton both solid and flexible. It protects the soft organs of the body, including the brain and lungs, and provides movement when muscles pull on the bones.

Bones make up 20 percent of the body's mass.

Where in the human body are one-quarter of all bones located?

The tibia (shinbone) extends from the knee to the ankle and supports the body's weight.

BONES ARE CONSTANTLY RESHAPING THEMSELVES

The entire human skeleton is replaced every 10 years. This gradual process involves teams of cells removing old bone tissue and making new bone tissue. In the process, bones are constantly reshaped to give them optimal strength.

ASTRONAUTS GROW TALLER IN SPACE

When the backbone is not exposed to the pull of Earth's gravity, it gets longer. This is because the disks that separate the backbone's vertebrae are no longer compressed (squashed). After an astronaut returns to Earth, it takes months for the backbone to return to its normal length.

COUGHING PUTS MORE STRAIN ON THE BACKBONE THAN WALKING

Coughing too hard can cause you to crack a rib! Laughing creates a similar strain on the backbone.

TRUE or FALSE? You use more **muscles** to **frown** than to **smile**

Frontalis muscle raises the eyebrows causing the forehead to wrinkle.

Keep smiling! Although smiling actually uses more muscles than frowning, it takes **less effort**. Most of us **smile much more often** than we frown, so our smile muscles stay in **better shape**.

Levator labii superioris muscle lifts and curls the upper lip.

Zygomaticus major and minor muscles pull the corner of the mouth upward, backward, and outward.

Risorius muscle pulls the corner of the mouth to the side and backward to create a smile.

MAKING MUSCLE

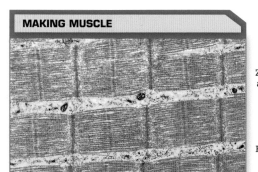

Scientists have found a way to regenerate human skeletal muscle using pig proteins. This can help people injured in accidents or wars avoid amputation. Proteins taken from pig intestines are placed inside the damaged tissue. Human stem cells move to the protein and begin to grow matching bone and tissue.

Is smiling really contagious?

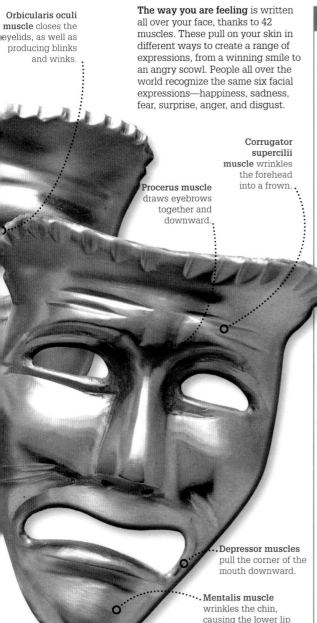

Orbicularis oculi muscle closes the eyelids, as well as producing blinks and winks.

The way you are feeling is written all over your face, thanks to 42 muscles. These pull on your skin in different ways to create a range of expressions, from a winning smile to an angry scowl. People all over the world recognize the same six facial expressions—happiness, sadness, fear, surprise, anger, and disgust.

Corrugator supercilii muscle wrinkles the forehead into a frown.

Procerus muscle draws eyebrows together and downward.

Depressor muscles pull the corner of the mouth downward.

Mentalis muscle wrinkles the chin, causing the lower lip to push out.

FAST FACTS

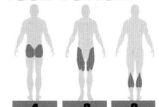

THE BIGGEST AND STRONGEST MUSCLE IN YOUR BODY SHAPES YOUR BOTTOM

1 GLUTEUS MAXIMUS (BUTTOCKS)

2 QUADRICEPS FEMORIS (THIGH)

3 SOLEUS (CALF)

The gluteus maximus fights against gravity to pull your body upward when you get up from a seat, run, or walk up stairs. Other strong muscles are found in the thigh, the calf, the jaw, and the tongue.

THE SMALLEST MUSCLE IS IN THE EAR

COCHLEA is a fluid-filled spiral chamber that detects sound vibrations

MIDDLE EAR

EARDRUM receives sound waves from ear canal

OSSICLES are three tiny bones that transmit sound waves to inner ear

STAPEDIUS MUSCLE

The stapedius, inside the middle ear, is about 0.04 in (1 mm) long and plays a part in sound transmission. It helps prevent loud sounds from damaging the ear's delicate receptors.

TRUE or FALSE? Birds are descended from dinosaurs

If a little bird told you our **feathered friends** were related to the great dinosaurs who roamed the earth **245–65 million years ago**, would you believe it? Recent **fossilized remains** discovered in **ancient rocks** have ruffled a few feathers. Birds are now known to be **descendants of the dinosaurs**, with many shared characteristics.

EXCEPTIONAL EVOLUTION

Evolution works in all kinds of interesting ways. Despite being a vulture, the palm-nut vulture eats mostly a vegetarian diet. The New Zealand kea (above) is a similar example. Instead of eating fruit and nuts like most parrots, the kea is an omnivore and will feed on fish, crabs, birds, and reptiles when plants are scarce.

- A feathered species named *Archaeopteryx* (meaning "ancient wing") had wings with the same basic shape as those of modern birds, so feathered wings probably first evolved for warmth and only later for flight.

SOME BIRDS STILL HAVE WING CLAWS

Clawed wing of the Hoatzin

The chicken-sized hoatzin lives in South American swamps, and its young have claws on each wing, just like the birdlike dinosaurs of the Cretaceous period. Hoatzin nests are built over water and the young dive in if danger threatens, then use their claws to climb back into the nest. The Hoatzin is the only bird with a digestive system like a cow's, allowing it to live exclusively on leaves and buds.

PSITTACOSAURUS 25 million years

HUMANS 200,000 years

■ DINOSAUR
■ HUMAN

THE LONGEST-SURVIVING DINOSAUR TYPE LIVED FOR 25 MILLION YEARS

The beaked herbivore *Psittacosaurus* holds this record. By comparison, modern humans have been around for only 200,000 years.

Where can reptilelike body scales still be seen on birds?

Many dinosaurs had small yet powerful three-clawed hands, similar to the three digits of modern birds, though these are not visible within the wing.

Most dinosaurs had teeth, claws, and a small, bony tail, but some features were lost as bird species evolved. Modern birds still have clawed feet and a tail called the pygostyle. ⋯⋯⋯⋯⋯

Anatomical similarities between some dinosaur species and modern birds include light, hollow bones and feathers. Over millions of years, the long arm bones of dinosaurs would evolve into wings. The behavior of dinosaurs and birds is also linked, since both make nests and lay eggs.

TRUE or FALSE? T-rex was the biggest dinosaur

Part of a vertebra from the backbone of a dinosaur called *Amphicoelias* was found more than a century ago. Its size suggested the species was a staggering 130–196 ft (40–60 m) long.

The tail, which was lined with muscle, acted as a counterbalance to the head and body when T-rex was in motion.

Tyrannosaurus rex may not have been the biggest dinosaur, but it was one of the biggest biters. Able to bite with about four times the strength of an alligator's jaws, this meat-muncher sealed the fate of its prey instantly. By ripping the skin apart, T-rex could feast on the juicy flesh underneath.

T-rex was 39 ft (12 m) in length.

Long, muscular legs and powerful thighs were built to run.

Large claws provided traction for stable movemen

FAST FACTS

THE LARGEST FLYING ANIMAL WAS THE SIZE OF AN AIRPLANE

With a whopping wingspan of 36 ft (11 m), the huge pterosaur *Quetzalcoatlus* was about the size of the Spitfire airplane used in World War II. Despite its size, it weighed no more than 550 lb (250 kg).

THE BIGGEST DINOSAURS WERE AS HEAVY AS SIX FIRE TRUCKS

Argentinosaurus, a massive sauropod from the Cretaceous period, was about 98 ft (30 m) long and weighed somewhere between 60 and 100 tons, as heavy as six fire trucks.

The **poster-boy predator** of the prehistoric period, *Tyrannosaurus rex* dominated the last age of the dinosaurs. But the "**tyrant lizard**" was surpassed in size by many **much bigger** species.

Forward-facing eyes provided binocular vision to launch attacks on prey.

Powerful jaws, lined with more than 60 spearlike teeth, were able to bite through solid bone.

When does a dog sound exactly like a T-rex?

Each strong arm had two or three claws.

Slim ankles suggest that T-rex could run very fast.

FOSSILIZED FINDS

Part of the border between Utah and Colorado is now called Dinosaur National Monument. This region is home to a big collection of dinosaur fossils, with one sandstone wall housing 1,500 bones. These fossils tell us what we know about dinosaurs today.

TRUE or FALSE? Crocodiles **cry** when they eat **prey**

Beware the **crocodile smile**, and watch out when it weeps! Crocodiles **tear off lumps of food** and **swallow them whole**. Glands to keep the eyes moist are near their throats, so feeding **produces tears**. But don't offer a tissue unless you want to be next on the menu…

Without sweat glands, **how do crocodiles release heat?**

JESUS LIZARD

The basilisk lizard is at home in the trees of Central and South America. Known as the "Jesus lizard," this reptile is able to run across water, thanks to big, fringed feet that create pockets of air around them. This generates forces sufficient to stay upright on water, a miraculous skill that comes in handy when escaping forest predators.

FAST FACTS

A TURTLE'S HEART
KEEPS BEATING
LONG AFTER ITS DEATH

In many animals, the beating of the heart is controlled by the brain, but special nerve cells in the heart can keep it beating even if it has been removed from the body. Usually, this phenomenon does not last long, but a turtle's heart can continue to beat for hours.

RATTLESNAKES
CAN KILL EVEN AFTER THEY HAVE DIED

Don't think for a second that chopping off a rattlesnake's head will be the end of it—that head can see, move, and bite with its deadly fangs up to an hour after the final blow!

One of the closest living relatives of dinosaurs, crocodiles are the most powerful reptiles. These skilled hunters can ambush, kill, and devour all kinds of prey. If a crocodile drowns a zebra, it can survive for months without needing to make another kill.

Stones are swallowed by crocodiles to help them grind up food inside their stomachs, and also act as ballast to stabilize them in the water.

A crocodile's tongue is connected to the roof of its mouth.

A range of fish, birds, and other creatures are eaten by crocodiles.

These reptiles can regrow a set of teeth to replace old or missing ones at least 40 times during their lives.

TRUE or FALSE? Elephants never forget

This is more than just mumbo jumbo. Elephants **recognize** old friends after long periods apart and **know the scents** of about 30 relatives. Grieving elephants **touch the skulls and tusks** of the deceased with their trunks and **return** to the site as if in mourning.

Elephants are sensitive and tactile, showing tenderness and concern when their babies are upset. They enjoy regular play time, which strengthens social bonds. As a form of greeting, two elephants may wrap their trunks together affectionately.

print safari pictures

CLEVER KANZI

Kanzi, a male bonobo, communicates with humans using lexigrams (symbols that represent words). He can also use tools, and even cook food over a campfire—showing a humanlike ability to think and express himself.

The trunk contains more than 100,000 muscles and the tip is dextrous enough to pick up a peanut.

pack trunk

Although the tough skin is 1 in (2.5 cm) thick, an elephant will still cover itself in mud to protect against biting insects and damaging sunburn.

check weight on scale

apply antiwrinkle creams

take a mud bath

How do elephants use their feet to detect sounds?

play squash on Friday

book jumbo jet flight

📊 FAST FACTS

KOALAS
SLEEP FOR UP TO
22 HOURS
A DAY

These sleepyheads are diet-conscious. Koalas eat only eucalyptus leaves, and these tough, fibrous, and not very nutritious plants require a lot of energy to digest. Sleeping for most of the day helps koalas conserve energy.

SOME ANIMALS DISCARD THEIR BODY PARTS

When threatened by a predator, some lizards will leave their tails behind to distract their attackers as they make a quick getaway. Stags often cast off their antlers after fighting over females, and snakes shed their skins when they outgrow them.

JAPANESE MACAQUES LOVE A
HOT BATH

In 1963 the first Japanese macaque (a type of monkey) ventured into the hot water springs at the Jigokudani Monkey Park in Nagano, Japan. Soon, all the macaques were warming themselves in winter by bathing regularly, showing that they learn by example.

TRUE or FALSE? Camels store water in their humps

Please, don't **get upset** if you thought this was true. A camel's hump is really a **huge lump of fat**. This is a food store, which allows the camel to **survive for long periods** in the desert.

A camel's nostrils trap and suck in the moisture in their breath so it is not lost.

Two rows of long eyelashes help prevent sand from entering the eyes during sandstorms.

Camels are resilient creatures, designed to cope with the difficulties of desert life. Their many adaptations include a long large intestine to ensure the maximum absorption of water in their food supply. When food or water is very scarce, fat inside the hump breaks down to give an energy boost.

FAST FACTS

SOME INSECTS SURVIVE BEING FROZEN SOLID FOR THE WINTER

The woolly bear caterpillar lives in cold regions, such as the Arctic. When winter comes, the caterpillar is frozen solid, causing its heart to stop beating. It has adapted to survive the cold, and thaws once the ice melts in the spring.

STARFISH CAN CHANGE GENDER

The *Asterina gibbosa* starfish is born male, but changes into a female as it gets older. Other starfish change their gender according to the availability of food and mates.

CHIPMUNKS STORE FOOD IN THEIR CHEEKS

Chipmunks use this special ability to transport peanuts and other food items. They have fur-lined cheek pouches that expand and keep the food fresh, allowing them to carry it to their burrows for safekeeping.

EVOLUTIONARY ECHIDNA

Australia's echidna has multiple adaptations for feeding and self-defense. A long snout and sticky tongue help it reach into anthills to devour insects. Attackers are caught off guard when the spiny echidna curls up into a spiky ball.

How long does a camel take to drink 26 gallons (100 liters) of water?

Long legs allow the camel to move easily over long distances, and also elevate the body high above the sand, which is blazing hot.

The fat in a camel's hump, its narrow back, and its thick coat all insulate its body against the sun's scorching heat.

HELPING HUMANS

Occasionally shark attacks result in dolphins coming to aid the victims. Surfer Todd Endris was bitten by a shark in California in 2007. A pod of bottlenose dolphins circled him and helped him to shore. He says they saved his life.

TRUE or FALSE?

Falling coconuts kill more people than sharks

Falling coconuts can kill, but it's an **urban legend** that they are more deadly than sharks. On average, **eight people** are killed by sharks annually. **Ten times** more are killed by nonvenomous insects, **30 times** more by dogs, and **60 times** more by hornets, wasps, or bees.

The most fearsome predatory fish, the great white shark has a reputation as the ultimate marine monster. However, most attacks on humans are accidental, often occurring when sharks mistake surfboards on the surface for sea lions and seals—their favorite food.

Great white sharks eat about 12 tons (11 metric tons) of food a year. They use and lose more than 1,000 teeth during their lifetime of at least 70 years.

The average length of a great white shark is 13 ft (4 m), but one of the biggest ever caught was 20 ft (6 m) long, off Prince Edward Island, Canada, in 1993.

Which amazing **sensory ability** do sharks and **tigers** have in common?

BOX JELLYFISH ARE THE REAL MARINE KILLERS

Don't underestimate the most venomous creature on Earth—it causes about 100 deaths per year. The venom attacks the heart, nervous system, and skin, with survivors still experiencing pain weeks after contact.

HIPPOPOTAMUSES ARE AFRICA'S MOST PROLIFIC KILLER CREATURES

HIPPOPOTAMUS 3,000 per year

CROCODILE 1,000 per year

ELEPHANT 500 per year

Despite looking cuddly and kind, hippos have powerful jaws and large, sharp teeth. On top of this, they are fiercely aggressive if threatened and kill about 3,000 people a year.

MOSQUITO BITES ARE ESTIMATED TO KILL 725,000 PEOPLE A YEAR

AREAS REPORTING DEATHS FROM MALARIA

Mosquito bites transmit a variety of deadly diseases, including malaria, dengue fever, and yellow fever. Malaria alone kills more than 600,000 people every year and infects many more.

TRUE or FALSE? Chameleons change **color** to match their **surroundings**

If chameleons had wardrobes, they would switch outfits all day long. But their **changing appearance** is not always about **blending in**. **Light** and **temperature** affect chameleon colors, or they may just be **in the mood** for a change!

> **Which animal has striped skin as well as striped fur?**

Science has shown that chameleons don't want to be par of a crowd. Blending in is beneficial only when resting or unde attack. Simple environmental changes, such as different lightin or temperature, can alter their skin color in just 20 second: Mood swings cause the biggest change. An irritable, angr chameleon displays the brightest, most vibrant colors of al

Males are more colorful than females, with most going from brown to green. They become more brightly colored when frightened, courting, or defending their territories.

Chameleon eyes move independently, and each can swivel nearly 180 degrees.

Skin layers below the outer skin have chromatophores, which contain color pigments that expand and contract to alter skin color.

MARVELOUS MIMICS

Some creatures closely resemble another species in order to confuse and deter predators. This is called mimicry. One example is the locust borer, an insect that looks and sounds like a bee, though it does not have the capacity to sting!

FAST FACTS

NO TWO ZEBRAS HAVE THE
SAME STRIPES

Each one has a unique set of stripes. When they group together, predators find it hard to target one in the sea of stripes. Also, stripes are a way to avoid being bitten by blood-sucking insects, which prefer solid colors.

THE ARCTIC FOX CHANGES
COLOR WITH THE SEASONS

In the winter, when everything is blanketed in snow, the Arctic fox has long, thick, white fur to blend in and keep warm. In spring, the fox molts, and is left with a shorter coat that is gray, brown, black, or blue.

Summer

Winter

TRUE or FALSE? If it's scared, an **ostrich** will bury its **head** in the **sand**

This is a bird-brained idea. Ostriches do stick their heads in the sand, but **not due to fear**. The world's **biggest bird** is **no chicken**. These **super sprinters** can escape danger by **fleeing at high speed** in the bushlands of their native Africa.

MANY-TONGUED MIMIC

Northern mockingbirds are not only able to imitate the songs of many birds; some can also re-create other sounds, including a squeaking door, car alarm, and meowing cat. They are so good at imitating sounds that this skill is reflected in their scientific name, *Mimus polyglottos*, which means "many-tongued mimic."

The long neck acts as a counterbalance to the weight of the body. Its length gives the eyes a good vantage point to spot and flee danger.

An ostrich eyeball is bigger than its brain.

Ostrich eggs are the biggest of any bird— each one weighs up to 5 lb (2.3 kg), the same as 24 chicken eggs.

Ostriches stand up to 9 ft (3 m) in height.

The confusion over this myth comes from ostrich breeding behavior. Once the female ostrich has laid her eggs, the male digs a hole in the sand, where he moves the eggs for safekeeping. Each parent takes turns sitting on the eggs and turning them over with their beaks during the day. Since the eggs are turned over up to 3 ft (0.9 m) below the surface, it can look as though the ostrich has buried its head in the sand.

An ostrich can weigh up to 400 lb (180 kg).

Ostriches have only two toes instead of the three or four toes of other bird species.

How fast can an ostrich can run in the wild?

📈 FAST FACTS

AN ALBATROSS FLEW AROUND THE WORLD IN
46 DAYS

An albatross from South Georgia Island flew more than 13,670 miles (22,000 km) around the Southern Hemisphere in only 46 days. These amazing birds can glide on wind currents for hours without flapping their wings and can even snooze while flying.

HUMMINGBIRDS ARE
ALWAYS HUNGRY

The energetic hummingbird has the fastest metabolism of any animal. It is so quick that despite the fact that it drinks more than its weight in nectar every day, it is always only a few hours from starving to death.

TRUE or FALSE? You can't boil water on top of a mountain

Forget enjoying a hot tea with a view. Water **does boil** at the top of a mountain, but at a **much lower temperature.** This is because **air pressure is much lower at high altitudes.** As a result, the water isn't hot enough, and **lukewarm liquid is no one's cup of tea.**

Cooking in warm water takes much longer, so at very high altitudes, mountaineers sometimes use pressure cookers to make up for the low atmospheric pressure.

Which country drinks the most tea per person?

SALTY SEA

Seawater is more dense than freshwater because it has salt dissolved in it. The Dead Sea contains so much salt that it is denser than the human body. This is why bathers float on the surface.

°C °F

50 — 120
40 — 100
30 — 80
20 — 60
10 — 40
     32
0 — 20
-10 — 0
-20 — -20
-30 — -20

the time. The rate of evaporation increases with temperature. Water boils when vapor is produced quickly enough to exert the same pressure outward as atmospheric pressure. Since atmospheric pressure decreases with altitude, water boils at a lower temperature at the top of mountains, such as the Matterhorn, shown here.

Water is the only substance that occurs naturally on Earth as a solid (ice), liquid, and gas (water vapor).

FAST FACTS

A FAUCET DRIPPING ONCE A SECOND WASTES ENOUGH WATER TO FILL 100 BATHTUBS

That's 2,200 gallons (10,000 liters) each year, and it shows why small changes can make a big difference when it comes to saving water. Two-thirds of water used in the home is used in the bathroom, and this is spread between flushing toilets, showering, and bathing.

MOST OF THE WORLD'S WATER SUPPLY IS USED FOR AGRICULTURE

DOMESTIC 8% **INDUSTRY 22%** **AGRICULTURE 70%**

Water usage around the world varies considerably. In Africa, agriculture uses 88 percent of all water, while in Europe most water is used in factories.

WATER EXPANDS AS IT FREEZES

Unlike nearly all other substances, water expands as it cools from 39°F (4°C) to 32°F (0°C). Ice takes up 9 percent more space than the same amount of cold water. This is why water pipes can burst on cold days.

TRUE or FALSE? All **light** travels at the **same speed**

Fasten your seat belts! Light travels **faster in a vacuum** (an area without matter) than anything in the universe, at a speed of about 186,000 miles per second (300,000 km/s). But whenever light **passes through matter**, such as air, water, or glass, it **slows down**, stopping this myth in its tracks.

FAST FACTS

NASA'S X-43 SCRAMJET CAN FLY FROM NEW YORK TO LOS ANGELES IN 20 MINUTES

That's 0.000405 percent of the speed of light! At approximately 7,000 mph (11,000 km/h), this is the fastest aircraft in history. It would take six hours for a normal passenger plane to make this journey.

WATER SLOWS THE SPEED OF LIGHT TO 75% OF ITS TOP SPEED IN A VACUUM

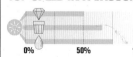

0%   50%   100%

Glass slows it to 66% and diamonds slow it to 50%. The molecules in these materials are so tightly packed that the light bumps into many molecules along the way, which means it takes longer to get from A to B.

AT THE SPEED OF LIGHT, YOU COULD CIRCLE THE EQUATOR 7.5 TIMES IN A SECOND

According to relativity, the speed of light is nature's ultimate speed limit—and only things with no mass, such as light, can ever travel that fast. To get *you* to light speed would require an infinite amount of energy.

ight can travel through a vacuum at breakneck peed because there is nothing to slow it down. f any matter is present, light interacts with it, nd this slows it down. Light travels at different peeds in different materials—and if it moves om one to another at an angle, the light changes direction. This is why light bends when it asses through a glass lens, for example.

The presence of air slows down light waves.

Different colors are produced by different wavelengths of light. Red light travels very slightly faster through air or glass than blue light.

Which country uses the most light, based on electricity per capita?

CALCULATIONS BY CANDLELIGHT

The intensity (brightness) of light is measured using a unit called a candela. It was originally based on the amount of light emanating from a single candle. A typical lightning flash produces light with an intensity of about eight trillion times that of a candle.

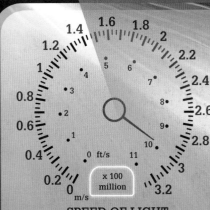

1.4 1.6 1.8
1.2   2
          2.2
1   5   6
    4   7   2.4
0.8   3   8   2.6
    2   9
0.6   1   10 2.8
0.4   0 ft/s 11
          3
0.2   x 100
       million   3.2
0
m/s

SPEED OF LIGHT

983,571,056 ft/s
299,792,458 m/s

TRUE or FALSE?

An opera singer can shatter glass

Italian opera singer Enrico Caruso claimed his **high notes** could **shatter champagne flutes**. He was right—ear-piercing tones have been known to break glass. A **powerful voice** producing a **very loud, pure tone** at a **perfect pitch** can break a wine glass. **Smash!** You'd be left picking up the pieces.

Glass has a natural resonant frequency—the speed it will vibrate when knocked by someone or disturbed by a sound wave. If a professional sings at the right pitch and volume to vibrate the air particles around the glass at its precise resonant frequency, the glass will vibrate. Raising the volume of singing can result in the glass breaking altogether.

SONIC BOOM

Speedy sound travels through the air at 1,130 ft/s (344 m/s). Some things move faster still, breaking the sound barrier and creating a shock wave called a sonic boom. The crack of a whip is a sonic boom caused by part of the whip moving faster than the speed of sound.

Fine crystal is the type of glass most likely to be shattered by sound waves.

Wine glasses are the best candidates because their tubular shape produces a ringing sound when clinked.

The singer's vocals displace surrounding air particles, sending them toward the glass at high speed.

Why should you avoid whistling at the end of an opera?

FAST FACTS

SOUNDS ABOVE 85 DB CAN DAMAGE YOUR HEARING

Sound intensity is measured in decibels (dB). The louder the noise, the more decibels it racks up. Listening to sounds above 85 dB for long periods can hurt your ears, while sounds louder than 120 dB are painful.

NOISY RESTAURANT (80 dB)

ROCK CONCERT (100 dB)

AIRPLANE TAKEOFF (130 dB)

NEARBY BLUE WHALE (180 dB)

NEARBY ROCKET LAUNCH (200 dB)

EPICENTER OF BIG EARTHQUAKE (300 dB)

SOUND TRAVELS ABOUT FOUR TIMES FASTER IN WATER THAN IN AIR

WATER

This is because water molecules in a liquid are much closer together than those in a gas, so it takes less time for the sound waves to pass through.

TRUE or FALSE? A **rainbow** has seven colors

All children know the **colors of the rainbow**, but the reality is not as black and white as **seven distinct colors**. Reflecting sunlight off water droplets, a rainbow **bounces back every wavelength** from infrared to ultraviolet, with **colors** running across **millions of kaleidoscopic shades**.

DEEP BLUE SEA

The sea isn't blue because it reflects the blue sky. An object looks a certain color because it absorbs some wavelengths of light and reflects others. We see only the reflected ones. Seawater absorbs all colors except blue, so we see only the reflected blue wavelengths.

It's impossible to reach the end of a rainbow—as you move and your perspective changes the rainbow moves too.

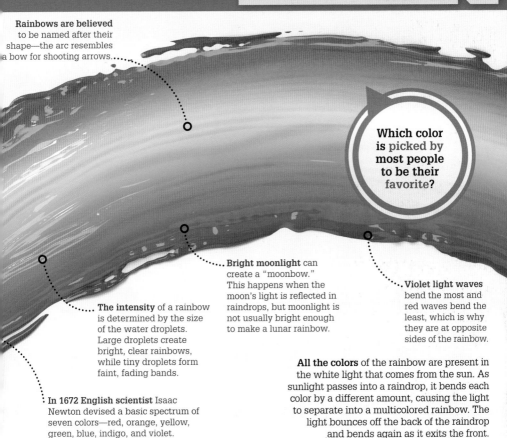

Rainbows are believed to be named after their shape—the arc resembles a bow for shooting arrows.

Which color is picked by most people to be their favorite?

The intensity of a rainbow is determined by the size of the water droplets. Large droplets create bright, clear rainbows, while tiny droplets form faint, fading bands.

Bright moonlight can create a "moonbow." This happens when the moon's light is reflected in raindrops, but moonlight is not usually bright enough to make a lunar rainbow.

Violet light waves bend the most and red waves bend the least, which is why they are at opposite sides of the rainbow.

In 1672 English scientist Isaac Newton devised a basic spectrum of seven colors—red, orange, yellow, green, blue, indigo, and violet.

All the colors of the rainbow are present in the white light that comes from the sun. As sunlight passes into a raindrop, it bends each color by a different amount, causing the light to separate into a multicolored rainbow. The light bounces off the back of the raindrop and bends again as it exits the front.

FAST FACTS

CHROMOPHOBIA
IS THE IRRATIONAL FEAR OF COLORS

Fear of a certain color can occur when a person experiences an extremely negative event associated with a particular color. Symptoms may include any of the signs of anxiety, such as heart palpitations, chest pain, or shortness of breath.

BEES CAN SEE COLORS THAT HUMANS CAN'T

WHAT A HUMAN SEES   **WHAT A BEE SEES**

Bees can see light in the ultraviolet (UV) spectrum, but this range is invisible to the naked human eye. Using special devices, scientists have discovered that the colored world these insects see guides them to target "landing strips" where they feed on nectar.

COLOR WHEEL

An artist's color wheel shows how different colored pigments mix together. Any color can be made by mixing the "primary colors"—red, yellow, and blue—in different proportions. Any two primary colors mixed together produce the "secondary colors."

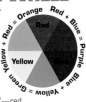

TRUE or FALSE? A coin dropped from a tall building can kill

Being **showered with money** sounds good in theory, but getting struck by a falling coin is said **to be fatal.** The truth is that a falling coin is small and flat, and its speed is **limited by air resistance.** Dropping one from a great height will **sting the skin** but not prove deadly.

LIFE IN THE FAST LANE

The front and rear wings of a Formula 1 race car create a huge downward force that stops the vehicle from overturning. The drag is so strong that, theoretically, it could counteract gravity, and these cars could be driven upside down when moving faster than 100 mph (160 km/h).

A coin dropped from the roof of the Empire State Building in New York would fall 1,250 ft (381 m) to the ground.

A coin's top speed, or terminal velocity, depends on its shape and size, as well as the density of the air. For a one euro coin, it is about 100 mph (160 km/h).

Some people assume that a falling coin will accelerate throughout its fall, at the mercy of gravity, until it hits the ground at high speed. However, repeated collisions with molecules in the air limit the coin's speed. This "drag force" increases with the coin's speed, eventually balancing the gravitational force, so the coin can no longer accelerate.

the air increases the air resistance, thereby slowing the downward motion.

What are the top speeds of a falling skydiver, a tennis ball, and a raindrop?

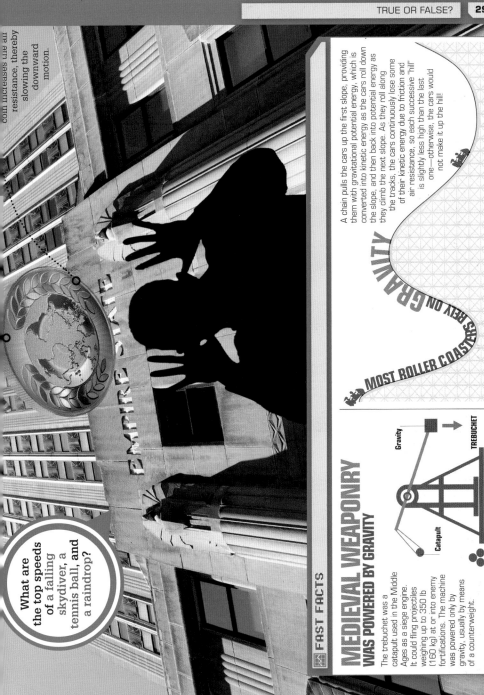

EMPIRE STATE

MOST ROLLER COASTERS RELY ON GRAVITY

A chain pulls the cars up the first slope, providing them with gravitational potential energy, which is converted into kinetic energy as the cars roll down the slope, and then back into potential energy as they climb the next slope. As they roll along the tracks, the cars continuously lose some of their kinetic energy due to friction and air resistance, so each successive "hill" is slightly less high than the last one—otherwise, the cars would not make it up the hill!

⊞ FAST FACTS

MEDIEVAL WEAPONRY WAS POWERED BY GRAVITY

The trebuchet was a catapult used in the Middle Ages as a siege engine. It could fling projectiles weighing up to 350 lb (160 kg) at or into enemy fortifications. The machine was powered only by gravity, usually by means of a counterweight.

Gravity

Catapult

TREBUCHET

TRUE or FALSE? Toast lands butter-side down

What are the **odds**? If you drop toast, **chances are** that it will hit the floor butter-side down. Splat! Similarly, a falling cat can thank its nine lives for landing safely on its feet **more often than not**. Although these are the **probable outcomes** of the two scenarios, there are reasons for both, and **no outcome is guaranteed**.

SHARED CELEBRATIONS

Sharing a birthday is often seen as a big coincidence, though it's anything but. In a group of only 23 people, there is a 50 percent chance that two share the same birthday. The probability is very close to 100 percent with 367 people, though it is 99 percent with just 57 people.

If the average kitchen counter was twice as high, toast would land butter-side up 95 percent of the time because there would be time for a complete rotation.

Toast lands butter-side down because of the height of a kitchen counter and the size of bread. There isn't enough time for toast to make a full rotation. The feline is built for free fall, with its highly flexible backbone enabling it to correct positions in midair. Neither situation is a miracle—they are just more likely to happen than not.

The cat will usually flip over during the fall, letting its four feet absorb the shock on landing.

Cats have 30 spinal vertebrae, compared to humans who have 26. This enables greater suppleness and versatility.

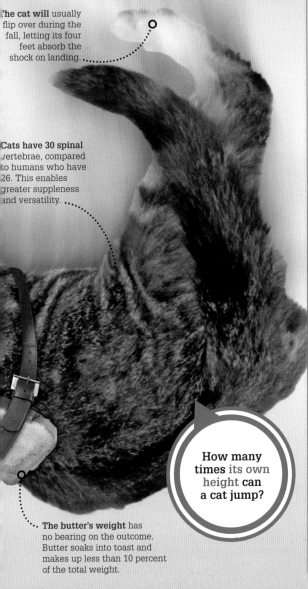

How many times its own height can a cat jump?

The butter's weight has no bearing on the outcome. Butter soaks into toast and makes up less than 10 percent of the total weight.

📊 **FAST FACTS**

DISEASES ARE THE MOST PROBABLE CAUSE OF DEATH

The chances of dying of heart disease are 1 in 5, with cancer close behind at 1 in 7. Only 6 percent of deaths are due to accidents, but this adds up to more than three million deaths a year.

WALKING INTO A LAMPPOST
360 MILLION TO 1

LIGHTNING STRIKE
10 MILLION TO 1

FALLING DOWN A MANHOLE
5 MILLION TO 1

COMPUTER GAME EXHAUSTION
1.5 MILLION TO 1

THERE IS ALWAYS A 1 IN 2 CHANCE THAT A COIN WILL LAND HEADS UP

It's tempting to think that if you have tossed two heads in a row, the next toss is more likely to be tails. In fact, it is equally likely to be heads again.

PYTHAGORAS THOUGHT OF ODD NUMBERS AS MALE AND EVEN NUMBERS AS FEMALE

This Greek mathematician lived in the sixth century BCE, but his calculations and theories are still used today. He wasn't alone on the male and female numbers, either—the Chinese philosophy of yin and yang holds the same view.

📊 FAST FACTS

AMERICA USES MORE THAN 77 TIMES AS MUCH ELECTRICITY PER PERSON AS KENYA

Electricity consumption is uneven around the world, with developed countries using the most. However, global electricity demand is expected to rise by 70 percent by 2035, partly because of the growth of emerging economies in Africa, Asia, and the Middle East.

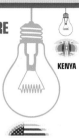

KENYA

USA

AN ELECTRIC EEL CAN DISCHARGE ELECTRICITY AT 600 VOLTS

Eels store electric charge in specialized cells that work like batteries. These cells all discharge at the same time when the eel is under threat, or attacking prey.

USA
120 VOLT PLUG

EUROPE
230 VOLT PLUG

EEL
600 VOLTS

The modern world relies upon electricity. Electric current is the flow of electric charge. In wires, it is electrically charged particles called electrons that move. This is achieved using huge electromagnetic machines called generators, which are typically powered by burning fossil fuels, such as oil or coal.

Leaving appliances off but plugged in is called vampire power because they still suck electricity from the wall socket.

Who invented the incandescent light bulb, fuses, switches, and sockets?

High-voltage electricity generated in power plants flows along cables attached to towers. Devices called transformers, at electricity substations, reduce the voltage so it is safe to use in the home.

TRUE or FALSE? A screen saver saves electricity

At offices around the world, screen savers are **part of a day's work**. **Taking a break** from the computer **starts the screen saver**, but the electricity supply is not reduced. Far from cutting costs, the computer is **still running a program**, going about **business as usual**.

A screen saver is usually activated for visual entertainment or computer security purposes.

GOING GREEN

Most electricity is generated in power plants burning coal, oil, or natural gas. But, increasingly, alternative sources, such as wind, water, and solar power are being used. In certain countries, notably in South America, some electricity is generated using ethanol, a renewable fuel made from sugarcane (above).

TRUE or FALSE? The **Big Bang** was loud

The universe began in an **explosive split-second** about 14 billion years ago, but it didn't go off with a bang! Sound must have a material through which to **transmit its vibrations**, so before everything started, there was no way to **"hear"** it. Instead, it was a silent spectacular we call the Big Bang.

Heat left over from the Big Bang is called cosmic microwave background radiation.

BEIGE UNIVERSE

Until the universe was three minutes old, its matter was nearly all hydrogen and helium atoms.

The universe's first starry galaxies developed in the most densely packed areas.

In 2002 American astronomers studied the average color of the universe and declared it to be… beige. From looking at all the light in space and surveying more than 200,000 galaxies, they compared the creamy beige results to milky coffee. The color of the universe is now called "Cosmic Latte."

Starting off quiet, hot, and smaller than a period, the universe has been getting noisier, cooler, and much, much bigger ever since. A trillionth of a second after the Big Bang, the universe grew supersized in a period called the inflation era. It then slowed down to expand more steadily.

The temperature of the early universe was a scorching 10 billion trillion trillion degrees Celsius.

What are the Big Rip, the Big Crunch, and the Big Freeze?

FAST FACTS

IN SPACE NO ONE CAN HEAR YOU SCREAM

Sound waves need a medium such as air or water to travel through. So, in the vacuum of space, screams cannot be heard.

THE SUN
9,900°F (5,500°C)

EARTH
59°F (15°C)

NEPTUNE
-330°F (-201°C)

SPACE DOESN'T HAVE A TEMPERATURE

Space doesn't have a temperature, but the objects within the universe do. Temperatures range from way below freezing to superhot.

90,000 FT (27,000 M) 20% GRAVITY

30,000 FT (9,000 M) 60% GRAVITY

ON EARTH 100% GRAVITY

THERE IS GRAVITY IN SPACE

Small levels of gravity can be found everywhere in space, but it weakens with distance. As a rocket travels farther and farther from Earth, it feels less and less of the planet's gravitational pull.

TRUE or FALSE? The **universe** is getting **bigger**

In the first **three minutes of existence**, the universe took off in a big way—from something billions of times smaller than a **tiny atom** to a **whopper** the size of our home galaxy, the Milky Way. It has been **expanding ever since**.

In the space beyond the Milky Way, there are about 10 dwarf galaxies orbiting it.

MISSING UNIVERSE

Matter we know and recognize, such as planets and galaxies, makes up less than five percent of the total universe. Most of the universe is unknown matter, called dark matter, and unseen energy, called dark energy. Neither are visible, but their impact on what we can see is clear.

Earth, the sun, and the stars we see at night are all part of the Milky Way. There are now about 400 billion stars in our galaxy. Although the first stars lived and died during the first billion years of the universe, the remnants led to the birth of billions of new stars.

How many planets are there in the Milky Way galaxy?

In addition to stars, the galaxy contains dust and gas, held together by gravity.

FAST FACTS

THE UNIVERSE IS EXPANDING BY ABOUT 72 KM (45 MILES) EVERY SECOND

That's a whopping 3.7 million miles (6 million km) every hour! While you are asleep at night, it grows by 30 million miles (50 million km).

ELLIPTICAL

SPIRAL

IRREGULAR

BARRED SPIRAL

THE BIGGEST GALAXIES LOOK LIKE SQUASHED BALLS

Galaxies can be one of four shapes—elliptical (oval-shaped), spiral (disk-shaped with bright, curving lanes of stars), irregular (no defined shape), and barred spiral (spiral with a bar shape in the middle).

The Milky Way is a barred spiral galaxy, seen as a bright path of stars in Earth's night sky.

Though the amount of material in the universe has stayed the same, the shape of the universe is spreading out.

In the galaxy's center is a supermassive black hole, named Sagittarius A*.

TRUE or FALSE? A **black hole sucks in** everything near it

This is not the whole story. The **gravitational pull** of a black hole is undeniably strong, but it **cannot absorb** all matter. Mysterious **dark matter** seems able to resist it.

The opening of the hole is called the "event horizon." If an object crosses this point, it can never escape.

SUPERMASSIVE HOLES

A basic black hole is just one collapsed star, but the center of a galaxy is home to a supermassive black hole. This is millions of times heavier and more massive, with far stronger gravitational force.

A **stellar black hole** forms when a massive star dies, but we don't know exactly how supermassive black holes are formed. These holes are black because no light can escape from inside. The first black hole to be discovered was Cygnus X-1 during the 1970s.

The ergosphere is the area around the event horizon. An object in the ergosphere can still exit the black hole.

What might happen if you fell into a black hole?

📊 **FAST FACTS**

YOU CAN'T SEE A BLACK HOLE

The powerful gravity pulls light into the middle of the black hole, so it's invisible. Scientists know black holes exist from watching how the gravity affects the stars and gas around them.

TIME STOPS IN

00:00

A BLACK HOLE

The black hole's gravity distorts time, which runs slower near the hole. Time appears to stop once an object has crossed the event horizon, and the object seems to become frozen in space.

THE BLACK HOLE IN THE MILKY WAY HAS THE MASS OF

4 MILLION SUNS

The smallest black holes may be a single atom, but with the mass of a large mountain. This shows how dense they are—so dense that nothing can escape their amazing gravitational pull.

TRUE or FALSE? Only Saturn has rings

Saturn is the solar system's **ring leader**, but all the other **gas giants** have rings, too. The rings of Jupiter, Neptune, and Uranus **contain less material**, so they are harder to spot.

Jumbo Jupiter is the fastest-spinning planet, whirling around at more than double the speed of Earth.

Great Red Spot

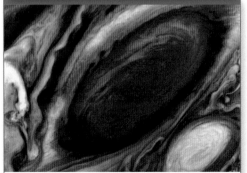

STORMY SPOTS

The biggest storm in the solar system is raging on Jupiter. Called the Great Red Spot, it is twice the size of Earth and has been there for at least 300 years. The combination of Jupiter's speedy spin and wild winds produce megastorms, creating spots on the surface.

Jupiter has more than 60 moons, including Ganymede, the biggest moon in the solar system.

It is often assumed that Saturn has a solitary ring, but up close there are hundreds of them. Each one consists of millions of bits of dirty ice. From tiny dust particles to huge rocks, these pieces whizz their way around the planet. The rings of the other three giants are similarly composed, though much less visible.

📈 FAST FACTS

URANUS
IS THE ONLY PLANET TO SPIN ON ITS SIDE

EARTH

URANUS

It's possible that an object the size of Earth crashed into Uranus in the past and knocked it over. All the other planets spin almost upright.

MARS   JUPITER   VENUS

EARTH   MERCURY

URANUS   NEPTUNE

SATURN

ALL THE PLANETS COULD FIT
INSIDE JUPITER

In fact, Jupiter is so huge you could put the other planets inside it, and there would still be room to spare.

JUPITER 11.86 YEARS   SUN

NEPTUNE 164.9 YEARS

EARTH 1 YEAR

IT TAKES NEPTUNE 164.9 EARTH YEARS TO ORBIT THE SUN

This is the longest planetary orbit of the sun. It takes Uranus about 84 Earth years, Saturn about 29.5 Earth years, and Jupiter about 12 Earth years.

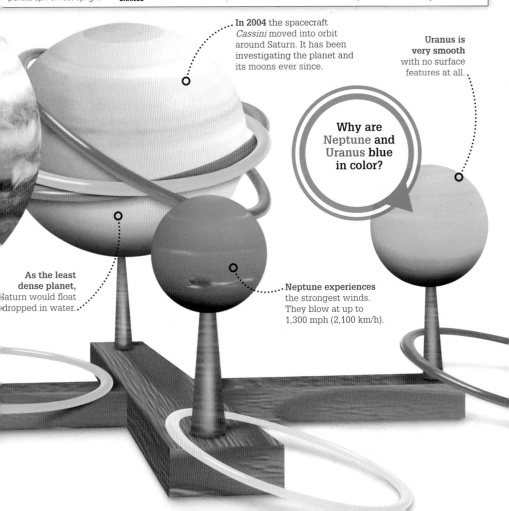

In 2004 the spacecraft *Cassini* moved into orbit around Saturn. It has been investigating the planet and its moons ever since.

Uranus is very smooth with no surface features at all.

Why are Neptune and Uranus blue in color?

As the least dense planet, Saturn would float dropped in water.

Neptune experiences the strongest winds. They blow at up to 1,300 mph (2,100 km/h).

TRUE or FALSE? There has **never been** life on Mars

Earth is the only place in the universe where life is known to exist, but fellow **rocky world Mars** may also have produced life. This **red planet** was once **warm and wet**. Where water flows, there is the **possibility of life**, though maybe not as we know it...

LONG-HAUL VOYAGERS

Even if we can't find life on Mars, it may exist elsewhere. Two Voyager spacecraft are on a mission to attract alien interest. On board is a golden record, detailing the history of humans. Launched by NASA in 1977, they'll arrive at the next planetary system in 80,000 years. So watch this space...

Mars is now cold and dry, with empty riverbeds and cracked floodplains, but the lakes and seas that formed in its craters three billion years ago would have been suitable environments for early life-forms to thrive. Only 100 years ago, some observers believed the network of barren canals on Mars was the result of hardworking aliens!

Wind blows dust into the air, making the sky red.

Giant volcanoes and deep canyons are surface features.

The robot rover *Curiosity* has been exploring Mars since 2012, looking for signs that it was once home to tiny life-forms.

The extendable arm of *Curiosity* stretches 7 ft (2 m) to study a rock at close range.

How fast does *Curiosity* **travel across the surface of Mars?**

Dusty red soil covers the surface of Mars.

📊 FAST FACTS

MERCURY IS BOTH HOT AND COLD

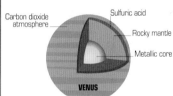

Nighttime
-290°F (-180°C)

Daytime
800°F (430°C)

SUN

MERCURY

The temperature on this rocky planet ranges from a fiery 800°F (430°C) in the day to a bitterly cold -290°F (-180°C) at night.

Carbon dioxide atmosphere

Sulfuric acid

Rocky mantle

Metallic core

VENUS

VENUS IS NAMED AFTER THE ROMAN GODDESS OF LOVE AND BEAUTY

This is an unlikely pairing, since Venus is a hot, hostile, rocky planet, surrounded by clouds of corrosive sulfuric acid.

MARS IS HALF THE SIZE OF EARTH

4,220 miles (6,800 km) in diameter

7,926 miles (12,756 km) in diameter

MARS

EARTH

But Mars has no oceans and is land all over, so its land covers about the same area as that of our home planet.

TRUE or FALSE? Pluto is a planet

Discovered in 1930, Pluto became the ninth honorary member of the **planetary party**. The party was over in 2006 when astronomers **reclassified it as a dwarf planet**. Now Pluto keeps company with the other dwarf planets, and **more are likely** to join them.

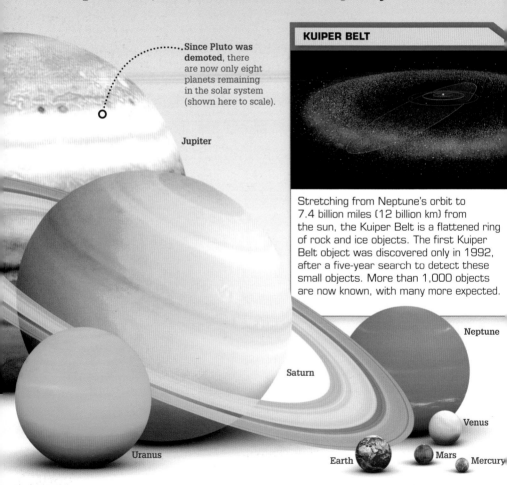

Since Pluto was demoted, there are now only eight planets remaining in the solar system (shown here to scale).

Jupiter

KUIPER BELT

Stretching from Neptune's orbit to 7.4 billion miles (12 billion km) from the sun, the Kuiper Belt is a flattened ring of rock and ice objects. The first Kuiper Belt object was discovered only in 1992, after a five-year search to detect these small objects. More than 1,000 objects are now known, with many more expected.

Neptune

Saturn

Venus

Uranus

Earth

Mars

Mercury

FAST FACTS

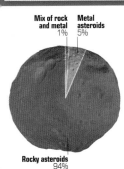

Mix of rock and metal 1%

Metal asteroids 5%

Rocky asteroids 94%

ASTEROIDS
COME IN DIFFERENT
VARIETIES

Billions of asteroids orbit the sun. Most are rocky, while the rest are made of metal, or a mix of rock and metal. Metallic asteroids are mostly made of iron, but may also include platinum and even gold.

2006 Left Earth

2007 Passed Jupiter

***New Horizons* probe**

2015 Reached Pluto

IT TAKES NEARLY A DECADE
TO REACH PLUTO

Launched by NASA in 2006, the *New Horizons* spacecraft is on a mission to explore the edge of the solar system. It traveled nearly 3 billion miles (5 billion km) to reach Pluto and sent back pictures of the dwarf planet and its moons. It is now heading to the Kuiper Belt, and will study objects in it.

In 2006 astronomers introduced the class of "dwarf planets." This new group consists of rocky balls much smaller than the main planets of the solar system but still planetlike in shape. They include Pluto, Eris, Haumea, and Makemake. All four orbit the sun as part of a gang of icy rock bodies and whizzing comets that live in the space neighborhood beyond the planets.

Pluto is smaller than Earth's moon. The surface temperature here is -380°F (-230°C), even in summer!

Covered in a thick coating of ice, Pluto has a rocky interior.

What is the story behind Pluto's name?

Makemake takes 310 years to go around the sun.

◀ PLANETS

NONPLANETS ▶

Haumea is egg-shaped.

Eris is the largest dwarf planet.

TRUE or FALSE? India was once joined to **Australia**

Earth's surface consists of **tectonic plates**, which fit together like a **jigsaw puzzle**. The continents we recognize today sit on six of these plates and were formed when large **supercontinents** broke up and **drifted apart**. The supercontinent **Gondwana** connected India and Australia, along with Africa, South America, and Antarctica.

AFRICA

FOSSIL FAMILIES

Newly discovered fossils on shorelines provide further evidence that the shifting continents were once joined. One example is *Mesosaurus* (pictured), a coastal marine reptile found in Africa and South America.

Scientists saw that the east coast of South America fitted the west coast of Africa almost perfectly.

SOUTH AMERICA

PLATES MOVE APART AT DIFFERENT RATES

EAST PACIFIC RISE

ARCTIC RIDGE

The slowest rate of plate separation occurs at the Arctic ridge, at 1 in (2.5 cm) each year. By contrast, at the East Pacific Rise near Easter Island, the plates are moving apart at the speedy rate of more than 6 in (15 cm) each year.

MOUNT EVEREST IS GETTING TALLER

Global positioning satellite (GPS) readings suggest that Mount Everest is growing by up to 0.0006 in (0.016 mm) every day, and that the Himalaya Mountains as a whole rise by 0.4 in (1 cm) each year. This is caused by the Indian tectonic plate moving into the Eurasian plate.

ASIA

NORTH AMERICA

BERING STRAIT

SOME OF TODAY'S CONTINENTS WERE ONCE LINKED BY LAND BRIDGES

These land bridges did exist for periods of time; for example, North America and Asia were linked intermittently by a land bridge over what is now the Bering Strait.

India and Australia began to split apart 140 million years ago, when dinosaurs roamed the earth.

Australia has been isolated for so long that it has developed unique flora and fauna, including marsupials such as kangaroos.

INDIA

AUSTRALIA

What is the average thickness of the tectonic plates?

ANTARCTICA

The theory of plate tectonics was developed in the 1960s to explain how the continents move across Earth. Geologist Alfred Wegener believed the continents once fitted together, and formed the theory of continental drift. It is now known that Earth's top layer, the lithosphere, has cracked into seven large plates carrying the continents, with many smaller plates. Heat currents under the surface power their gradual movement.

TRUE or FALSE? There are seven seas

This expression comes from sailors thousands of years ago, but it is as **mythical as mermaids**. In truth there are **five oceans** and more than **50 seas** that make up our **saltwater world** today.

Adriatic Sea

Black Sea

Caspian Sea

Mediterranean Sea

Persian Gulf

Red Sea

Arabian Sea

DEEP DIVE

Only five percent of the ocean has been explored, while the rest is a vast unknown. In 1960 a specially built bathyscaphe named *Trieste* descended to the Mariana Trench—the deepest point on Earth at 35,797 ft (10,910 m). The bathyscaphe resisted pressures of up to 200,000 tons.

NORTH AMERICA

The Atlantic Ocean is, on average, the saltiest ocean.

The Pacific Ocean is almost as large as all the other oceans combined.

SOUTH AMERICA

The original seven seas referred to in early European and Islamic texts encompassed the Mediterranean, Adriatic, Arabian, Black, Red, and Caspian Seas, along with the Persian Gulf. But this was because sailors had not traveled beyond their immediate waters. Oceans and seas are often used to mean the same thing, but oceans are open expanses of water, while most seas are partly enclosed by land.

📊 FAST FACTS

OCEANS CONTAIN
97% OF EARTH'S WATER

The largest ocean, the Pacific, houses nearly half of this saltwater. The remaining 3 percent of Earth's water is freshwater.

OCEANS 96.6%

TOTAL GLOBAL WATER

FRESHWATER 2.5%
OTHER SALINE 0.9%

GROUNDWATER 30.1%

GLACIERS AND ICE CAPS 68.7%

SURFACE/OTHER FRESHWATER 1.2%

FRESHWATER

ATMOSPHERE 3.0%

SOIL MOISTURE 3.8%

LAKES 20.9%

GROUND ICE AND PERMAFROST 69.0%

LIVING THINGS 0.26%

RIVERS 0.44%

SWAMPS, MARSHES 2.6%

SURFACE WATER AND OTHER FRESHWATER

Which countries border three different oceans?

The Arctic Ocean is not only the coldest ocean; it is also the smallest and the shallowest.

EUROPE

ASIA

The Indian Ocean is the warmest ocean in the world.

AFRICA

AUSTRALIA

Pirate stories in the past referred to seven seas.

The Southern Ocean is geologically the youngest ocean. It was formed about 30 million years ago.

The Amazon River is home to an incredible variety of creatures. Species include the anaconda, river otter, and Amazon river dolphin. There are 2,000 types of fish, more than the number in the Atlantic Ocean. The deadly piranha is one of them.

TRUE or FALSE?

Earth's longest river is the Amazon

The Amazon in South America is by far the largest and widest river, but it falls short in the long run. The Amazon comes a close second to the Nile in northeastern Africa.

0 km   1,000   2,000   3,000

AMAZON RIVER

Lake Victoria is the largest tropical lake in the world.

NILE RIVER

The name *Nile* comes from the Greek for "river valley."

The Amazon River flows through Peru, Columbia, and Brazil.

With its lakes and tributaries, the Nile connects 11 African countries, flowing northward from Burundi to Egypt.

Thousands of tributaries (streams) flow into the main river course.

WHITE NILE

BLUE NILE

The Nile has two major tributaries: the White Nile, which originates in Burundi, and the Blue Nile, which originates

0 miles   200   400   600   800   1,000   1,200   1,400   1,600   1,800   2,00

CHINA'S YELLOW RIVER IS THE MUDDIEST IN THE WORLD

Huang He, which means "Yellow River," is the second-longest river in Asia. About 1.6 billion tons of sediment is washed down it every year, giving the water a yellow color.

THE AMAZON HOLDS 20% OF THE PLANET'S FLOWING FRESH WATER

It carries more water than the Nile, Mississippi-Missouri, Yenisey-Angara, and Yangtze Rivers combined. The volume of water carried by each river is measured by how much water it discharges into the ocean every second.

NILE
180,100 ft³
(5,100 m³)

MISSISSIPPI-MISSOURI
572,100 ft³
(16,200 m³)

YENISEY-ANGARA
671,000 ft³
(19,000 m³)

YANGTZE
1,094,800 ft³
(31,000 m³)

AMAZON
7,733,900 ft³
(219,000 m³)

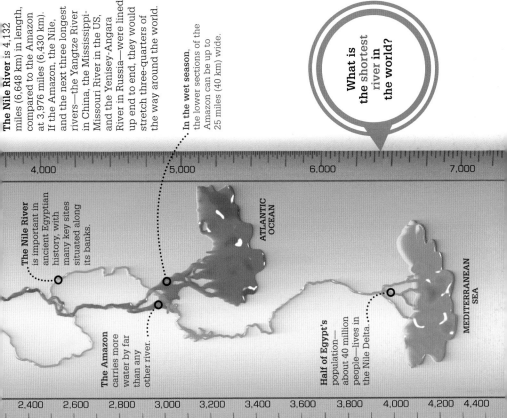

The Nile River is 4,132 miles (6,648 km) in length, compared to the Amazon at 3,976 miles (6,430 km). If the Amazon, the Nile, and the next three longest rivers—the Yangtze River in China, the Mississippi-Missouri River in the US, and the Yenisey-Angara River in Russia—were lined up end to end, they would stretch three-quarters of the way around the world.

In the wet season, the lower sections of the Amazon can be up to 25 miles (40 km) wide.

What is the shortest river in the world?

The Nile River is important in ancient Egyptian history, with many key sites situated along its banks.

The Amazon carries more water by far than any other river.

Half of Egypt's population—about 40 million people—lives in the Nile Delta.

ATLANTIC OCEAN

MEDITERRANEAN SEA

4,000 5,000 6,000 7,000

2,400 2,600 2,800 3,000 3,200 3,400 3,600 3,800 4,000 4,200 4,400

TRUE or FALSE?

Mount Everest is the world's tallest mountain

Everest is topped by another **mighty mound**, which is often overlooked because so much of it is **hidden under the sea**. The lesser-known **Mauna Kea** triumphs over Everest easily if measured **base to peak**.

Although the top of Mauna Kea is only 13,796 ft (4,205 m) above sea level, it is the tallest mountain on Earth in total base-to-peak height.

FAST FACTS

As you go up a mountain, the air pressure decreases. This makes it harder to breathe because oxygen can't pass through the lungs into the blood as easily as at sea level. The body responds by making more red blood cells to carry more oxygen and keep you healthy.

PEOPLE LIVING AT HIGH ALTITUDE HAVE MORE

RED BLOOD CELLS

ABOUT 70 MILLION

HIMALAYAS 70 million people

FRANCE 67 million people

PEOPLE LIVE IN THE HIMALAYAS

This giant mountain range is an inhospitable place, yet a population greater than that of France lives in the Himalayas. Despite the harsh weather and lack of flat ground, most mountain communities rely on agriculture to sustain them.

MOUNTAINOUS MARS

Bigger than any mountain on our planet is Olympus Mons on Mars. Formed about three billion years ago, this shield volcano towers almost 14 miles (22 km) high—more than two times higher than the tallest mountain on Earth.

In ideal weather conditions, it is possible to see for 100 miles (160 km) from the top of Everest.

More than 3,000 climbers have reached Mount Everest's summit.

Mauna Kea in Hawaii is a dormant volcano, which last erupted 4,500 years ago. Measured from its underwater base in the Pacific Ocean, it stretches 32,000 ft (9,750 m) to the top. This makes Everest in the Himalayas appear small by comparison at 29,035 ft (8,850 m).

At what **height** does **a hill** become **a mountain?**

More than one million years old, Mauna Kea is sinking slowly at a rate of 0.25 in (5 mm) a year as the seabed sags under its heavy weight.

TRUE or FALSE? Deserts are always hot

This fact is a lot of hot air. In reality, **deserts can be hot or cold**. Any area that receives **less than 10 in (25 cm) of rain** a year is a desert, so there are deserts all around the world, from blazing Africa to icy Antarctica!

Temperatures in Antarctica can dip to -80°F (-62°C) but the lack of rainfall means it is still classified as desert land.

SANDS OF TIME

Deserts are expanding as time goes on because of overfarming, deforestation, and climate change. This process is called desertification. Asia's Gobi Desert is growing at a rate of 1,390 square miles (3,600 sq km) each year.

Plants in hot deserts must survive extreme temperatures, high winds, and arid conditions. Plants like this cactus can store water in their stems, but other plants can survive only for a short period after it rains.

It is a myth that all deserts are sandy. Only 20 percent of the world's deserts are sand.

Which are the hottest and coldest deserts in the world?

Deserts can never be permanently hot. Even those located in the hottest parts of the world get very cold at night without the heat of the sun. This is why it is hard for people to live in the desert and cope with the extremes of temperature. The priority is being near a water source, so inhabitants lead a nomadic existence, moving from place to place for survival.

TRUE or FALSE? If a **volcano** does not produce **lava**, it isn't **dangerous**

This is a dangerous assumption! All volcanoes are **deadly**. Giant ash clouds, treacherous mudflows, hazardous gases, and rocky landslides are all released when they **erupt**. Another bombshell is that about **300,000 people** have been **killed by volcanoes** in the last 400 years.

Four-fifths of Earth's surface is volcanic rock, but much of it is hidden under the ocean. Liquid magma rising from deep within Earth is spewed out by volcanoes as incandescent lava. This may be accompanied by spectacular gas and ash plumes, as seen here.

POMPEII CASTS

The city of Pompeii in Italy was destroyed when Mount Vesuvius erupted in 79 CE. Buried under ash and rock, 20,000 citizens died. Archaeologists found remains of the victims buried in the ash and made lifelike casts of them.

MAGMA'S

- SMOKY BURGERS
- BBQ RIBS
- EXTRA HOT CHILI

OPEN

In addition to water vapor and carbon dioxide, deadly sulfur dioxide fills the air with poisonous gas.

What was the world's largest volcanic eruption?

Ash clouds can cover vast areas, forming a suffocating blanket overhead.

Over time lava and ash may build up to form a cone-shaped volcanic mountain, where it breaks through a weak point in the crust.

FAST FACTS

THE LOUDEST SOUND IN RECORDED HISTORY WAS THE KRAKATOA ERUPTION

Erupting in Indonesia in 1883, the explosion reached 180 decibels and was heard up to 2,970 miles (4,782 km) away on the island of Rodrigues, near Mauritius. Sounds above 110 dB can cause lasting hearing damage if listened to for more than a minute.

VOLCANOES RANGE FROM NONEXPLOSIVE TO MEGA-COLOSSAL

STROMBOLI
VEI 1 gentle

ST. HELENS
VEI 5
paroxysmal

KRAKATOA
VEI 6 colossal

YELLOWSTONE
VEI 8 mega-colossal

The volcanic explosivity index (VEI) measures volcanoes from zero (nonexplosive) to eight (mega-colossal mass ejections, erupting about every 10,000 years). Each interval on the scale represents a tenfold increase in criteria, such as volume of ash, eruption, cloud height, and explosivity.

90% OF ALL VOLCANIC ACTIVITY OCCURS IN THE OCEANS

90%

10%

Underwater vents or fissures in Earth's surface, called submarine volcanoes, are mostly found at ocean ridges, where tectonic plates are moving apart. They are estimated to account for 75% of magma output each year.

TRUE or FALSE? Neanderthals were really hairy and spoke in grunts

This unflattering description comes from **media stereotypes** of early peoples. Science reveals that Neanderthals were not overly hairy and spoke similarly to people today. **DNA** studies show they were a **separate evolutionary line** from humans, dying out 30,000 years ago.

GENOME PROJECTS

In the Human Genome Project, scientists mapped more than 20,000 genes that make up human DNA (shown)—the design for life. Then it was time for the Neanderthal Genome Project, using genetic material (or DNA) extracted from fossil bones. It is now possible to clone a Neanderthal and bring it to life, though this would be costly and open to ethical debate.

They hunted prey with spears and used a range of stone tools to cut up carcasses.

The icy climate about 200,000 years ago was tough. Neanderthal noses were bigger to warm the cold air.

Computer models show that if Neanderthals had been really hairy, they would have sweated excessively. This sweat would have frozen, bringing the risk of death by hypothermia. The notion of grunting was also dispelled by scientists in 1983 when a Neanderthal hyoid bone (part of the vocal system) was found in a cave in Israel. Identical to a human one, it proved that their capacity for speech resembled our own.

📊 FAST FACTS

PREHISTORIC PEOPLE WERE ARTISTIC

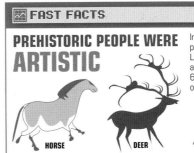

In 1940 prehistoric cave paintings were discovered in Lascaux, France. Dating back at least 15,000 years, the 600 pictures depict a variety of different animals.

HORSE

DEER

COW

Neanderthals were very strong and powerful, though much shorter and more heavily built than humans today.

How do we know Neanderthals enjoyed music?

Cave dwellings were strengthened with branches and bones, and covered in animal skins.

Neanderthals did not hunch over like chimps, but walked upright like humans.

TRUE or FALSE? The **pyramids** were built by slaves

One of the **Seven Wonders** of the World, the **Great Pyramid** at Giza was slaved over by a workforce of willing men from **all walks of life**. Rather than a cruel endeavor ordered by the Pharaoh, it was a **labor of love** for the community.

The King's Chamber is the actual burial room, which is lined with granite.

This abandoned burial chamber was mistakenly named the Queen's Chamber by early explorers.

Original burial chamber is carved into bedrock.

PRESERVATION PROCESS

In ancient Egypt the bodies of the deceased were preserved by mummification. This process was meant to take them safely to the afterlife. Internal organs were cut out, dried, and wrapped in linen before being stored in special containers called canopic jars (above).

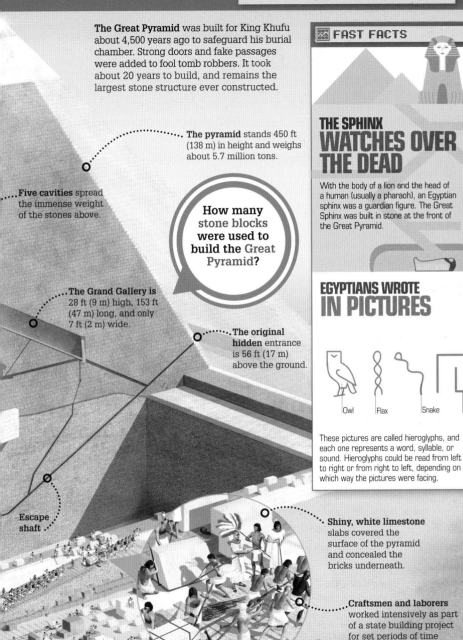

The Great Pyramid was built for King Khufu about 4,500 years ago to safeguard his burial chamber. Strong doors and fake passages were added to fool tomb robbers. It took about 20 years to build, and remains the largest stone structure ever constructed.

The pyramid stands 450 ft (138 m) in height and weighs about 5.7 million tons.

Five cavities spread the immense weight of the stones above.

How many stone blocks were used to build the Great Pyramid?

The Grand Gallery is 28 ft (9 m) high, 153 ft (47 m) long, and only 7 ft (2 m) wide.

The original hidden entrance is 56 ft (17 m) above the ground.

Escape shaft

Shiny, white limestone slabs covered the surface of the pyramid and concealed the bricks underneath.

Craftsmen and laborers worked intensively as part of a state building project for set periods of time without paying taxes.

FAST FACTS

THE SPHINX
WATCHES OVER THE DEAD

With the body of a lion and the head of a human (usually a pharaoh), an Egyptian sphinx was a guardian figure. The Great Sphinx was built in stone at the front of the Great Pyramid.

EGYPTIANS WROTE
IN PICTURES

Owl | Flax | Snake | House

These pictures are called hieroglyphs, and each one represents a word, syllable, or sound. Hieroglyphs could be read from left to right or from right to left, depending on which way the pictures were facing.

TRUE or FALSE? Greek statues are white marble

The classical world was home to **true masters of art**. They pioneered developments in painting and sculpting, leaving a legacy of **fine work** behind. But the white marble statues we associate with Greece are a bit **off-color**. The originals were actually **brightly painted**, but the pigments have **worn away** over time.

According to ancient Greek artists, statues left plain were considered ugly.

GREEK DRAMA

Most ancient Greek cities had a theater because plays were part of religious festivals. Crowds of up to 18,000 people would gather in the open air to watch the drama on stage. Only men and boys were allowed to act, and they wore masks to express character and feelings.

Why was some paint in ancient Greece **dangerous?**

The colored version uses the tempera technique (grinding powder pigments by hand) on artificial marble.

Under ultraviolet light, tiny remnants of pigment glow, illuminating detailed patterns and colors that can be revived.

The Greeks created statues of their gods, leaders, and warrior heroes.

Original colors came from plant- and animal-based pigments, crushed stones, or broken shells.

In addition to marble statues, celebrated buildings such as the Parthenon in Athens received the full-color treatment. Today, scientific researchers use infrared, ultraviolet, and X-ray spectroscopy techniques to help analyze which colors and designs were once painted on antique art and architecture. They then re-create the originals using authentic materials.

FAST FACTS

ANCIENT GREECE
WAS NOT A NATION

Instead, it was a collection of city-states, each with its own way of governing and waging wars. But although the city-states competed with one another, their inhabitants spoke the same language and worshipped the same gods.

BEANS WERE OFF
THE MENU

Unlike most modern vegetarians, some ancient Greeks, led by the philosopher and mathematician Pythagoras, refused to eat—or even touch—beans. They believed that beans contained the souls of the dead.

CRETE HAD
FLUSH TOILETS

Home to the ancient Minoans, the Greek city-state of Crete was the first place to have flushing toilets. In the palace of Knossos, water was poured into the lavatory from storage tanks to wash away royal deposits.

Drain

Water channel

TRUE or FALSE? Roman emperors gave a **thumbs-up** to save a **gladiator**

Bloodthirsty battles between **trained fighters** called **gladiators** took place in the **huge arenas** of ancient Rome. There was **no rule of thumb**, though. The emperor held the gladiators' lives in the palm of his hand. An **open palm** meant "**Spare him**," while a closed one meant "**Kill him**."

The word *gladiator* comes from the Latin for "sword."

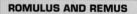

ROMULUS AND REMUS

The city of Rome was founded in 753 BCE by its first king, Romulus. Legend says that Romulus had a twin named Remus. Abandoned as babies, a she-wolf raised them in the wild. When they grew into men, Romulus killed Remus in a battle to become Rome's sole ruler.

Slaves and criminals were usually chosen as gladiators because they had nothing to lose. Trained in special schools called *ludi*, they learned how to use different weapons. Gladiators often fought in pairs. Death rates were high, though some gladiators survived more than 50 combats. Other fighters battled wild animals such as lions or bears.

📈 FAST FACTS

CENTRAL HEATING WAS INVENTED BY THE ROMANS

Floor

Furnace   Hot air

The comfort-loving Romans were a skilful bunch. Not only did they install under-floor heating in their homes and public buildings; they also invented cement and built the first proper roads—and very straight they were, too.

DURING A LIFE IN SERVICE, AN AVERAGE ROMAN SOLDIER MARCHED 226,800 MILES (365,000 KM)

x9

That amounts to walking around the world nine times! Soldiers were all male Roman citizens, age 20 or older, and they weren't allowed to get married. They had to serve for 25 years.

THE ROMANS ATE ROASTED PARROTS

They also dined on such exotic delicacies as dormice, storks, flamingos, lark's tongues, and sea urchins. Ingredients were shipped to Rome from all over the empire.

If a gladiator killed his opponent before the emperor gave his permission, the gladiator would be put on trial for murder.

The Colosseum in Rome held the largest gladiator games, in front of more than 50,000 spectators.

On special occasions, as a mark of his status, the emperor wore a laurel wreath—the Roman symbol of victory.

What was special about the color purple in ancient Rome?

TRUE or FALSE? **Vikings** wore **horned** helmets

Experts once **locked horns** on this subject, but it is now known that Viking helmets were **cone-shaped**. If horned helmets ever existed, they were only used for **ceremonial purposes**.

Which popular winter sport was enjoyed by the Vikings?

The Vikings were farmers-turned-raiders from Denmark, Norway, and Sweden. From the 790s onward, they invaded Britain, Ireland, and France, causing chaos as they conquered. Some Vikings traveled to Iceland and Greenland, where they set up colonies, while others navigated the rivers of Russia to trade with the Arab and Byzantine Empires.

Instead of horned helmets, Vikings usually opted for basic leather and metal-frame helmets, or just went bareheaded.

The idea of horned helmets came from the 19th century, when idealized paintings of the Vikings grew popular.

The freezing cold Scandinavian winters would have made fur hats far more practical than horned ones.

LONGSHIPS ALIGHT

Vikings traveled in longships, or dragon ships, decorated with fearsome, carved animal heads. These shallow oar- and wind-powered vessels were fast and strong enough to cross the stormy Atlantic Ocean. Dead Viking leaders may have been cremated inside their ships.

📈 FAST FACTS

VIKINGS BATHED ONCE A WEEK

SCRAPER

COMB

TWEEZERS

As a result, these fearsome warriors were much cleaner than other Europeans at the time. Excavations of Viking settlements have uncovered tools for personal hygiene crafted from animal bones and antlers.

THOR WAS THE VIKING GOD OF THUNDER

He had a magic belt, iron gloves, and a hammer. The Vikings had their own pagan religion, and worshipped many gods. Their tales of gods, giants, monsters, and elves are known as the Norse myths.

VIKING RUNES HAD MAGICAL PROPERTIES

ᚠ ᚱ ᛘ ᛒ ᛋ ᛏ

A   R   M   B   S   T

The Vikings used an alphabet of 16 symbols called runes to label their belongings, decorate gravestones, or write poems. Discovered by the god Odin, runes were said to have special powers, but only rune masters could cast spells or curses.

📊 FAST FACTS

MEDIEVAL PEOPLE USED
SLICES OF
BREAD
AS PLATES

They weren't a very well-mannered bunch, by modern standards. They ate with knives and fingers, rather than forks, and threw their chewed bones on the floor. Still, at least there weren't many dishes to wash!

WOOL WAS WASHED IN PEE

Before a greasy, grubby fleece could be turned into wool, it had to be washed. The most effective way to do this was to scrub it in urine diluted with water.

A GRAND HOUSEHOLD COULD BURN
100 lb (45 kg) OF WAX
AND TALLOW IN A SINGLE NIGHT

The equivalent of 1,300 candles, this might be used to light a lavish banquet in a dark medieval castle, at which swans and peacocks were served, feathers and all.

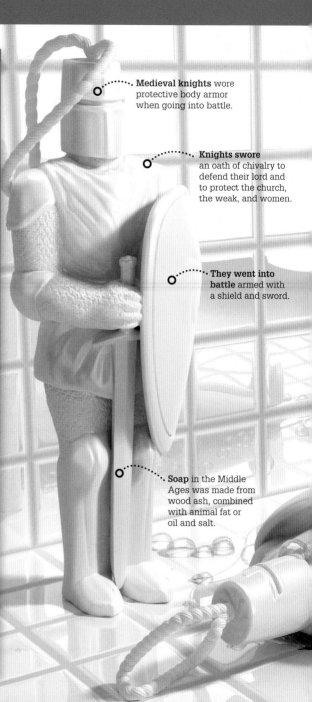

Medieval knights wore protective body armor when going into battle.

Knights swore an oath of chivalry to defend their lord and to protect the church, the weak, and women.

They went into battle armed with a shield and sword.

Soap in the Middle Ages was made from wood ash, combined with animal fat or oil and salt.

TRUE or FALSE? Medieval people didn't bathe

This is just a **dirty lie**. Medieval people were **clean-living** folk, washing their hands before and after meals. Soap was so popular by the 13th century that it was produced on an **industrial scale** in Britain, France, Italy, and Spain.

Medieval life was based on a feudal system, in which land was given in exchange for service. The king was at the top, passing land to his noblemen, who provided soldiers in return. These were knights (pictured) who fought on horseback. Many won prestige and recognition in battle. At the bottom were the peasants who farmed the land, keeping a share of the harvest for themselves.

What did most people drink in the Middle Ages?

ROUTE TO KNIGHTHOOD

The sons of noblemen started training for knighthood at the age of seven. Known as pages, the boys learned how to fight and ride into battle. At 15 years old, they were assigned knights to serve, and became squires. Intensive "on the job" training was given until they were ready for the special ceremony in which they became knights themselves.

TRUE or FALSE? Rats spread the plague

What method of plague prevention actually made it worse?

For centuries, we've been blaming these rodents for one of history's **worst diseases**. The plague or **Black Death** of the 1340s killed **half the population** of Europe and millions more in Asia and Africa. Eventually it was discovered that the **fleas on rats** were the true cause, but rats still played their part in **spreading the disease**.

HEALTH AND HYGIENE

In the 1860s the medical industry at last focused on hygiene and sanitation to improve healthcare standards. Surgeons washed their hands to prevent infection and cleaned wounds with carbolic acid to kill bacteria. Sewers were built to prevent bacteria from human waste polluting drinking water.

People believed they could catch the plague by breathing bad air. In reality, the true cause of the disease was bacteria, passed on by flea bites. Sufferers tried in vain to find cures, such as drinking urine, spreading butter on their sores, or putting toads on them.

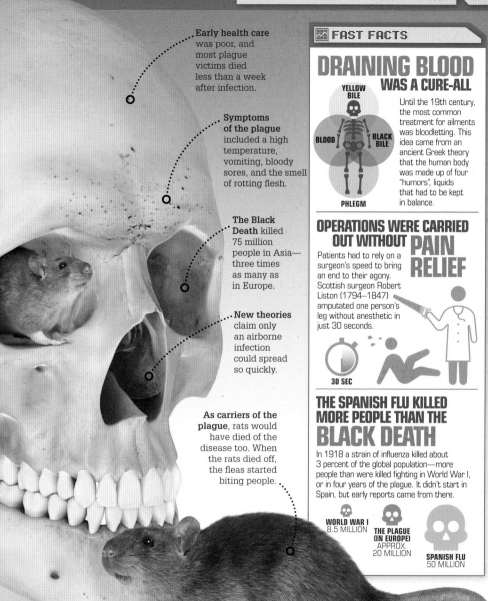

Early health care was poor, and most plague victims died less than a week after infection.

Symptoms of the plague included a high temperature, vomiting, bloody sores, and the smell of rotting flesh.

The Black Death killed 75 million people in Asia— three times as many as in Europe.

New theories claim only an airborne infection could spread so quickly.

As carriers of the plague, rats would have died of the disease too. When the rats died off, the fleas started biting people.

FAST FACTS

DRAINING BLOOD
WAS A CURE-ALL

YELLOW BILE

BLOOD

BLACK BILE

PHLEGM

Until the 19th century, the most common treatment for ailments was bloodletting. This idea came from an ancient Greek theory that the human body was made up of four "humors", liquids that had to be kept in balance.

OPERATIONS WERE CARRIED OUT WITHOUT PAIN RELIEF

Patients had to rely on a surgeon's speed to bring an end to their agony. Scottish surgeon Robert Liston (1794–1847) amputated one person's leg without anesthetic in just 30 seconds.

30 SEC

THE SPANISH FLU KILLED MORE PEOPLE THAN THE BLACK DEATH

In 1918 a strain of influenza killed about 3 percent of the global population—more people than were killed fighting in World War I, or in four years of the plague. It didn't start in Spain, but early reports came from there.

WORLD WAR I
8.5 MILLION

THE PLAGUE (IN EUROPE)
APPROX. 20 MILLION

SPANISH FLU
50 MILLION

TRUE or FALSE? Columbus discovered America

In 1492 Christopher Columbus **sailed west** from Spain looking for Asia. He landed in the Bahamas on a journey that **opened up the Americas** to other explorers. But someone always gets there first! Native people already lived in the **New World**, and a Viking had **beat him to the punch** 500 years before.

EXOTIC GOODS

During the great age of exploration, European travelers returned with a growing menu of new foods. Potatoes, tomatoes, pineapples, and cocoa were introduced from the New World. Asian spices were so valuable in the 15th century that they were used as currency.

FINISH LINE

Columbus landed on an island in what is now the Bahamas, and called it San Salvador.

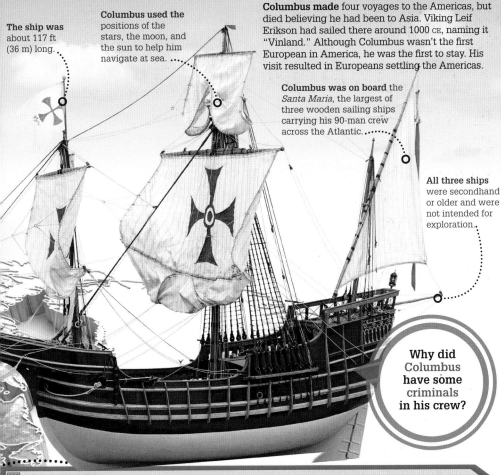

The ship was about 117 ft (36 m) long.

Columbus used the positions of the stars, the moon, and the sun to help him navigate at sea.

Columbus made four voyages to the Americas, but died believing he had been to Asia. Viking Leif Erikson had sailed there around 1000 CE, naming it "Vinland." Although Columbus wasn't the first European in America, he was the first to stay. His visit resulted in Europeans settling the Americas.

Columbus was on board the *Santa Maria*, the largest of three wooden sailing ships carrying his 90-man crew across the Atlantic.

All three ships were secondhand or older and were not intended for exploration.

Why did Columbus have some criminals in his crew?

FAST FACTS

BRAZIL WAS DISCOVERED BY ACCIDENT

Portuguese explorer Pedro Alvares Cabral stumbled across the country on his way to India in 1500. This explains why Brazilians speak Portuguese, while Spanish is spoken in most other South American countries.

LANGUAGES
PORTUGUESE ▌
SPANISH ▌
ENGLISH ▌
DUTCH ▌
FRENCH ▌

EUROPEAN DISEASES WIPED OUT THE LOCALS

The Spanish soldiers not only imported horses, cattle, pigs, wheat, and guns to Central America. They also brought deadly European diseases such as smallpox, which had a devastating effect on native populations.

NATIVE POPULATION OF CENTRAL AMERICA

POPULATION IN 1519
25 MILLION

POPULATION IN 1565
2.5 MILLION

EXPLORATION WAS A RISKY BUSINESS

92.4% DIED
7.6% SURVIVED

In 1519 Portuguese explorer Ferdinand Magellan set sail around the world with a crew of 237. Only 18 survived the voyage. Magellan himself was killed in the Philippines after becoming embroiled in a battle between local chieftains.

ANSWERS

258–259 BODILY FLUIDS
Yes. Water intoxication causes the brain to swell, with potentially fatal consequences.

260–261 THE BRAIN
No. There is no proof of this.

262–263 NERVOUS SYSTEM
90 percent.

264–265 CIRCULATION
Yes. When you have a hot drink, nerve receptors in the tongue signal to the brain that something hot is entering the body, so it can prepare to start sweating.

266–267 DIGESTION
Yes, but only in an extreme situation of overeating.

268–269 BONES
The feet. Each foot consists of 26 bones.

270–271 MUSCLES
Yes. When you see someone else smiling, your brain's mirror neurons will stimulate a sensation that is associated with smiling, so you smile immediately.

272–273 ANIMAL EVOLUTION
On their legs.

274–275 DINOSAURS
When it's on screen. In the movie Jurassic Park, some of the main noises for the T-rex came from the sound designer's tiny Jack Russell terrier, Buster. The sounds were slowed down.

276–277 REPTILES
Heat is released through the crocodile's mouth.

278–279 ANIMAL BEHAVIOR
Elephants can hear low-frequency calls of other elephants that are up to 6 miles (10 km) away. The calls are too low for humans to hear but the elephants can "hear" the sounds through their feet.

280–281 ANIMAL ADAPTATIONS
10 minutes.

282–283 DANGEROUS ANIMALS
Their ability to see very well in low light.

284–285 ANIMAL MARKINGS
A tiger.

286–287 BIRDS
Although they can't fly, ostriches can run at speeds of 40 mph (60 km/h), which is as fast as a horse.

288–289 WATER
Morocco.

290–291 LIGHT
Iceland.

292–293 SOUND
At many European operas, whistling means "Boo!"

294–295 COLOR
Blue. In a survey of people around the world, 40 percent of people chose blue. The second favorite was purple, which was chosen by 14 percent of people.

296–297 GRAVITY
A skydiver reaches 130 mph (210 km/h), a tennis ball 60 mph (95 km/h), and a raindrop 15 mph (25 km/h).

298–299 MATH AND PROBABILITY
Up to five times!

300–301 ELECTRICITY
American inventor Thomas Edison (1847–1931).

302–303 BIRTH OF THE UNIVERSE
Theories about how the universe might end—in a Big Rip (torn apart), a Big Crunch (stops expanding and collapses), or a Big Freeze (a long, slow fade-out).

304–305 EXPANDING UNIVERSE
There are up to 100 billion planets in the universe including Earth.

306–307 BLACK HOLES
As you get close to the hole you feel its pull. If you are going in feet first, the pull is stronger on your feet than your head. You get stretched lengthwise and squashed sideways, becoming increasingly long and thin—a process known as spaghettification. You are spaghettified until your body can take no more and rips apart.

308–309 GAS GIANTS
The blue comes from methane gas in their atmospheres.

310–311 ROCKY PLANETS
1.5 in (3.8 cm) per second.

312–313 SPACE BODIES
In 1930, 11-year-old Venetia Burney from Oxford, England, suggested the name Pluto to her grandfather, who passed it on to the Lowell Observatory in the United States. When Pluto was chosen as the name, he gave Venetia five pounds (about three dollars) as a reward.

314–315 PLATE TECTONICS
The average thickness of a tectonic plate is 50 miles (80 km).

316–317 OCEANS
Russia, the United States, Canada, and Australia.

318–319 RIVERS
In 1988 students in Montana successfully campaigned to have their local North Fork Roe River recognized as the world's shortest. It is just 59 ft (18 m) long.

320–321 MOUNTAINS
A peak above 2,000 ft (610 m) is a mountain, while anything smaller is a hill.

322–323 DESERTS
The hottest desert by average temperature is the Danakil in Ethiopia, while the coldest is Antarctica.

324–325 VOLCANOES
Volcano Toba exploded 73,000 years ago in what is now Indonesia.

326–327 PREHISTORIC PEOPLE
Flutes made of bones and tusks have been discovered, showing that Neanderthals played music.

328–329 ANCIENT EGYPT
A total of 2,300,000 stone blocks make up the Great Pyramid.

330–331 ANCIENT GREECE
Some paint was made of lead, and this is hazardous. It can cause damage to the nervous system, kidney failure, and stunted growth.

332–333 ANCIENT ROME
Purple was considered the color of status and authority, so only the emperor could wear it. The purple dye came from the shell of a sea snail called a murex.

334–335 THE VIKINGS
Skiing. The Vikings enjoyed skiing and worshipped a god of skiing named Ullr.

336–337 THE MIDDLE AGES
Water. This mostly came from wells, so would have been relatively clean. Peasants also drank beer, which was much weaker than it is today. Wine was the drink of choice in noble households.

338–339 DISEASE AND HEALTH CARE
Some villages killed off all their cats because they were supposedly associated with witchcraft. Without cats to keep rat numbers down, the population grew and the plague spread even more quickly.

340–341 EXPLORATION
Amnesty (an official pardon) was granted to criminals who went on the dangerous journey. At least four men are known to have taken advantage of the offer.

ACKNOWLEDGMENTS

Dorling Kindersley would like to thank: Andrea Mills for authoring text; Helen Abramson, Carron Brown, Rishi Bryan, Monica Byles, Steven Carton, Jessica Cawthra, Linda Esposito, Charlie Galbraith, Matilda Gollon, Ciara Heneghan, Wendy Horobin, Rob Houston, Aashirwad Jain, Tina Jindal, Katie John, Gareth Jones, Ashwin Khurana, Bahja Norwood, Victoria Pyke, Vicky Richards, Steve Setford, Jenny Sich, Rona Skene, Caroline Stamps, Fleur Star, and Alka Thakur for editorial assistance; David Ball, Romi Chakraborty, Sheila Collins, Paul Drislane, Michael Duffy, Mik Gates, Rachael Grady, Jim Green, Spencer Holbrook, Shipra Jain, Kit Lane, Peter Laws, Philip Letsu, Clare Marshall, Isha Nagar, Jeongeun Yule Park, Stefan Podhorodecki, Mary Sandberg, Anis Sayyed, Deep Shikha Walia, Jemma Westing, and Steve Woosnam-Savage for design assistance; Hazel Beynon, Kim Bryan, Jack Challoner, Robert Dinwiddie, Derek Harvey, Chris Hawkes, Simon Holland, Katie John, Susan Kennedy, Ben Morgan, Martyn Page, Carole Stott, Richard Walker, and Chris Woodford for fact checking; Sumedha Chopra, Martin Copeland, Nic Dean, Aditya Katyal, and Sarah Smithies for picture research; Chrissy Barnard, Adam Benton, Stuart Jackson Carter, Anders Kjellberg, Simon Mumford, and Michael Parker, 385Jon@KJA-Artists.com for illustrations; Steve Crozier and Steve Willis for creative retouching; Simon Mumford for maps; Stefan Podhorodecki for photography; Hazel Beynon, Carron Brown, Neha Gupta, and Samira Sood for proofreading; Helen Peters for indexing; John Searcy for Americanization; Jessica Bentall, Laura Brim, Mark Cavanagh, Suhita Dharamjit, Claire Gell, Manisha Majithia, Priyanka Sharma, Saloni Singh, Sophia M Tampakopoulos Turner, Surabhi Wadhwa, Jemma Westing, and Maud Whatley for assistance with Jackets; Nityanand Kumar and Pankaj Sharma for assistance with hi-res work; Harish Aggarwal, Neeraj Bhatia, Nikoleta Parasaki, Rebekah Parsons-King, and Jacqueline Street for assistance with pre-production; and Mandy Inness, Ben Marcus, Gemma Sharpe, and Vivienne Yong for assistance with production.

The publisher would like to thank the following for their kind permission to reproduce their photographs:

(Key: a–above; b–below/bottom; c–center; f–far; l–left; r–right; t–top)

1 Science Photo Library: Mark Garlick (b). **2 Getty Images:** Michele Falzone (cra, tr). **2–3 123RF.com:** Derege (b). **Getty Images:** Volanthevist (bc). **3 Getty Images:** Katsumasa Iwasawa (ca). **5 Getty Images:** Bence Mate / Nature Picture Library (cla). **SeaPics.com:** James D. Watt (br). **6–7 Getty Images:** Michele Falzone. **8 Corbis:** Ulises Rodriguez / epa (br). **8–9 Tormod Sandtorv. 10 Alamy Images:** age fotostock (bl). **10–11 Corbis:** Kazuyoshi Nomachi. **12–13 Getty Images:** Mark D Callanan. **13 Alamy Images:** adp-stock (br). **Dreamstime.com:** Jesús Eloy Ramos Lara (tr). **14 Alamy Images:** All Canada Photos (bl). **14–15 Corbis:** Gunter Marx Photography. **16 Alamy Images:** National Geographic Image Collection (bl). **16–17 National Geographic Creative:** John Stanmeyer. **18–19 123RF.com:** derege. **19 Alamy Images:** Sergey Podkolzin (tc). **20–21 Corbis:** Imaginechina. **20 Corbis:** Viking 1 (bl). **22 Corbis:** Michele Falzone / JAI (b). **23 Fotolia:** janmiko (bl). **Getty Images:** Suzanne and Nick Geary (cr). **Masterfile:** Frank Krahmer (tr). **24–25 Alamy Images:** blickwinkel. **24 NASA:** JPL / Space Science Institute (bl). **26–27 AWL Images:** Max Milligan. **27 DK Images:** Angela Coppola / University of Pennsylvania Museum of Archaeology and Anthropology (bc). **28–29 Alamy Images:** Paul Springett 10. **28 Rex Features:** Imaginechina (bl). **30 Alamy Images:** dpa picture alliance archive (b). **Corbis:** Wolfgang Rattay / Reuters (cl). **31 Corbis:** Wolfgang Rattay / Reuters (br). **Getty Images:** William West / AFP (tl). **TopFoto.co.uk:** ullsteinbild (cl). **32–33 Stuart Jackson Carter. 33 Corbis:** Marc Dozier (bc). **34 Alamy Images:** Blaine Harrington III (cr). **34–35 Getty Images:** Moment Open. **36–37 Getty Images:** Feature China / Barcroft Images / Barcroft Media. **36 Alamy Stock Photo:** Simon Rinderer (tl). **38 Getty Images:** Timothy Allen (bl). **38–39 Frederic Buyle:** (tr). **40–41 Getty Images:** Timothy Allen. **40 Rex Features:** HAP / Quirky China News (bl). **42 Alamy Images:** Pacific Press. **42–43 Dima Chatrov. 44–45 Alamy Images:** Prisma Bildagentur AG. **45 Getty Images:** Sergio Camacho (br). **46–47 Corbis:** Alcibbum Photography. **47 Andrea Moro:** (tr). **48–49 Science Photo Library:** Dr Morley Read. **48 laajala/flickr:** (bl). **50 Caters News Agency:** Eeerkia Schulz (b). **51 Alamy Images:** age fotostock (bl); David Bigwood (cr). **NOLEHACE Orchid Photography:** (tr). **52 FLPA:** Photo Researchers (l). **52–53 FLPA:** Photo Researchers (b). **53 Corbis:** Ch'ien Lee / Minden Pictures (br). **FLPA:** Photo Researchers (r). **54–55 Rex Features:** Amos Chapple. **54 Pooktre / Peter Cook and Becky Northey:** (tl). **56–57 SuperStock:** Sara Janini / age fotostock. **56 SuperStock:** Morales / age fotostock (bl). **58 Corbis:** Michael Durham / Minden Pictures (bl). **58–59 Caters News Agency:** Gary Tindale. **60–61 Caters News Agency:** Antero Topp. **61 Photoshot:** NHPA (br). **62 Alamy Images:** Ethan Daniels (b). **63 Corbis:** Juan Medina / Reuters (tl); Michael Edwards / Great Stock (br). **Rex Features:** Mint Images (cl). **64–65 FLPA:** Frans Lanting. **65 Alamy Images:** Marvin Dembinsky Photo Associates (cr). **66–67 Corbis:** Department for International Development / Russell Watkins (b). **67 Corbis:** Stephen Frink (br). **68–69 Jurgen Otto. 69 Corbis:** Tim Laman / National Geographic Creative br). **70 Corbis:** Dr. David Phillips / Visuals Unlimited (br). **70–71 Science Photo Library:** Eye Of Science. **70** Science Photo Library: Eye Of Science (br). **72 Alamy Images:** Ethan Daniels b). **73 Alamy Images:** Frank Hecker cl); Michael Doolittle (tr). **FLPA:** Gianpiero Ferrari (br). **74–75 Science Photo Library:** Eye Of Science. **75 Alamy Images:** Science Photo Library (br). **76–77 Corbis:** Mark Comalty / Aurora Photos. **76 SuperStock:** Prisma (bl). **78 Dreamstime.com:** Sean Pavone cr). **78–79 Alamy Images:** Carver Mostardi. **80–81 Press Association Images:** Jad Saab / AP. **81 Alamy Images:** John Warburton-Lee Photography (tr). **82–83 Alamy Images:** imageBROKER. **82 Corbis:** Tourism Ministry / Xinhua Press (tl). **84–85 Stephen Locke. 85 Alamy Images:** Thierry Grun (cr). **86 Corbis:** Mike Theiss / Ultimate Chase (cl). **86–87 Corbis:** Reuters (t); Wave (b). **87 Corbis:** Eric Nguyen (tr). **Press Association Images:** Stephen B. Thornton / AP (br). **88–89 Martin Rietze. 88 NASA:** JPL / University of Arizona (bl). **90 Dreamstime.com:** Matt Dobson (bl). **90–91 Brian Middleton. 92–93 Getty Images:** Katsumasa Iwasawa. **94–95 Alan Friedman / avertedimagination.com:** c). **94 Institute for Solar Physics:** SST Göran Scharmer / Mats Löfdahl (bl). **95 NASA:** GSFC / F. Espenak (cl/Reproduced five times). **96 NASA:** Hinode / XRT (clb). **97 Dreamstime. com:** Elisanth (cra/Reproduced four times, cr/moons); Stanalin (tr, crb, cr). **98–99 Pascal Henry,www.lesud.com. 98 NASA:** (clb). **100–101 Pascal Henry,www.lesud.com:** (c). **101 NASA:** JPL / Space Science Institute tc). **102–103 Science Photo Library:** Mark Garlick. **102 Dorling Kindersley:** London Planetarium (fcl). **Dreamstime.com:** Elisanth (cl). **103 NASA:** (bc). **104 Dreamstime.com:** Vmeeds (clb). **106 NASA:** ESA and H. Hammel, MIT (cl). **108 Dreamstime. com:** Jabiru (bl). **113 NASA:** ESA, J. Hester, A. Loll (ASU) (tl). **115 NASA:** CXC / SAO / F. Seward (tc). **117 NASA Goddard Space Flight Center:** Tom Zagwodzki (tr). **119 Corbis:** Visuals Unlimited (cr). **120 NASA:** (bl). **120–121 Science Photo Library:** Chris

Butler (c). **121 ESA / Hubble:** S. Beckwith (STScI) and the HUDF Team (br). **Getty Images:** Azem Ramadani (tl). **Science Photo Library:** Mark Garlick (cr). **126 Science Photo Library:** Geoeye (bc). **128 NASA:** Visible Earth / Jeff Schmaltz (cr). **131 Dreamstime.com:** Asdf_1 (tc). **132 Dreamstime.com:** Ericsch (bl). **134 Dreamstime.com:** Maxwell De Araújo Rodrigues (cla/Reproduced seven times). **135 Getty Images:** National Geographic (cr). **136 Corbis:** Galen Rowell (bl). **138 NASA:** JPL / University of Arizona (clb). **140 Corbis:** Arctic-Images (clb). **142 Corbis:** Charles & Josette Lenars (bc). **143 Getty Images:** Mike Copeland (crb). **144–145 Getty Images:** National Geographic. **146 Corbis:** Paul Souders (clb). **148 Corbis:** Science Faction / Norbert Wu (clb). **151 Corbis:** Nippon News / Aflo / Newspaper / Mainichi (clb). **152 Getty Images:** Paul Souders (bl). **154 NSIDC:** USGS, W.O. Field (1941) and B. F. Molnia (2004) (clb). **155 Dreamstime.com:** Maxwell De Araújo Rodrigues (cr/Reproduced five times). **158 Getty Images:** Katsumasa Iwasawa (clb). **158–159 Dreamstime. com:** Stockshoppe (c). **159 Dreamstime.com:** Laraslk (crb). **160 Corbis:** Visuals Unlimited (clb). **161 Dreamstime.com:** Pictac (bc). **164 Getty Images:** (bl). **164–165 Getty Images:** Hulton Archive. **166 Corbis:** epa / Michael Reynolds (bl). **168 Corbis:** Ocean (clb). **168–169 Corbis:** Ikon Images / Jurgen Ziewe (c). **170 Dreamstime.com:** Mantinov (clb). **171 Corbis:** Jurgen Ziewe / Ikon Images (cr). **172 Dreamstime.com:** 1enchik (cb); Diego Barucco (clb); Mopic (bl). **174–175 Dreamstime.com:** Rawpixelimages (t/Used multiple times on the spread). **174 Dreamstime.com:** Monkey Business Images (crb/Used multiple times on the spread); Hongqi Zhang (aka Michael Zhang) (cra/Used multiple times on the spread); Get4net (cr/ Used multiple times on the spread). **175 Dreamstime.com:** Elena Elisseeva (cl/Used multiple times on the spread); Alexander Raths (cla/Used multiple times on the spread, c/Used multiple times on the spread); Andres Rodriguez (clb/Used multiple times on the spread); Itsmejust (cr); Tmcphotos

(cb/Used multiple times on the spread). **176 Getty Images:** Greg Wood / AFP (br). **180 Corbis:** Michael Macor / San Francisco Chronicle (clb). **183 Dreamstime.com:** Kevin Panizza (bl). **184–185 Dreamstime. com:** Dzmitri Mikhaltsov (c). **184 Alamy Images:** blickwinkel (bc). **185 Dreamstime.com:** Tracy King (cl). **188–189 Dreamstime.com:** Rakjung2 (c). **189 123RF.com:** Aaron Amat (r). **Dreamstime.com:** Jacek Sopotnicki (br). **190 Corbis:** William Radcliffe / Science Faction (clb). **191 Dreamstime.com:** William Roberts (cla, tc). **195 Getty Images:** Thomas Kokta (tr). **196–197 Dreamstime.com:** Glenn Price (c). **197 Alamy Images:** Wayne Farrell (tr); The Oxfordshire Chilli Garden (r/Chilli). **Dreamstime. com:** Ron Sumners (r/Flame). **198–199 Alamy Images:** Arterra Picture Library (c). **198 Alamy Images:** Arterra Picture Library (cra). **Dreamstime.com:** Kevin Carden (clb). **199 Alamy Images:** Hemis (bl); Arterra Picture Library (cla, tl, tc, ca). **200 123RF.com:** Evgeny Karandaev (bl); nito500 (bc); Thanakrit Yomthaisong (br). **Dreamstime.com:** Baibaz (fbl). **200–201 123RF.com:** zdravinjo (b/All sugar cubes used on the spread). **201 123RF.com:** bagwold (bc); Evgeny Karandaev (bl). **Dreamstime.com:** Lasse Kristensen (br). **202 Alamy Images:** dbimages (clb). **Dreamstime.com:** Roman Samokhin (br). **202–203 123RF.com:** Natalia Merzlyakova. **205 Getty Images:** STR / AFP (crb). **208 Alamy Images:** GL Archive (clb). **208–209 Alamy Images:** Stefan Hofecker. Christophe Dedieu: (b/Harmony Of The Seas). **209 Rex by Shutterstock:** Erik Pendzich (b). **211 Getty Images:** Obank / Connellan / Barcroft Media (br). **212 Getty Images:** Mike Hewitt / Allsport (clb). **214–215 Dreamstime.com:** Konstantinos Moraitis (All mini cars used on the spread). **Getty Images:** Peter Endig. **215 Alamy Images:** SPUTNIK (tr). **216–217 Jani Bryson:** (Photo of children used multiple times in the spread). **SD Model Makers:** (c). **217 Alamy Images:** LondonPhotos - Homer Sykes (bc). **219 TopFoto.co.uk:** PA Photos (tr). **221 Alamy Images:** Michael Jenner / Robertharding (crb).